Punishment without Walls

A Volume in the

Crime, Law, and Deviance Series

Punishment
without Walls
Community Service Sentences
in New York City
Douglas Corry McDonald

Rutgers University Press

New Brunswick, New Jersey

Library of Congress Cataloging-in-Publication Data

McDonald, Douglas, 1946–
  Punishment without walls.

  (Crime, law, and deviance series)
  Includes index.
  1. Community-based corrections—Law and legislation—
New York (N.Y.) 2. Sentences (Criminal procedure)—
New York (N.Y.) I. Title. II. Series.
  KFX2093.M38 1986   364.6'8   85–26185
  ISBN 0–8135–1147–X

For Mary Elizabeth and Corry

Contents

List of Tables and Figure

Foreword

The United States has been emulative rather than innovative in devising effective and humane criminal punishments; with *Punishment without Walls* Douglas McDonald and the Vera Institute of Justice break new ground.

Based on the long-established theme of restitution and the fact that a crime is an injury to the community and not only to the victim, community service sentences were first used widely in California, then introduced systematically in Great Britain, and more recently have been adopted in other parts of this country. In one legal form or another, they now form part of the punishment armory of most criminal courts. They have proved particularly useful with white collar offenders; what had never been tested was their applicability to the persistent property offenders who crowd the jails and clutter the prisons. The Vera Institute has now demonstrated that community service sentences, if intelligently applied, vigorously enforced, and closely supervised, "can be imposed in large numbers not only upon the relatively well-to-do first offenders who possess valuable skills, but also upon those chronic property offenders who are generally not violent but who nonetheless present the courts with difficult problems." It is an important demonstration that should be neglected by no one concerned with the imposition and enforcement of criminal sanctions.

The right and left of crime control—those who favor increased severity and those who deplore the brutality of our crowded prisons and jails—should unite in welcoming this book. It is common ground between them that rational, fair, and effective sentencing requires more than our present over-reliance on imprisonment, which is itself a product of the unavailability of effective alter-   xiii

natives. *Punishment without Walls* demonstrates that community
service sentences have an important role to play in filling this gap.

It is a hopeful book at a time when gloom characterizes most
scholarship on crime control. But it is not foolishly euphoric. The
story of the Vera Institute's establishment of three substantial community service projects in three New York boroughs, of 2,400 men
strictly supervised in labor crews, each required to perform seventy hours of community service work as punishment for his crime,
is precisely and critically told. Students of court reform efforts,
who have become aware of the difficulties faced by programs that
aim for changes in sentencing patterns, will find intriguing and
hopeful the strategies and techniques the Vera Institute employed
to encourage the courts to use this new sentence—and to use it in
the jailbound cases for which it was intended.

Let me oversimplify the problem as a foreword to its more precise definition by McDonald. American criminal justice systems—
federal, state, and local—have well demonstrated that they know
how to imprison. What has not been demonstrated is that they
know how to impose and collect fines, how to provide probation
with effective and firm supervision, how to ensure that conditions
of probation are fulfilled, and how to impose community service
sentences that are rigorously enforced against the offender to the
benefit of the community. Our alternatives to imprisonment too
often are seen as "letting off"—and, in general, that is a correct
perception. Too many city courts fail to collect a substantial portion of collectible fines they have imposed; too often convicted
offenders are put on probation to probation officers with case loads
of two hundred (to say nothing of their obligations of pre-sentence
reports to their judges), so that supervision becomes an unreality.
There can be no political dispute concerning the need to rectify
this situation.

It is of first importance to a rational criminal justice system that
the law should keep its promises; that what judges order should in
fact be carried out. Too frequently in criminal courts this is not so.

Central to the Vera Institute project was a Vera-appointed court
representative's careful selection of the chronic petty offenders
most likely to go to jail, the negotiation with counsel and judge of

community service sentences in those cases, and then the determined insistence by Vera-employed site supervisors that the work be done, or else that the offender be resentenced—mostly to jail. The law kept its promises and carried out its threats. It was by no means a sentimental project; rather it was hard-headed and cost-conscious.

The Vera Institute became an innovative force in law enforcement with the success of its early efforts at reforming the money bail system, which were widely copied and eventually adopted, universally I think, in federal and state legislation. None has since then doubted the Vera Institute's force for humane reforms. Over the years, the Vera Institute has added a capacity for critical evaluation of its own projects that is unique among criminal justice reform agencies in this county—or anywhere else I know of. Institute-supported studies the Manhattan Bail Project, the Court Employment Project, the Victim Services Project, and the Felony Mediation Project have all demonstrated that a reform agency can mount evaluative studies critical of its own work. Now, with this analysis of the New York City Community Service Sentencing Project, they have gone further and shown that they can evaluate an ongoing effort, assess some of its weakness, and in midstream correct them.

McDonald's book also explores the effect of community service sentences on the petty recidivists who were required to serve them. His examinations of how offenders viewed their crimes and their sentences, and of the effect jail terms and community service sentences had on subsesquent criminality, pose some troubling questions as well as some neat solutions.

In sum, a rarity: an innovative plan, flexibly applied, and critically evaluated—a lesson for every criminal court in the land.

Norval Morris
Professor of Law and Criminology
University of Chicago

Preface

This book is the product of a fortunate intersection of my own interests in criminal sentencing and the needs of the Vera Institute of Justice, a private not-for-profit research and development organization in New York City. In 1981, I was asked to join the institute's Research Department and evaluate a small experimental project that was operating in the Bronx Criminal Court but was to expand into other city courts as well. The offer was enticing for several reasons. Since its establishment in 1961, the institute had acquired a reputation for instigating imaginative reforms in the courts and other institutional domains, and the chance to sit in the front row and watch an ambitious project either succeed or fail appealed to my curiosity. I had been studying and writing about the courts, criminal sentencing practices, and the politics of sentencing reform for a number of years, and the opportunity to explore further some ideas that had intrigued me was a hard one to pass up.

At least as appealing was the prospect of directly contributing to something that could turn out to be useful. Over the past twenty years, the institute has pursued a distinctive reform strategy. One division designs, creates, and manages numerous demonstration projects that test innovative policy solutions to a variety of problems in governmental administration. Professional social scientists working out of another division, the Research Department, evaluate these projects with an eye to determining whether they are successful, desirable, and effective. This marriage of action and research under a single roof produces its expected tensions, although when it works best, it provides excellent opportunities for social scientists.

In my case, I was given not only broad access to the community service project staff, but also an open door to the courts, largely because of the institute's excellent reputation there. I was given substantial support for my research, both financial and colleagial. I encountered no real constraints (apart from the normal ones of money, time, and imagination) on my ability to frame the inquiry and answer the questions as I posed them. Best of all, this freedom was not purchased through isolation from the world I was studying. My findings were eagerly consumed by the institute's managers and used by them to redirect the course of their reform efforts. I found this mix of quasi-academic freedom and programmatic engagement enormously satisfying.

At all stages of this project, I have benefited greatly from the generous assistance of many people. I am especially grateful to my research assistants for their stubborn attention to data collection and analysis. These include Selma Marks and Sam Blackwell, both of whom performed a wide variety of tasks at all stages of the project; Ashbel T. Wall, who interviewed dozens of judges, prosecutors, and defense attorneys in three New York City borough courts; and Antonio Valderrama, who interviewed eighty-one criminal offenders sentenced to community service sentence and thereby provided the channel for them to speak to us. Others— Connie Chin, Patty Giovenco, Charles Priester, and Camilla Dunham—coded data drawn from court records so that sentencing patterns could be analyzed by computer. Todd McDaniel provided me with very valuable assistance in programming a number of different tasks on the City University of New York's computer, not the least of which was the construction of what turned out to be a very complicated data set. James Cataldo assisted with the analysis of recidivism and some other miscellaneous programming. Scott Sparks, Darlene Mejias, Gricet Otero, and Jayne Chamberlin typed thousands of pages of draft manuscript and interviews, and their patience with my obsessive rewriting is much appreciated. I am also grateful to several readers for their comments on early drafts— David Beier, David Greenberg, Milton Heumann, Sally Hillsman, Jerome McElroy, David Nee, and Susan Rai—and Cynthia Perwin Halpern for her editorial assistance.

Those who were the subjects of this research were extraordinarily giving of their time and were remarkably open to me and my assistants. These included dozens of judges, prosecutors, and

Legal Aid Society attorneys in the three boroughs of Brooklyn, Manhattan, and the Bronx. Especially cooperative were the staffs of the institute's Community Service Sentencing Projects and their citywide director, Judith Greene. They opened their files to us, let us look over their shoulders as they went about their work, and told us what was on their minds. Most importantly, they went to great trouble to fill out thousands of detailed forms for the better part of three years so that we could analyze decision patterns. Even though they undoubtedly felt the strain of being evaluated closely for such a long period of time, they were always hospitable and helpful. I am also indebted to the staff of the New York City Criminal Justice Agency for providing records of court proceedings for several thousand defendants.

Michael Smith, the Vera Institute's director, deserves special thanks here. Not many managers ask a professional skeptic/social scientist to evaluate closely a project that they have spent years creating and nurturing. Even fewer would be willing to do so knowing that the results of that investigation would be placed in the limelight for all to see. Whatever anxiety I had in the beginning about biting the hand that feeds me was misplaced. Michael wanted to know whether his efforts had succeeded or failed and whether the policies embodied in the project made sense. Working with him has been a rewarding and intellectually stimulating experience.

Support for this study was provided by grants from the Florence V. Burden Foundation and the Charles E. Culpeper Foundation. Additional support was provided by The Ford Foundation and The Edna McConnell Clark Foundation, and the costs of data collection were borne in part by the governments of the City and State of New York. The generosity of the individuals and agencies involved is very deeply appreciated.

And finally, I am grateful to Nancy Porter for her being there throughout this long and arduous project. Trying to complete a book while balancing other professional activities left precious little time for our life together. I look forward to having a new schedule.

Punishment without Walls

Introduction

This study examines what happened when a new criminal sentence—an order to perform unpaid service to the community—was introduced by the Vera Institute of Justice into three different New York City courts between 1979 and 1981. It also explores the effect this new punishment had upon those given it and upon the larger community as well. Although my focus here is on a single city's experience, I have written it with an eye to illuminating broader terrain.

Sigmund Freud, in one of his discourses on the organization of the human psyche, remarked that the structure of a crystal is best revealed when cracked. He therefore chose to examine pathologies in order to learn more about the general organization and development of personality. For similar reasons, attempts to reform institutions can be strategic sites for exploration, if one is interested in determining how those institutions are structured. Everyday routines are shaken up; working accommodations that individuals reach with one another are thrown into question and subjected to reexamination; and lines of cleavage become more readily apparent to the outside observer. Some reform initiatives provoke no such changes at all, which also reveals something important about the institution in question, as well as about the particular reform strategy adopted.

The Vera Institute's experience is especially interesting because it tried to dislodge a well-established convention: the practice of sentencing chronic property offenders to jail. With the backing of important sponsors, the institute set out to pursuade prosecutors and judges to substitute community service sentences for short jail terms. This study examines the results of this experience in order to assess whether the use of these punishments makes sense as a matter of public policy and to see what this particular experiment reveals about how the courts work.

The Vera Institute's Community Service Sentencing Project is one of a larger family of similar reforms being tried here in this country and abroad. The British government established community service orders in the mid-1970s and was beginning to reappraise them in 1984. In 1983, the French government initiated the use of community service orders, a development that remains unstudied. The progress of community service sentencing in this country has followed a more erratic course, largely because of the decentralized character of government here. Nonetheless, the sentence has made a strong impact. It is increasingly being touted as a sensible and cost-effective means of sanctioning criminal offenders who are not violent, but are still deserving of punishment.

There exists, however, a good deal of controversy regarding the appropriateness of this kind of sentencing. One current of opinion, running strongly in this country, favors stiffer and more controlling penalties for convicted criminals. An opposing current advocates reducing our reliance on expensive jails and prisons and expanding the use of substitute punishments, such as unpaid community service. Unfortunately, the debate over these alternatives has generally gone forward without much analysis of how the courts have used the community service sentence, what effect these punishments have had upon those ordered to serve them, and how public safety has been affected. This study examines these and other questions so that policy decisions may be more informed.

Some may wonder whether an examination of one project in New York City is really relevant to our understanding of similar practices elsewhere. In conversations with criminal justice professionals and policymakers elsewhere in the country, I frequently hear words such as, "You can't compare our situation with New York's." This sentiment comes from the perception that New York City is different from most other parts of the nation, not only in scale but also in kind, so much so that New York City is seen as almost another country altogether. In many instances, I suspect that this is a manifestation of an admirable local pride: "Where I make my home is special and unlike anywhere else." But how different, really, are New York City's courts and criminals from those found in other sections of the country?

With respect to its courts, the difference is not one of type. The structural similarities among all local American criminal courts are so strong that it is accurate to speak of "the urban criminal court" as a distinct institutional form. The significant differences are really between upper and lower courts ("lesser and superior jurisdictions"), and between rural and urban ones, rather than between New York City's courts and all others. All are united by an essentially similar law of criminal procedure. Police make arrests; district attorneys' offices charge defendants and prosecute them on behalf of the public and the state; defense attorneys represent defendants. Judges manage the adjudication process, take convictions, and pass sentences. And, most importantly for our purposes here, plea bargaining practices found in New York City courts resemble those found elsewhere. Although the guilty plea rate is high in New York City, it is high in most places throughout the country, especially in the lower-level urban courts. In short, New York's courts are more similar to those elsewhere than they are different.

Instead of dismissing what happens in New York as irrelevant to other localities, innovations germinated in the city's courts deserve close scrutiny because they have frequently been copied nationwide. Moreover, the Vera Institute's role in creating many of these innovations has been central. In the mid-1960s, the institute's Manhattan Bail Project experimented with the greatly expanded use of release-on-recognizance (ROR) in lieu of bail, a reform that soon swept the country, culminating in the federal 1966 Bail Reform Act. In the early 1970s, the institute, in partnership with the Washington D.C. Bail Agency, kicked off what became another national reform movement: the pretrial diversion of youthful offenders. The institute's Court Employment Project sought to divert from further prosecution young defendants who might benefit from counselling and various forms of social assistance, and this innovation was copied in jurisdictions large and small across the United States. The institute also pioneered the Desk Appearance Tickets—issuing summonses to rather than arresting people suspected of committing lesser crimes or violations—and this tool has been adopted by police departments elsewhere. The Victim Witness/Assistance Project, also a Vera Institute creation, stimulated the nationwide growth of government services extended to victims of crimes. Other much-imitated innovations, developed not by the institute but by others in the New York court system, have included the establishment within prosecutors' offices of specialized bureaus for the handling of major offenses (from which career criminal bureaus have evolved) and units called "early case assessment" or "felony screening" bureaus, which screen incoming cases to determine which are to be selected for aggressive prosecution. This list of "Made in New York" court innovations could be much expanded, but the point is clear: New York has been a leader in court reform, rather than an island isolated from the rest of the country's practices.

Largely because of its visibility and reputation, the Vera Institute's experiment with community service sentencing is being watched to see if the received wisdom of the skeptics is being confirmed: that there exist iron laws that inevitably doom attempts to substitute nonincarcerative alternatives to prison and jail. This skepticism has its roots in the failure of pretrial diversion programs to accomplish their goals and in the difficulties reformers have faced in getting other community-based alternatives accepted by the courts as viable sentencing options. The institute's success or failure in this venture is likely to reverberate widely throughout this country and perhaps abroad as well.

The analysis presented in subsequent chapters follows several different tracks. It is primarily an in-depth examination of one particular experiment. I think that these findings have relevance for more general issues, however, and therefore I follow what I think are their implications for our knowledge of how the courts work, how sentencing and plea bargaining decisions are made, how and why reforms succeed and fail. Throughout I try to pull together two lines of contemporary research that have tended to run in separate directions: examinations of plea bargaining and court organization on the one side, and studies of judicial sentencing decisions on the other. Our capacity to understand and to change sentencing practices has been handicapped by the tendency to treat sentencing decisions separately from the process of guilty plea negotiation. A more powerful analytic approach draws upon and integrates both streams of research.

To determine how the introduction of the community service sentencing option affected the courts' sentencing practices, statistical models of actual sentencing decisions were constructed and then used to project how offenders' cases would have been resolved had the community service sentence not been available. These models yielded estimates of how often the community service sentence was used as a substitute for short jail terms. Information drawn from observation and from interviews with judges, attorneys, and project personnel was then examined to develop both a description of how and an explanation of why the reform initiative fared as it did in each of three different New York City courts.

This research strategy is a little used one, even though it relies upon statistical modelling techniques that are well established. It overcomes some of the limitations that have plagued attempts to assess a variety of different court and sentencing reforms. Evaluators have generally not been able to impose rigorously controlled experimental designs on the courts because they require some measure of randomized decision making. Before-and-after studies have also been difficult to implement because interest in evaluating policy reforms usually develops after reforms have occurred. All one can observe directly is the "after" state of affairs, and reconstructing a picture of how the courts worked before the reform was instituted is often difficult and very expensive. By developing statistical models of post-reform decision making, controls approximating those afforded by experimental methods can be imposed. By coupling these statistical techniques with ethnographic material derived from interviews and observation, one can develop not only good estimates of reform outcomes, but also a rich understanding of how courts accommodate, subvert, or otherwise respond to attempts to change them. This research strategy could be used to great advantage, I believe, in examinations of other types of reforms in the courts and in other institutional domains as well.

This book is organized in the following fashion. Chapter 1 describes the development of community service sentencing in this country and abroad, with special attention given to several important questions about the use of the sentence. The Vera Institute's Community Service Sentencing Project in the New York City courts is then described in chapter 2. Chapters 3 and 4 explore the impact this project has had upon the courts in three different boroughs of the city. The statistical methods used for this examination are described in plain English so that the lay person can easily understand them. A more technical description of the methods and assumptions used is reserved for the Appendix. Our study then turns to the persons who were given the sentence. More than eighty were interviewed at length to ascertain their views about the crimes they had committed and the sentences they had been ordered to serve. Their responses are analyzed in chapter 5. In chapter 6, we look at the question of whether public safety was affected by the use of the sentence. The recidivism of offenders sentenced to community service was measured and comparisons were drawn with other types of offenders to determine whether imposing jail sentences would have enhanced the courts' ability to prevent crime. Finally, the conclusion pulls together findings developed in the earlier chapters and summarizes the various costs and benefits resulting from the use of the sentence, which provides us with a basis for evaluating the wisdom of the experiment. We end with a discussion of the implications of our findings for our understanding of court reform strategies more generally.

Chapter One

Community Service Sentences in American Courts:
Promises and Problems

In 1966, municipal court judges in California's Alameda County instituted a program that was new to the American scene: large numbers of people convicted of traffic offenses were sentenced to perform unpaid labor, or "community service," as punishment.[1] Since then, judges across the country have imposed a variety of community service orders upon people convicted of many different kinds of crimes. For example, six Nebraska contractors, all convicted in federal court of rigging their bids for highway construction jobs, were given community service sentences as part of their punishment. One was ordered to establish a program to create jobs for released prisoners; another had to plan road improvements on a local Indian reservation.[2] Elsewhere, executives of a meat packing firm who were convicted of criminal violations were ordered to donate two hundred hours of service to a youth training project and to hire a specified number of paroled felons in their own company.[3] In Washington, D.C., a partner in a lobbying and public information firm was convicted of passing insider information about plans for a corporate takeover, permitting friends to make nearly a million dollars of profit in stock trading, and the judge imposed three hundred hours of community service and a ten thousand dollar fine.[4] The head of a major motion picture studio in Hollywood, convicted of cocaine possession, was ordered to make and distribute an educational film about drug abuse and its dangers.[5]

7

Although such sentences are most likely to make the newspapers if the crimes and the criminals are of the white-collar variety, community service orders have also been imposed upon poorer and less glamorous offenders. In the Vera Institute's project, for example, thieves, burglars, shoplifters, pickpockets, small-time drug peddlers, and other persons convicted of similarly minor offenses, paint nursing homes, repair park benches, do heavy manual labor in preparation for converting dilapidated ghetto buildings into low-income housing, and perform similar jobs without pay.

Such sentences extend and mix two much older traditions: ordering offenders to make restitution to victims for their offenses, and requiring convicts to undertake uncompensated labor. Ancient Babylonian, Greek, Roman, and Jewish law all contained provisions for calculating the compensation to be paid by offenders to their victims or their kin.[6] The Alameda county court's innovation was to make offenders repay the community at large rather than the specific victim, a twist that made it possible to apply the sanction in instances where there were no victimized persons (such as motoring offenses).

In creating their community service program, Alameda's judges also sheared the provision of uncompensated labor from its traditional connection to imprisonment sentences. Labor was a common feature of the early American workhouses and then of prisons as well; in warmer regions, chain gangs were also taken out of prison during the day to work the roads and fields.[7] But labor in and of itself was not generally considered the sentence. Rather, it was almost always used as an auxilliary to the deprivation of liberty, which was the principal punishment.[8] The California program was really the first to consider unpaid labor as a discrete sentencing option. A special agency was established to administer the orders, and it was designed to operate apart from the conventional correctional institutions. The provision for labor was thus no longer a supplement to one of the traditionally available sentences, but was considered a punishment in its own right.[9]

This Alameda program established the basic framework for the developments that followed. Its two essential features—service to the community rather than to victims, and the provision for unpaid labor outside custodial settings—have come to define community service as a distinct penal sanction available to the courts.

This development is significant because, since the introduction of probation during the first two decades of this century, there have been no enduring additions to the repertoire of criminal sanctions used by the courts. Community service may now be on the threshold of becoming a permanent institution. During the past decade, the use of this kind of sentence expanded quickly with much fanfare. Reports of the British experience spurred this development. In 1973, England's Home Office instituted a nationwide community service sentencing reform, demonstrating that the use of the sanction for offenders convicted of relatively serious crimes was feasible on a large scale.[10] (Earlier American usage of this kind of sentence was generally limited to very minor offenses, many of which were not even serious enough to be ranked as crimes.) In the mid-seventies, funding for community service projects on this side of the Atlantic began to flow in earnest, and enormous amounts of money were given for start-up costs. In 1976, the Law Enforcement Assistance Administration undertook a national effort to promote the sanction, and it provided the seed money for about 60 percent of all the adult community service programs that were to open their doors in the following years.[11] The Office of Juvenile Justice and Delinquency Prevention undertook in 1978 a massive initiative to do the same in the juvenile field. Over the next three years, it spent approximately $30 million to set up programs in eighty-five counties and states.[12]

By the late 1970s, specific statutory authorizations for community service existed in about a third of all the states in the United States,[13] and well over a hundred formally organized projects had been established. Surveys conducted in 1977 and 1978 counted fifty-eight organized community service programs for adult criminal offenders and another seventy for juveniles.[14] Whether the number has grown or declined since then is difficult to determine. When the federal funds dried up, more than half of the community service programs for juvenile offenders died.[15] No similar survey has been conducted to document the current state of programs in the adult courts. Some private foundations have come into the breach to aid existing programs and to start new ones, and some projects have managed to win a place in the budgets of their state and local governments. But a great many of the programs that were begun in the middle to late seventies have probably collapsed altogether or grown smaller.

These developments have had an impact beyond the formal establishment of community service programs, however. With increasing frequency, judges are fashioning community service sentences on their own, without having specially organized programs in their localities.[16] One survey, conducted in 1977, found that 46 percent of the sampled juvenile court judges imposed community service sentences of some sort, and the majority did so without relying on established programs.[17] (Most were probably supervised by local probation departments.) There may be a similarly broad diffusion of judge-made sentences for occasional offenders in the adult courts as well, but no one has yet documented how widespread this has become. The number of jurisdictions in which the sentence is used must number well into the hundreds.

The methods of imposing the sentence in the United States vary greatly from one courthouse to another, because the existing programs are home-grown rather than the offspring of a national policy decision, as they are in England. A wide diversity of schemes exists for determining how many hours of labor should be imposed for different kinds of offenses. Procedures for administering, monitoring, and enforcing the service obligation also differ.[18] In some jurisdictions, community service programs are operated by private agencies; in others they are established within existing probation departments.[19] Some are run out of sheriffs' departments.[20]

The statutory status of the sentence also varies greatly from one part of the country to another. In some states, community service is authorized only as a condition of probation. In others, it is a sentence sui generis; in still others it is imposed as a condition of a suspended sentence, of a discharge, and even as an obligation to be fulfilled before the imposition of formal sentences.[21] The actual practices of imposing the sentence are even more varied than the written laws suggest. In some states, judges can resentence offenders to community service after they have served time behind bars, even though the judges lack the legal authority to do so.[22] Trial courts across the nation have been remarkably creative in working with and around the legislatively established rules of criminal procedure, and there are probably dozens of extra-legal procedures that have emerged to accomodate judges' willingness to impose community service sentences.

The movement to expand the use of community service sentencing is now at a critical point in its development. A fast-growth period that was fed by federal funds has ended. If the existing community service projects are to be kept alive, and if judges are to rely upon the sanction more heavily in the future, local supporters are going to have to be convinced that this new sentencing practice makes sense. As long as the seedling projects had their bills paid by funds from the federal government or from private foundations, they enjoyed a kind of privileged status in their communities. Not having to compete for local tax dollars, they were often held to standards of performance that were more relaxed than might have been the case had they had to fight with other local agencies for funding. Their existence was not readily threatened if their caseloads were lower than originally hoped for or when the costs per sentence were higher than expected. In other words, they had time to prove themselves.

The sledding got rougher when the money ran out, however. The demise of the federal funding initiatives meant that managers of community service projects had to turn to state and local governments for their support. Unfortunately, the fiscal pressures on these governments have been intense since the mid-seventies, the result of several deleterious trends that have left many cities and counties close to bankruptcy. Bridges, highways, water, sewage, and transportation systems are literally falling apart across the country for lack of maintenance and replacement. Operating budgets of city and state governments have suffered deep cuts in most regions of the country, and many essential services have been declining.[23] This is a tough environment in which to survive, especially for new programs that lack well-established constituencies.

The future course of community service sentencing could run in either of two directions. Looking back from a vantage point of five or ten years hence, we might see it as but another of the fads California periodically sends out to the nation, which, after enjoying great popularity for a brief period, falls into disuse and disfavor. Of course, the opposite could also be true. Community service could become as common a sentence as probation or a fine. In Great Britain, upwards of eight hundred convicted criminals are performing community service throughout the country on any given Saturday.[24] In France, the government established a target of sentencing several thousand persons to community service during 1984.[25] Because the criminal courts in this country convict millions of people each year,[26] it is possible to imagine a future in which criminals numbering in the thousands would be working off their sentences on any particular day.

Substitutes for Imprisonment Sentences?

The most powerful impulse animating the creation of community service programs across the country came from the desire for a new sanction to be used in place of locking up offenders. By the late sixties and early seventies, policymakers and opinion leaders had grown skeptical about the ability of prisons to rehabilitate criminal offenders. The National Advisory Commission on Criminal Justice Standards and Goals declared in its 1973 report that "the institutional model for corrections has not been successful in curbing potential crime."[27] But not only were prisons failing to do good, many thought; they were also places of destruction.

The effectiveness of the prison as a school for crime is exaggerated, for the criminal can learn the technology of crime far better on the streets. The damage the prison does is far more subtle. Attitudes are brutalized, and self-confidence is lost. The prison is a place of coercion where compliance is obtained by force. The typical response to coercion is alienation, which may take the form of active hostility to all social controls or later a passive withdrawal into alcoholism, drug addiction, or dependency.[28]

To minimize the damaging effects of institutionalization, reformers argued that, whenever possible, criminals should not be placed in prisons. The principle that nonincarcerative programs should be preferred was endorsed by numerous prestigious commissions and standard-setting bodies.[29]

By the early 1970s a preference for "community-based corrections" had become a central tenet in the liberal creed prevailing in many policymaking circles. Even though crime rates had been rising steadily since the early 1960s and "law and order" rhetoric had played a crucial role in electoral campaigns, and even though new fads had appeared (preventive detention, for example) the interest in alternatives to incarceration remained strong. Liberal Democratic congressmen and women sat on the committees overseeing the Law Enforcement Assistance Administration and dominated the formulation of the priorities that governed its grant making decisions in corrections. These priorities embodied a clear preference for nonincarcerative alternatives.[30] In a booklet published by the Law Enforcement Assistance Administration describing its 1976 program objectives, the agency said "it places a high priority on community-based corrections—programs that appear to offer more hope of rehabilitation because they keep certain types of offenders in their community where they have family or social ties."[31] This priority was translated into millions of dollars given out that year and in the following years to establish community service sentencing projects across the nation. The eighty-five community service sentencing programs for juveniles created and supported by the U.S. Office of Juvenile Justice and Delinquency Prevention were expressly intended to serve as alternatives to incarceration.

But do judges actually use such sentences in the way that the liberal reformers had hoped, as substitutes for jail or prison sentences? Unfortunately, there have been only a few attempts to answer this question, despite the very large amount of money spent to achieve this objective. Of the four federally sponsored evaluation studies that examined the adult and juvenile community service and restitution programs, none addressed this central question in a satisfactory manner. (Indeed, three of the four were not expected to.)[32] This is partly because of an enormous difficulty in logic and method: How can one determine what judges would have done had they not sentenced offenders to community service? If the programs had not existed in the jurisdictions where they did in fact operate, the range of sanctions available to the judges at each sentencing decision would have been different and the constraints on their decisions would have been different.

Whether judges would have incarcerated more or fewer offenders is hard, if not impossible, to determine simply by looking at their decisions sentencing people to community service.

Although no researchers in this country have reported the kind of sophisticated investigation of this question that is needed, some have already drawn conclusions based on their rather impressionistic observations of several different programs. For example, James Beha and his colleagues, working under a grant from the Law Enforcement Assistance Administration, examined several community service programs and concluded in 1977 that:

The record of community service programs to date in the United States indicates that they have been used primarily for cases that might otherwise be handled by fine or probation, rather than for cases in which a jail sentence is the traditional alternative. In some situations this is an explicit facet of the program; elsewhere, it is simply a characteristic of the caseload.[33]

Alan Harland came to much the same conclusion in his review of statutory provisions for community service in this country. Drawing upon this review and a reading of the existing program descriptions, he wrote:

it is possible to conclude with considerable assurance that the offender sentenced to community service does not typically avoid incarceration thereby: instead the service is imposed in addition to his normal penalty, or, at best, in lieu of monetary sanctions.[34]

Eugene Doleshal added that the evaluations have demonstrated that:

community service is only marginally effective, if effective at all, as a means of reducing institutional overcrowding, correctional costs, recidivism, or probation caseloads. The reader may be left wondering what it is good for except to widen the net of social control.[35]

Judging from the writing on the subject, the jury seems to have returned its verdict: reforms that attempt to substitute community service sentences for imprisonment sanctions have failed. Looking at the failure of pretrial diversion programs to achieve their objective of shunting away from prosecution defendants who would otherwise have suffered significant penal consequences,[36] and what appear to be the similar failings of the community service programs, Doleshal concluded pessimistically that "there is a dynamic equilibrium in criminal justice which prevents those attempting to reform criminal justice by reducing penalties or incarceration rates from succeeding."[37] He saw that similar efforts in other countries had also failed, a finding that he used to buttress his proposition.

Little has emerged from research to encourage a belief in the possibility of success for criminal justice reforms that aim to divert offenders from institutional confinement, whether the attempt is made at the pretrial or at the post-conviction stage. But can one say that such efforts must fail? Are there iron laws that necessarily kill or at least subvert these reforms? I believe an affirmative answer to these questions is premature, for several reasons.

First, definitive judgments about community service orders cannot be made without methodologically sophisticated examination of actual sentencing practices in jurisdictions where community service programs exist. The studies of sentencing that have been done in this country are impressionistic at best. To date, the British government has published the most rigorous evaluations of community service sentencing, but even these are too limited for their findings to be seen as anything more than suggestive.[38] (Indeed, different readers have drawn different conclusions from them.)[39]

Secondly, we know too little about the relationships that almost certainly exist between the way community service sentencing reforms have come into being and operate and their success or failure at reducing the courts' reliance on imprisonment sentences. In their review of the literature on community service and restitution projects for the National Institute of Justice, Joe Hudson, Burt Galaway, and Steven Novack found very few reports in which the problems and processes of implementation were discussed. "The picture is that of vaguely conceptualized projects being implemented exactly as intended."[40] If we are to understand why the courts do or do not employ community service as an alternative to incarceration, we need case studies of these reform efforts that focus on the workings of the courts and on the process of implementation itself. In most jurisdictions, the question of success is not generally a matter of complete success or failure. Rather, it is a matter of degree: some judges probably do use the sanction in some instances in which the offender otherwise would have been incarcerated, and what varies is the proportion of cases where this occurs. By examining why some offenders bound for prison or jail are given community service and why others are not, one can begin to disentangle the processes that produced these results. If these processes were better understood, program design and implementation could better suit the reformers' aim to have community service used, when it is imposed, as a substitute for imprisonment. But none of the research published to date has paid close attention to the actual decision making processes in the courts in which community service sentences have been imposed. Consequently, we are far from being able to explain either how these courts respond, or why the courts respond as they do, to the introduction of the community service alternative.

Should Community Service Sentences Be Encouraged?

Beyond the question of whether community service sentences are used as substitutes for terms of imprisonment are more fundamental issues: Should this society endorse, as a matter of public policy, their use in lieu of jail or prison sentences? Should such a substitution be demanded of the courts? For some, there is no question. As Anne Newton declared:

Sentencing to community service or restitution provides an alternative to imprisonment which is positive from every point of view: It avoids the destructiveness of imprisonment, it is less costly than imprisonment, it holds the possibility of helping the offender, and it helps compensate the victim of crime for his loss.[41]

Others are less given to seeing such sentences as a panacea and question whether there are other penal concerns that are not being satisfied. For example, is a community service sentence punishment enough for the crimes that the offenders sentenced to it have committed? Does its use in lieu of imprisonment reduce public safety? As with other public policy issues, this one forces trade-offs among several different and perhaps even competing goals and principles.

Judgments about the propriety of sentencing particular kinds of offenders to community service ultimately turn on three primary considerations. (1) What are judges trying to achieve by imposing the sentence? (2) Do the judges' sentencing objectives, when they impose such sentences, conform to our own ideas of what we think the court should be trying to do? (And do those objectives square with what we deem to be legitimate principles for governing judges' sentencing decisions?) (3) Even if we agree that the sentencing objectives are sensible and just and are appropriately applied to specified kinds of offenders, do we have any evidence that the imposition of community service sentences achieves these objectives? Can we justify its use if it is not found to be a device for achieving the chosen objective?

A Practice In Search Of Theory?

Lacking a national policy to guide development of the community service sentence, program administrators and judges set their sights on many different goals. By the time the federal government assumed an active role in supporting the new reform, a decade had passed since the earliest of the community service programs had opened its doors, and a variety of different homegrown practices had already emerged. The federal government attempted to bring greater uniformity to the use of the sentence when it began dispensing grant money though the Law Enforcement Assistance Administration and the Office of Juvenile Justice and Delinquency Prevention, but this attempt met with limited success. Both agencies aimed to have the community service sentence used only as an alternative to incarceration. Unfortunately, such loose strings were attached to the grants that local decision makers were given great latitude in shaping their own particular programs and practices. The result was that local courts were effectively freed to use the new sanction for just about any purpose they chose.

The federal government's attempt to impose a uniformity of practice in sentencing was also hindered by the absence of a well-developed rationale supporting its stated objectives with regard to the sentence. Rather than articulating a persuasive answer to the question of why the courts should impose community service sentences instead of jail or prison, the federal agencies simply relied on the argument that community-based alternatives were more effective than imprisonment sentences in rehabilitating offenders. To be sure, such beliefs did command a following among many in the criminal justice community, but by the late seventies, these kinds of pronouncements were increasingly being seen as hollow rhetoric by large numbers of influential decision makers.

Some of the more theoretically minded advocates of the sentence sought to place it on a sturdier legal foundation by formulating a rationale linking its goals to the established principles and goals of more conventional sentencing options. All of this is still in a relatively tender stage of development, however, and community service sentencing is very much a practice in search of a theory. This complicates the task of assessing the sanction, because one cannot simply examine whether it fulfills its principal objectives.

This condition is not unique to this particular sanction or to this country. There is currently a great deal of controversy in the United States about why we sentence criminals at all and why any one sanction is to be preferred over another. Community service is thus a somewhat ill-defined sanction being introduced to the courts during a period when little consensus exists regarding sentencing and its goals. Even in Britain, where the sanction was introduced as a matter of national policy, a deliberate ambivalence pervaded the government's reasons for adopting the sentence. For example, the report of the Home Secretary's Advisory Council on the Penal System (commonly known as the "Wootton Committee" for its chairwoman, Baroness Wootton), which recommended the establishment of community service sentences, stated:

The proposition that some offenders should be required to undertake community service should appeal to different varieties of penal philosophy. To some, it would be simply a more constructive and cheaper alternative to imprisonment; by others it would be seen as introducing into the penal system a new dimension with an emphasis on reparation to the community; others again would regard it as giving effect to the old adage that the punishment should fit the crime; while still others would stress the value of bringing offenders into close touch with those members of the community who are most in need of help and support.[42]

Commenting upon the British use of community service, Kenneth Pease and his colleagues in the Home Office noted that "the penal theory underlying the scheme is thought by some to be uncertain. . . ."[43]

Rehabilitation

A rationale commonly given by judges for imposing community service sentences is that offenders may be rehabilitated. For example, Judge Dennis Challeen, a Minnesota county court judge who was an early advocate of the sentencing practice, argued that these sentences made sense because they "require offenders to make efforts toward self-improvement, thus removing them from their roles as losers and helping them to address their personal problems and character defects that alienate them from the mainstream of society."[44] The British policy was also powerfully motivated by a theory of offender rehabilitation in the community. Reformers there thought that by putting convicted criminals in voluntary service organizations, where they would work side by side with public-spirited citizens, a greater sense of civic responsibility might be instilled in them.[45]

Some argue that the rehabilitative effect of community service derives from its restitutive character. Joe Hudson, Burt Galaway, and Steve Novack, all of the University of Minnesota (and influential advocates for the sanction) wrote:

Restitution may be more rehabilitative than other correctional measures because it is rationally related to the amount of damages done, is a specific sanction which allows the offender to clearly know when requirements are completed, requires the offender's active involvement, provides a socially appropriate and concrete way of expressing guilt, and creates a situation in which an offender is likely to elicit a positive response from other persons.[46]

But does community service really rehabilitate offenders? The large body of studies that have examined the rehabilitative effects of other correctional "treatments" provides little reason for optimism regarding the power of the penal sanction to change peoples' lives.[47] With respect to the community service sentence, few studies have been published that offer any good evidence either suporting or rebutting the propostion that serving the sentence rehabilitates offenders.[48] Judge Challeen, for example, reports that the recidivism rate of offenders sentenced to community service in his court was 2.7 percent, compared to a 27 percent rate for persons released from jail.[49] But seemingly conclusive statements such as these actually tell us very little.

Comparisons of recidivism rates, however they are defined, are of little value unless they are based on rigourous comparisons between similar groups of people. Persons sent to jail are typically more persistant lawbreakers than those give lesser sentences, and this undoubtedly explains most if not all of the observed difference in post-sentencing criminality. Unless we are told that recidivism studies explicitly account for such differences in the composition of their comparison groups, we have little reason to grant their findings much significance. To be sure, community service may indeed produce some measure of reform, but we need much better research studies if we are to base our claims on anything more than faith.

Restitution

Another commonly given objective of the community service sentence is to make offenders pay the community back. Asked why his office supported the use of community service sentences, one high-level prosecutor pointed out his office window to New York City's South Bronx and said, "That neighborhood needs a lot of fixing up, and it's right that these guys be made to do it." One may wonder what kind of penal theory underlies this goal, however. Many proponents and observers have classified community service as a form of restitution, thereby tying it to a penal practice with a longstanding tradition.[50] Although this may suffice to endow the community service order with a halo of legitimacy and respectability, one can question whether it really does constitute restitution. Historically, restitution has involved compensating directly the crime victim or the victim's kin. Persons sentenced to community service almost never provide that, which is why their service to the community at large is sometimes called "symbolic restitution." Paying back someone other than the victim might be seen as restitution, if one conceives of the community in general as being the victim of crime, but this stretches, I think, the concept of restitution pretty thin.

How to categorize community service is largely a semantic issue, a matter of theoretical definition, but it does raise important policy-related questions. If community service is a form of restitution, is the pay-back perceived by the larger society, and by the victims, as adequate compensation for the crimes that were committed? Is the exchange a fair and just one? Is the obligation to perform unpaid labor for fifty, three hundred, or even a thousand hours an appropriate penalty for a public official convicted of abusing the peoples' trust by accepting a bribe for favors? For a young thief who breaks into someone's house at night and steals valuable belongings while the owners are asleep in bed? For someone convicted of roughing somebody up and stealing her pocketbook? If unpaid labor is to be conceived as a restitutive exchange, how does one translate into hours of community service the sense of violation that burglary victims feel or the trauma experienced by a banged-up victim of a purse snatching? The absence of readily discernable equivalencies in nature requires that they be established by agreements among people. Such agreements, either in the form of guidelines or more hardened policies, are needed if the courts are to avoid imposing community service sentences thought to be either inappropriately lenient or excessive. (The absence of clearly established guidelines has resulted in some exceedingly punitive sentences for relatively trivial offenses—requiring thousands of hours of community service for littering public parks with beer cans, for example.[51])

If offenders are sentenced to community service as payment for their crimes, do they really perceive their labor as restitutive? Is it more clearly restitutive, from their perspective, than "paying one's debt to society" by being locked up would be? The offenders' perceptions in this regard are certainly important, especially if we hang hopes for rehabilitation upon the restitutive nature of the sanction. Do offenders really see the connection between their victims' suffering and their labor? An even more basic question is whether they see their crimes as involving victims at all. One New York City thief, convicted of stealing a radio from a car and sentenced to community service, said there was no victim to his crime because:

I don't be pulling knives on people or stealing from their apartments. I don't steal from poor people. I steal from people who have a little extra and I take the little shit.[52]

Another shoplifter denied he had victimized anyone, saying "the glasses were in the store and I took them. He [the owner] didn't even know until someone told him."[53] Is the connection between their unpaid labor and their crime too tenuous in the offenders' minds for them to perceive it as restitution? Is the sentence seen merely as another harrassment visited upon them by the government? If it is, does this mean that the objectives of restitution are being frustrated? Must there be a subjective recognition of this compensatory act for community service to be embraced as a desirable penal sanction?

Inflicting the Least Harm

For some advocates, then, the objective of getting community service sentences accepted and used as substitutes for imprisonment is not an end in and of itself, but rather a means of achieving other more conventionally defined penal goals—rehabilitation or restitution, for example. But for many others, achieving this substitution is itself the goal. The posture of these advocates is not derived from the penal goals that moral philosophers have discussed for centuries, but from a principled position regarding the use of state power. The issue was elegantly framed by Francis Allen, the former dean of the University of Michigan Law School. In his effort to rescue thinking about the criminal sanction from those scientific criminologists dedicated to the rehabilitative ideal, he wrote:

[I]f the function of criminal justice is considered in its proper dimensions, it will be discovered that the most fundamental problems in these areas are not those of psychiatry, sociology, social case work, or social psychology. On the contrary, the most fundamental problems are those of political philosophy and political science. The administration of the criminal law presents to any community the most extreme issues of the proper relations of the individual citizen to state power. We are concerned here with the perennial issue of political authority: Under what circumstanes is the state justified in bringing its force to bear on the individual human being? These issues, of course, are not confined to the criminal law, but it is in the area of penal regulation that they are most dramatically manifested.

The criminal law, then, is located somewhere near the center of the political problem, as the history of the twentieth century abundantly reveals. It is no accident, after all, that the agencies of criminal justice and law enforcement are those first seized by an emerging totalitarian regime. In short, a study of criminal justice is fundamentally a study in the exercise of political power. No such study can properly avoid the problem of the abuse of power.[54]

Throughout most of the history of our republic, the balance of power and right in the penal realm has been struck far in the state's favor. For example, a ruling in 1871 by a Virginia court declared that a prisoner "is for the time being the slave of the state."[55] Although this ruling applied only to prisoners, a similar spirit infected the treatment of other convicted criminals as well, for they were stripped of many of their legal rights of citizenship. Since the mid-sixties, however, this balance has been shifted considerably. The courts have much expanded the rights of prisoners, charged defendants, and convicted persons generally.[56]

This development has affected discussions of sentencing. Several prestigious commissions and standard-setting bodies have articulated a preference for imposing the least severe sanction, other considerations being equal. For example, the American Bar Association's standards, promulgated in 1968, include the following provision as one of the four general principles to govern sentencing: "a sentence not involving confinement is to be preferred to a sentence involving partial or total confinement in the absence of affirmative reasons to the contrary."[57] Thus, community-based correctional programs such as community service were recommended not only because they were thought to be more effective vehicles for the rehabilitation of criminal offenders, but also because they protected the offender from the overly harsh use of state power. This is why the concern for how the sentence is actually being used is of such central importance for many observers. If it has not been used in place of imprisonment sentences and has been used as an additional penalty levied on top of other nonincarcerative sanctions, it would be condemned as an unwarranted and unwanted intensification of the state's social control powers.[58]

These three objectives—rehabilitating criminal offenders, obtaining restitution for the community, and restraining the punitive power of the state—motivated most of those who advocated community service sentencing during the first decade of the reform. This agenda also established the terms of the debate about the use of the sentence. Evaluating the success or failure of the reform focused upon whether the net of social control was being intensified or extended and whether offenders were really being rehabilitated by the sanction. That it was a restitutive sanction was typically taken for granted.

The Reemergence of Crime Control and Punishment Doctrines

The policy and political environment in which the community service sentence was marketed and evaluated has been changing dramatically, particularly during the past half-decade or so, and many would argue that the objectives of rehabiliting offenders and restraining the state's coercive powers are no longer relevant to debates about what should be asked of the courts. For most of this century, up until the mid-seventies, there prevailed a relatively stable consensus regarding the use of the criminal sanction by the courts and corrections. Our preeminant national objective in penal matters was to rehabilitate criminal offenders. The three main correctional institutions—prisons, parole, and probation—were oriented toward this end, and the sentencing laws established by legislatures were designed with this object in mind.

In the late sixties and early seventies, however, faith in our ability to do this waned. Influential criminologists, surveying the research literature that had been accumulating over the years, concluded that "nothing works" in the rehabilitation of offenders.[59] This was dismaying news, especially in the face of crime rates that were escalating higher and higher as the baby boom generation came of age. Civil libertarians, shocked by the increasingly publicized abuses of prison and parole systems, and especially by the Attica riots in 1971 and their aftermath, attacked the principles that were being used to justify the relatively unfettered discretionary power of the courts and correctional officials—primarily the rhetoric of rehabilitative penology.[60] The consensus that had prevailed for decades was shattered and rehabilitative principles were dethroned. Since the mid-seventies, the arena of sentencing policy has been riven by deep conflicts as proponents for one or another principle jockey for dominance.[61] No new consensus has emerged to replace the reign of rehabilitation in sentencing and corrections.

Even though many judges remain interested in rehabilitation, most legislators and penal theoreticians, in their recent works on sentencing policy, have turned their attention to justifying punishment and constructing rules for its imposition, and to crime control objectives. Retribution, long viewed with distaste and seen as a "primitive" motivation running contrary to enlightened penology, became fashionable once again in the mid-seventies. Ironically, the concept was resurrected first by liberals interested in establishing a limiting principle for sentencing decisions. That is, the "desert theory" of justice prescribed that punishments be proportionate to the crimes committed. This suggested an alternative justification for sentencing people to community service and for imposing other nonincarcerative punishments: less serious crimes deserve to be punished by penalties that are less coercive and less painful than imprisonment.[62] Talk of punishment is back in style and community service is now being advertised as a punitive sanction. "The most common political problem during the early life of the community service and restitution was that it was driven by a social premise, that work was good for the offender," said Mark Corrigan, the director of the National Institute for Sentencing Alternatives at Brandeis University. "That was a liability, because there's been a disenchantment with doing things for the offender. . . . Now we're seeing a second wave in the growth of programs, because it's looked upon as a good way to punish. That makes it ideologically attractive to many people."[63]

With regard to sentencing decisions, the principle of retribution is backward-looking: judges are asked to calculate how much punishment should be imposed by looking at the gravity of the crime. But the courts are also expected by many to do something about the future, to do something in order to reduce crime. The answer to that concern used to be rehabilitation. Confidence in our ability to achieve that has declined however, and more attention is now being paid to crime control via deterrence and incapacitation. Penal codes across the country have been stiffened in the hopes of deterring would-be criminals. Now, perhaps because the crime control gains (if there have been any) from this deterrent strategy are hard to see, penal codes in many places are being made tougher still—not for more deterrence, but in an attempt to control crime through incapacitation. Even if imprisonment does little else to reduce crime, at least it incapacitates criminals for the duration of their stay, thereby eliminating their opportunities for committing further crimes in the larger society. The recent emergence of incapacitation as a principal goal of sentencing has led many legislatures to promulgate laws that give sentencing judges no alternative but imprisonment for all persons convicted of certain specified crimes—violent crimes in most jurisdictions, but also drug and handgun-related offenses in others. Repeat offenders, whether violent or not, are also subjected in many states to mandatory minimum prison sentences.[64]

This turn of events and opinion has important implications for our thinking about community service sentences. To the extent that these concerns for punishment as an objective in its own right, and for crime control as the desired result of sentencing practice, weigh on the minds of judges as policy makers, community service will be measured according to its ability to inflict punishment and to reduce crime. It is probably not enough these days to argue that the sanction should be used because it offers some promise of rehabilitation, or because the community gets something back, or because nonincarcerative penal sanctions are to be preferred over more coercive ones as a matter of principle. Those who take responsiblity for the use of the sentence will want to know whether the sentence is perceived as being a punitive enough response to crime, whether relying on it significantly weakens the deterrent power of the law, and whether the loss of the incapacitating capability of prisons and jails is worth whatever positive benefits the sentence may afford. Unfortunately, these questions lie on the frontiers of our knowledge. Very few studies have addressed them and none have done so satisfactorily.

The Question of Costs and Resources

During the decade from the early sixties to the early seventies, before the abandonment of the rehabilitation ethos, this country was reducing its use of imprisonment. The number of persons sentenced to jail or prison declined steadily, as did the incarceration rate, measured as the proportion of the U.S. population under the jurisdiction of correctional authorities. By 1973, the incarceration rate for state and federal prisons had dipped lower than it had been since the mid-1920s. In 1974, when the widespread faith in criminal rehabilitation was being shattered, both the total population incarcerated and the incarceration rates began to rise precipitously.[65] Stiffer laws were passed; judges in many states lost the option of imposing nonincarcerative sanctions for various kinds of offenses; and parole boards turned more conservative as they faced a public calling more stridently for the abolition of their functions. By 1980, the incarceration rate had surpassed the previous peak, which had been reached in the 1930s. Each year since 1980, incarceration rates have set new records.[66] At no time in the history of the American republic has there been so large a proportion of its citizens in jail or prison.[67] By midyear 1983, 432,000 people were being held in state and federal prisons, and about half as many more were held in local jails across the country.[68] This is more than twice the number behind bars in the late 1960s and early 1970s.

The impact on prison conditions and government financing has been calamitous. Prisons and jails have become severely crowded, and by 1983, facilities in thirty-three states had come under court orders to rectify conditions found to be in violation of the Constitution's prohibition against cruel and unusual punishment.[69] With prison populations chalking up growth rates in excess of 10 percent a year, state and local governments have been spending more and more of their tax dollars to construct new prisons at a cost of thirty-four thousand to one hundred and ten thousand dollars per cell (which does not include the cost of financing this amount if the funds are borrowed by means of bonding).[70] Beyond these steep construction costs, very high operating costs are also at stake. In New York State, for example, the direct operating cost to the taxpayer of locking up one state prisoner for one year averaged about twenty-three thousand dollars in 1983. In New York City's jails, the average annual cost that year was thirty thousand dollars.[71] These costs vary widely from one jurisdiction to another, but New York's costs are probably not terribly different from what the rest of the country pays.[72] Imprisonment is a very costly method of control and punishment, and governments (especially at the state and local level) have been badly squeezed by the declining economy.

It is this fiscal pressure that has rekindled interest in community-based corrections. Whereas community service was favored in the late sixties and early seventies because it was less onerous than imprisonment, it has found new fans because it promises to be less expensive. Even U.S. Attorney General William French Smith, a member of an administration that came into power calling for law and order, has endorsed the concept of cost-effective alternatives to incarceration. "We must recognize that we cannot continue to rely exclusively on incarceration and dismiss other forms of punishment," he said in a speech delivered in 1983. Alternatives to prison, such as community service, "should be available only in limited cases for nonviolent criminals where the sanction is sufficient to punish the offender. . . . We simply cannot afford to ignore alternative forms of punishment."[73]

But will a policy of encouraging community service sentences actually save governments and taxpapers money? It will not if those given the sentence would not have received more costly punishments in its absence. And even if offenders otherwise bound for prison or jail are sentenced to community service, will their numbers be large enough to generate real savings in prison and jail budgets? Diverting a few people from custody does not incur a savings of twenty or thirty thousand dollars (or whatever the average annual cost per prisoner happens to be in a particular locality). Patterns of staffing the prisons and jails do not change radically with a drop of a few dozen in the prisoner population (or even a few hundred, in some institutions). Depending upon how the courts actually use the sanction and upon the nature of the alternatives available in each locality, sentencing offenders to community service may bring about enormously worthwhile benefits or may amount to a costly and foolish policy. The following chapters examine one city's experience with this new practice with an eye to making such an assessment.

Chapter Two

The New York City Community
Service Sentencing Project

In the closing days of 1978, after two years of negotiations and planning, the Vera Institute of Justice launched its Bronx Community Service Sentencing Project in the Bronx County Criminal Court. Within three years, similar units had been established in the lower courts of Brooklyn and Manhattan. By 1983, the city-wide project stabilized at its desired intake level, which was about one thousand sentenced offenders per year.[1]

This chapter describes the early development of the project and its expansion into three borough courts, the kinds of unpaid services that the offenders perform, the rationale for the project that guided its design, the active role that its staff plays in the plea negotiation process, and the way the project managers and the courts enforce the sanction. Rather than giving a month-by-month account of the many issues that were raised and resolved, this chapter is intended to serve as a general introduction to the project and as a backdrop for more detailed analyses of the topics that follow in subsequent chapters.

The Bronx Project Opens its Doors

By Christmas of 1978, the groundwork had been completed for the Community Service Sentencing Project (which was often referred to by Vera Institute officials as the "pilot project," a choice of words that indicated their expectation that similar units would be created elsewhere after the bugs had been ironed out). An office was found in the Bronx County courthouse and the project was in-

30

stalled there. This choice of headquarters was a revealing one. Rather than simply announcing to judges that they would supervise offenders ordered to perform community service, the institute's managers chose a more active stance. Full-time court representatives, or "court reps" for short, were hired and given the job of identifying prospective candidates for the sentence (and screening out inappropriate ones) even before they were convicted. They were to involve themselves actively in guilty plea negotiations because decisions reached in these negotiations often determine what the sentence will be.

During the second week of 1979, these new court representatives began to screen case files in the district attorney's office in search of prospective candidates for the sentence. Several defendants were rejected by the prosecutors because they wanted jail sentences. Others were rejected by defense attorneys because they hoped to obtain less onerous dispositions. A few days before the end of January, all parties to the negotiations agreed to take a plea from a thirty-one year old thief, whom we shall call "Warren."[2]

Warren had been arrested for stealing a twenty dollar pair of pants from Alexander's, a large department store. He claimed that he was going to sell them in order to support his infant child. This was not his first arrest; he had been arrested twenty-three times before, mostly for petty crimes such as shoplifting and possession of illegal drugs. Seventeen of these had resulted in convictions, four of them for burglary and one for robbery and assault. This latter conviction had earned him a five-year prison sentence in 1966. More recently, his crimes had gotten him a number of shorter sentences in the fifteen- to forty-five-day range.

The charge for stealing the pants was a minor one, and the assistant district attorney handling the case agreed to the community service sentence. Warren's attorney thought that he faced a strong chance of getting yet another jail term because of his record. Eager to avoid this, he agreed to recommend that Warren take a plea to the project. The court representative then interviewed Warren to see if he might be a problem on the work site. Warren admitted that he had a fifteen-year problem with drug addiction and had recently been hospitalized for alcohol detoxification. He was currently enrolled in a methadone clinic, where he reported daily for his dosage. His wife was also a drug addict and was about to go to the hospital. Warren was anxious to avoid a jail sentence because he wanted to care for their child. A call to the methadone clinic established that he was at least regular in his attendance there; his criminal record also revealed that he had never missed a scheduled day in court, despite his long string of arrests. The project accepted Warren, and the judge pronounced the sentence: an order to perform seventy hours of unpaid community service in the Vera Institute project. (More precisely, the judge imposed a conditional discharge, with the requirement that Warren perform the unpaid community service.[3])

Warren presented project officials with a preview of what would happen frequently during the coming months with subsequently sentenced offenders. Due to report to the project the next morning, he didn't show up. Project staff searched for him for the next two days (a weekend) and finally found him at his methadone clinic on Monday. He thought that community service was a light slap on the hand, not to be taken seriously. "I never thought you'd come looking for me," he said. "I just didn't think it mattered." Afraid that he would be sent to jail, he agreed to come back to project headquarters and begin his work.

Warren did report afterward but he needed a good deal of support to finish his sentence. His home life was chaotic; he had spent all of his public assistance funds and was without money until the next month's check arrived. Project officials provided him with emergency funds and spent a good deal of time counseling him on his family troubles. Despite the turmoil in his life and because of the staff support, Warren worked very hard cleaning up a senior citizens' center. He completed his required seventy hours, returned to court, and his sentence was changed to an unconditional discharge.

Slowly, the courts agreed to sentence others to community service. During the first three months, between five and seven persons were sentenced in this way each month. The project began to build a track record, however, and the numbers began picking up. Twelve months after Warren was sentenced, the project had supervised 120 offenders. The tally had risen to 331 by the end of the second year and to 508 by the end of the third.

Moving into Brooklyn and Manhattan

In December of 1980, twenty-two months after the Bronx project began full operations, a separate project was opened by the Vera Institute in the Brooklyn Criminal Court. By the end of the first year's operation, 110 offenders had been sentenced by the Brooklyn Criminal Court to the institute's project. By the end of the second year, 294 persons had been sentenced to community service in this borough.

A third unit was then established in the Manhattan Criminal Court in September 1981, and it "took off like a rocket," in the words of one of the people who had planned the project. Within three months of getting its first sentenced offender, fifty-nine persons had been given community service orders, compared to twenty-one the first three months in Brooklyn and seventeen by that time in the Bronx. Within six months, 138 offenders had been sentenced to the Manhattan unit. By the end of September 1982, twelve months after opening its doors, a total of 354 offenders had been sentenced to Manhattan Community Service Sentencing Project, more than had been sentenced during a two-year period in either the Bronx or Brooklyn courts.[4]

Services Performed

Those sentenced to community service work in crews were supervised by institute-employed foremen, a practice different from that found almost everywhere else in the world where the sentence is used. In England, for example, judges order local probation and after-care committees to place offenders in either voluntary service or public organizations.[5] Elsewhere in this country, offenders are typically placed in existing organizations (such as public parks departments).[6] The Vera Institute's planners thought this arrangement unlikely to win broad acceptance in New York City because they believed it would be difficult to find agencies willing to take on the responsibility for supervising thieves with poor work habits. The institute's earlier supported work program showed that small and closely supervised work teams were the most reliable and most easily accepted in community workplaces.[7] Because project foremen could ensure that offenders would not be left to wander about and get into trouble, the institute's planners adopted this small-team model for the community service project. Institute-employed site supervisors were hired to work as foremen to monitor attendance, direct the work, and move offenders from one work site to another during working hours.

Because criminal offenders are forbidden by New York statute to provide unpaid services to profit-making enterprises while working off their sentences, the institute's project managers located their different work sites in public or not-for-profit agencies.[8] During the first few years, these included community-owned nursing homes, city parks, churches, local YMCA branches, an organization restoring run-down and abandoned buildings for low-income housing, senior citizens' centers, day care centers, Salvation Army centers, and community gardens, among others.[9] Most of the work done in the Bronx and Brooklyn, however, involved maintenance tasks at a few large agencies. Bronx teams concentrated their efforts at two senior citizens' centers, and even had a small office and meeting room in one. Offenders mopped and waxed floors, moved boxes of food and furniture, shoveled snow in the winter, and performed a variety of other upkeep tasks. In Brooklyn, crews did similar kinds of work at a large community-owned nursing home in the Bedford-Stuyvesant area. They also painted walls and ceilings, installed smoke detectors, and sorted clothes there.

The kinds of work performed by the crews changed in October 1981 as a result of the project's obtaining federal community development funds. These federal funds are restricted to the rehabilitation of indoor and outdoor locations or to the remedying of blighted conditions within certain areas designated by New York City's government. Regular maintenance work cannot be supported by these funds. As a consequence of this changed pattern of revenues, project managers almost completely abandoned maintenance tasks for their work crews and directed their energies to community development work. This included making abandoned buildings useable or transforming them from one use to another and clearing rubbish from abandoned lots in the city so that they could be used for recreational space. Crews went into buildings and removed debris, insulated pipes, plastered, installed sheetrock, removed and replaced tiles, tore down wallpaper, did light carpentry work and painting, and other similar tasks. In Manhattan, the crews worked almost exclusively with a non-profit community corporation that is restoring West Harlem neighborhoods. Buildings that have been abandoned or neglected are taken over by this organization, renovated, and then either sold or rented to low-income residents of the community. Construction teams are employed by the organization to do the major renovation work, but the Vera Institute community service crews do a good portion of the less skilled but nonetheless demanding physical labor.

These work crews have been well received, by and large, in the communities. No systematic survey was made of agencies using the community service crews, but our researchers picked up comments and impressions in a somewhat haphazard way as they were collecting other kinds of information. There have been remarkably few complaints of theft from agency sites, quite a surprise given that the work crews are comprised of convicted thieves, often with very long records. This is largely attributable to the close supervision offenders are given by the site foremen. Many of the recipient agencies have given the offenders very high praise for their work. It is clear that the benefit to these agencies is often substantial, because the dollar value of the offenders' contributed services has sometimes been quite high.

The most serious constraint on placing offenders in the community has not been people's worries about having criminals in their midst, but rather the competition with other paid workers. In the mid-1970s, New York City's government suffered a severe crisis in its revenues and responded by cutting back services and laying off a very large proportion of its public employees workforce. Not surprisingly, many of those workers remaining on the payrolls were worried about whether they would be displaced by unpaid laborers working off their sentences. On one occasion in Brooklyn, for example, the project in that borough was asked by a city agency to put offenders in one of the local parks to help with clean-up and light maintenance tasks. Regular Parks Department employees balked at this and halted the offenders the first morning they arrived ready for work. Negotiations were undertaken that same day between management of the project, the Parks Department, and the officials of the employees' union. An agreement was reached to permit offenders to do some limited work. Few such collisions have occurred, simply because project managers are careful not to place crews in work situations in which they may appear to be displacing other paid employees, or where they may appear to be threatening such a displacement. At the current level of the institute's projects' operations, it is not difficult to find any number of public and private not-for-profit agencies that need tasks performed that are not being done by any other employees.

By the end of 1983, about twenty-four hundred offenders sentenced by the courts in the three boroughs to the Vera Institute's projects had worked without pay for approximately 142,800 hours, or the equivalent of about seventy-eight man/years.[10]

The Seventy-hour Requirement

All persons convicted and sentenced to community service in the institute projects are ordered to perform seventy hours of unpaid labor, even though they have committed different crimes and, it could be argued, are deserving of differing degrees of punishment. In setting this fixed schedule for all offenders, the institute diverged again from practices that prevailed elsewhere in this regard. In England, for example, judges are permitted by law to set the number of hours to be served anywhere between forty and two hundred and forty.[11] This enables judges to try to scale the penalty to the gravity of the offense. Early in the planning stage, the institute's managers rejected this approach, despite the preference for it expressed by the Bronx District Attorney's office. They thought that a fixed number of hours would minimize disparities in the way the courts used the sentence. Because the sanction was a new one, the courts had no experience in developing standards to match offenses with hours worked. For example, is three hundred hours an impossible requirement to fulfill or is it a mere slap on the hand? Is seventy hours? Some jurisdictions have tried to establish standards by creating what amounts to an exchange rate: one day worked equals a ten dollar fine, two days equals twenty dollars, etc.[12] One possibility would have been to construct a similar scale for jail sentences and work obligations: for example, one day in jail could have been made equivalent to two or three days of unpaid community service. In the end, the institute planners cast their votes against such a strategy. What was needed was a work obligation that was, in the words of one planner, "more positive, less burdensome and less costly than jail time, but more burdensome, more likely to be enforced, and thus, more credible than the present alternatives to jail."[13] Planners hoped that a seventy-hour term of continuous, unpaid work would be seen as punishing to persons not accustomed to regular and disciplined labor, yet it would not be such a crushing burden as to seem impossible to complete, inviting failure. The choice of seventy hours was somewhat arbitrary, but it was not quite pulled out of thin air; this was the average amount of time that English offenders were ordered to give at the time the Vera Institute was designing its own program.[14]

Why Encourage Community Service Sentences at All?

The institute created its community service project with the hope that the courts would use it as a substitute for short jail sentences. In addition, the institute's managers sought to provide a new sentence that would be used as a substitute for lesser sanctions as well. This was less an indication of schizophrenic ambivalence than a consciously designed two-pronged strategy (although this dual aim did generate tensions that significantly affected the way the project operated, as shall be discussed more fully in subsequent chapters). Explaining why these particular objectives were chosen requires some backtracking.

The definition of the project's basic mission evolved in the course of discussions during 1976–1977 among several different persons in New York City. The director of a South Bronx redevelopment organization proposed to the institute that arrangements be made to put convicted offenders to work in her organization to serve out their sentences, a suggestion that was resurrected several months later in discussions between Vera Institute planners and the New York City mayor's office. The main proponents of the plan in the mayor's office saw that the proposed sanction might alleviate a pressing problem. The city's jail system was badly overburdened, and a community service sentence used by the courts in lieu of a jail sentence would help to hold down escalating correctional costs.[15] A federal judge had ruled a few years earlier that one of the city's jails—"The Tombs" in Manhattan—had been operating in violation of the U.S. Constitution's Fourteenth Amendment, chiefly because of its overcrowded conditions.[16] This jail was closed and all prisoners being brought into the Manhattan criminal courts had to be held in other facilities on Rikers Island, a large city-run penal colony located in the Long Island Sound offshore from Queens. This exacerbated overcrowding in the city's remaining facilities, which in turn generated enormous pressures within city government to find solutions.

The mayor's assistants also liked the concept because it held some promise for solving another perceived problem. They thought that thousands of offenders were escaping punishment for lesser but nonetheless serious crimes because the overburdened courts lacked appropriate sanctions for them.[17] Offenders charged with unauthorized use of automobiles ("joyriding") and various other property crimes often avoided jail unless they had relatively heavy previous criminal records. The other available sanctions were seen as being far less than perfect instruments of justice. In these cases, city government officials worried that imposing fines on unemployed thieves only drove them to steal more. Assigning petty criminals to the already over-burdened probation departments for long periods of surveillance and counseling seemed to make little sense in many cases, because a punishment rather than rehabilitation-oriented social service was needed. Imposing conditional or unconditional discharges was thought to be insufficient punishment for offenses needing more burdensome sanctions. In short, the courts and the city corrections agencies had a very limited menu.[18] Community service orders might help to fill in the gaps.

The Vera Institute decided, therefore, to create a community service project that would address two objectives. It would aim to draw half of its project's participants from that group of offenders who would otherwise have gone to jail. The other half would include offenders not headed for jail but charged with offenses requiring some punitive response. The leader of the institute's planning team addressed this issue in a memo, responding to a question from a potential funder of the project, which is worth quoting at some length for what it reveals about the effort's overall design.

The conventional view, these days, is that programs should be avoided to the extent that they increase either the number of people who are under the net of social control or the intensity of that control (its burdensomeness, for example). This is an appealing view, and I share it to some extent. . . .

But this by no means disposes of the issue. There is another view, which might be stated as follows: the net of social control is presently inadequate—society does not even attempt to control the great bulk of offenders who are brought before the courts, but releases them after dismissal of the cases, or upon illusory sentences such as probation or conditional discharge, or (stated a bit more moderately) the formal process is not equipped with effective sanctions short of incarceration with which to signify to offenders that violation of laws will not be tolerated.

It seems to me that this second view has too much merit to be ignored when concerns are raised about widening the net of social control. Empirically, is our net of social control too wide or not? Reasonable men can and do differ, but I think it clear that, in New York and other urban centers with overburdened criminal justice systems, the system's response to admitted or proven violations of law—even quite serious and injurious violations—is often insufficiently burdensome for intelligent citizens to take the prospect of arrest and prosecution very seriously. Sadly, our repertoire of sanctions for crime is poorly designed to meet this problem. Those who feel the net of social control to be too limited call for more prison space and more prison sentences, or, even less acceptably, make use of system inefficiencies (delays between arrest and arraignment, for example) to make the process punitive because the dispositions are not.

Philosophically, the proposed community service sentencing project aims at the middle ground. Clearly, it assumes that some short jail sentences are imposed not because the behavior deserves imprisonment nor because the offender is perceived to be a danger to society unless incapacitated, but because no other disposition available to the court imposes any enforceable burden or punishment on the offender as a consequence of the offense. And the project aims to offer a punishment which has certain (stated) advantages when compared to imprisonment.

Up to this point, it is fair to say that the project aims to reduce the net of social control, at least by making use of a sanction less onerous than maximum security confinement in certain cases where that would otherwise be the disposition. . . .

But the proposed project is also expected to lead to the imposition of enforceable community service obligations on persons who would otherwise have been given sentences of probation or fine. Inevitably, some of those sentenced to the project would otherwise have received a conditional or unconditional discharge (although the frequency of this cannot be very great unless legal aid attorneys completely abdicate their responsibilities to their clients). As the proposal indicates, the program objective is to draw 50 percent of its participants from jail and 50 percent from the non-custodial sanctions. . . .

Given these program objectives, however, the question remains whether it is possible in good conscience to introduce a new penal sanction, designed to be at least as burdensome as probation (although the nature of the burden is different in important ways) and more burdensome than the various discharges and fines (unless, as is sometimes the case, the fine is enforced and non-payment leads to jail). The answer, I think, depends on a balancing of value judgments. If one believes that the less consequence there is to criminal conduct the better—and that view is, in my view, irrational—then the proposed project is 50 percent a mistake even in its design. If, however, one takes the view—which I do—that there are important social utilities to due process punishment for violation of criminal law, the proposed project makes sense by reducing the punitive aspect of the sanction in jail-bound cases, by preserving or increasing the punitive element of the other sanctions in cases not headed to jail, and—most importantly—by giving positive content to the sanction, regardless of whether it would otherwise have been jail. From this perspective, the community service sentence is but one of what should be a series of graduated punishments to fill the present void between no-sanction-at-all and imprisonment.[19]

In their discussions, the institute's planners often used the imagery of "driving a wedge into the seam of the tariff schedule," which is to say, into that "void between no-sanction-at-all and imprisonment." Doing so, it was hoped, would give judges greater flexibility in tailoring punishments to offenders for their crimes. Conceiving of their mission in such a fashion had important consequences for the way offenders were to be selected for community service, for the choice of the order's legal status, and for how the order would be justified, advertised, and enforced.

Regulating the Mix

Because the institute aimed to achieve a fifty/fifty mix, with half of the community service participants drawn from the stream of jail-bound offenders, project managers chose to intervene directly in the courtroom proceedings at the early stages of guilty plea negotiations. The institute's planners had been wary of simply informing judges that the option was now available to them. If this were done, there would be no way to regulate how the new sanction was used. Some consideration was given to assigning the preliminary screening duties to persons employed by existing courthouse agencies, but the planners quickly decided that this task should be performed by persons undistracted by other responsibilities. Thus, the position of court representative was created.

The principal job of these representatives was to identify defendants for whom they thought the new community service sanction was appropriate. To achieve their objective of drawing a large proportion of jailbound offenders, court representatives were asked to identify defendants who seemed likely to receive jail sentences of ninety days or less. These offenders constituted the target group. Several rules were developed to guide these court representatives: defendants without any prior adult criminal convictions were not to be considered for the sentence, because research had shown them to be the least likely to receive short jail terms in the lower criminal courts. Furthermore, the court representatives were to screen out all persons charged with crimes against a person or persons whose criminal records indicated past crimes of violence. Defendants without verified addresses, or with severe drug, alcohol, or mental or emotional problems were to be ruled ineligible, because project officials believed that such people would be hard to manage in a work setting.

The selection process also included several features designed as failsafes. To guard against the sentence being used only for offenders not otherwise bound for jail, defense attorneys were to be encouraged to exercise their right to veto defendants who might be able to win more favorable dispositions. Court representatives were also asked to protect the administrators of the work program, weeding out offenders who seemed more likely to commit violence against others on the work site and who appeared to be less likely to fulfill the conditions imposed by the courts. The success or failure of the project rested in large part on the shoulders of these court representatives, because they exercised considerable control over intake. Although the courts held the ultimate responsibility for the way the sentence was used, it was generally the court representatives who focused the court's attention on some defendants, while ignoring others.

(This brief description obscures not only the complexity of the selection process and sentencing decisions, but also the differences in how these decisions were made in the three boroughs. Chapters 3 and 4 examine in great detail these decision making procedures and their effects on how the project was used by the courts.)

The Legal Vehicle for the Sentence

At the time when the institute began planning its community service project, no clear statutory authority existed for the practice. After consideration of several alternatives, planners finally decided to have the community service obligation imposed as part of a conditional discharge, a statutorily defined sentence used frequently by the criminal courts in New York. This was not the only possible solution, and a number of key players in the early negotiations preferred other arrangements. In the end, however, the conditional discharge was designated as the legal vehicle, and this choice revealed a good deal about what the planners wanted to achieve.[20]

Early discussions among planners focused on the possibility of ordering community service in connection with an adjournment in contemplation of dismissal (ACD) because earlier pretrial diversion projects had used this legal device.[21] The ACD is available to the New York courts, and some people (primarily judges) preferred to graft the community service conditions onto this pretrial diversion model because of its administrative ease. If offenders refused to perform their court-ordered work satisfactorily, their cases could be restored to full prosecution without necessitating the more cumbersome due-process hearings required to modify already imposed sentences.

Planners rejected this approach quite early. Linking community service orders to dismissals would dilute their status in the eyes of judges, they decided. If community service was to be used in lieu of jail, it would have to be seen as a punishment; associating it with a dismissal or an ACD would define it as something other than a punishment. Moreover, relying on the ACD risked having the project seen as yet another diversion project. The Vera Institute's Court Employment Project, established in 1968, sought to divert young defendants from prosecution and conviction, but had been turned into a soft option by the courts, a placement for persons whose cases would in many cases be dismissed.[22] This was exactly what the institute planners hoped to avoid in its community service project. Better to avoid any association with the ACD than to risk the same fate for it as the pretrial diversion effort of the Court Employment Project.[23]

Linking community service to an ACD would also have raised Thirteenth Amendment problems. That amendment states that "Neither slavery nor involuntary servitude, except as a punishment for a crime whereof the party shall have been duly convicted, shall exist within the United States, or any place subject to their jurisdiction." Ordering an ACD averts a conviction, which is constitutionally necessary for the imposition of unpaid labor.

Planners had also rejected having community service tied to probation. To some, the probation sentence seemed the logical home for the community service order; indeed, this was the practice in England. But planners sought a clear demonstration that unpaid work in and of itself could suffice as a sentence. The clearest test of community service would be to require unpaid labor as a sole obligation and to enforce its performance in isolation from other demands.

There was yet another reason for rejecting the probation option. One of the institute's most successful early reforms, the Manhattan Bail Project, had been was turned over to the New York City Department of Probation three years after its inception. (This project set up a mechanism to give judges information at arraignment about defendants' likelihood of appearance at trial, so that judges would release greater numbers of persons on their own recognizance.) The experience had not been a happy one, however, because the project's momentum had faltered under the Probation Department's leadership. After nine years, the project had been returned to the institute's management. It stayed there for four years, before being turned back yet again to city government, this time as a new and discrete organization with its own management: the New York City Criminal Justice Agency.[24] One lesson the Vera Institute learned from this experience was that institutional reforms are sometimes more likely to succeed if they are managed by organizations dedicated to a single sharply focused purpose. Folding them in with already existing public service bureaucracies risks failure when the agencies' other well-established missions compete with the new project for money and managerial attention.

Even though the Vera Institute preferred to have its proposed community service sentence imposed in conjunction with a conditional discharge, there was some question as to whether the law permitted such a match. The laws that were on the books at that time authorized the courts to require an offender sentenced to conditional discharge (or to probation, for that matter) to "make restitution of the fruits of his offense or make reparation, in an amount he can afford to pay, for the loss or damage caused thereby." Community service was not explicity authorized. It could be considered a form of restitution payment, but there was some influential opposition to this. A few years earlier, in 1972, New York State's attorney general issued an opinion in connection with another matter in which he argued that the existing law did not permit a sentence conditioned upon the performance of unpaid labor.[25] Because of this, the chief administrative judge of New York City believed it inadvisable for the Vera Institute to rely upon the conditional discharge. To remedy this, the counsel to the courts (which is to say, the State Office of Court Administration), with assistance from the institute's lawyers, drew up an amendment to the penal law, which was submitted and passed in June 1978. Unpaid community service was now authorized explicitly in the laws of New York State. Offenders convicted of misdemeanors would be ordered to perform unpaid community service as a condition either of probation or of a conditional discharge.[26] (The law was subsequently amended to permit such sentences for lesser felons (classes D and E) as well.)[27]

Community Service as Punishment

Although the legislature gave community service its blessing with these amendments, it did not establish the reasons for which the sentence should be imposed. However, the planners who designed the Vera Institute project and the managers who later operated it were quite clear about their objectives. Their community service sentence was to be first and foremost a punishment. It is worth noting that this orientation sets the Vera Institute project apart from most others developed elsewhere in this country and abroad, for many of these programs employ the rhetoric the offender rehabilitation to justify their programs.[28] The Vera Institute planners and managers chose to downplay this aim in favor of more explicitly punitive ones, partly as a matter of strategy. If they wanted to have the sentence used as a substitute for jail, then it needed to be advertised to the court as a punitive sanction, because, they assumed, judges were sending people to jail for short terms primarily out of a desire to punish them. This choice of design was also a matter of values. Planners believed that "there are important social utilities to due process punishment for violation of the criminal law," as the author of the memo we have quoted at length declared. It was seen as a matter of honesty and believing in truth-in-advertising. Performing unpaid labor under court order may have some beneficial effects on those so sentenced, but the principal reason for requiring it of them is that they deserve it because of their crimes.

Nonetheless, planners did not eschew completely all considerations of offender rehabilitation. In one of the early proposals for funding written in 1978, planners stated:

It is not anticipated that two weeks of work would have a long-term impact on the offender's employment prospects or criminal activity. It is hoped, however, for certain offenders, the opportunity to work for the community in structured, visible jobs would begin to change their image of themselves and their role in the community. This in turn might motivate them to seek jobs or job training, to channel energy away from criminal activity and into constructive activities.[29]

For those offenders who wanted some form of assistance in getting more firmly planted on a law-abiding path, each of the borough units employed a social services coordinator, who acts as a broker for already existing service agencies in the community. Project participants are referred to jobs, job training organizations, employment agencies, drug and alcohol counselling, and public assistance agencies. Like Warren (the first project participant), many of the persons sentenced to community service live lives that are extremely unstable and need a good deal of support just to get through their seventy-hour obligations. These social services coordinators not infrequently help offenders find a place to live for at least the period during which they are under project supervision, help them find day care services if they have young children who need attention while they are working off their sentence, and assist them in other ways.

Enforcing the Sentence

The project's managers have always seen strict enforcement as crucial to the courts' acceptance of the community service sentence. They designed a tight system for enforcing attendance and performance, and violators are returned to court for resentencing. This has been a very important factor in gaining acceptance for the sanction, according to the judges we interviewed.

If offenders do not show up at work without having been previously excused for that day, project managers attempt to locate them and bring them to the worksite. (So that this can be done, one of the requirements for entry into the Vera Institite project is a fixed address.) If the offender cannot be found, a letter is sent to his or her address warning that the case will be referred back to court if the assigned hours are not completed. If this is not successful in producing the individual, a formal letter is sent by the project staff to begin resentencing proceedings. In the Bronx and Brooklyn projects, the letter is sent to the district attorney's office, so that the offender's case can be restored to the court calendar. A summons is sent out, and if the offender fails to appear, the judge can order a warrant for the person's arrest. In the Manhattan project, the letter is sent directly to the sentencing judge. These letters detail the efforts that have been made to contact offenders, and judges often bypass the summons and order an arrest warrant directly. In all boroughs, project officials often work with the warrant squads to locate the offender and bring him or her back to court.

The proportion of people failing to complete their assigned community service obligation has remained relatively low throughout the project's history. Prior to the end of June 1983, 86 percent of the offenders sentenced to the Bronx project had completed their imposed service orders. Eighty-five percent of all persons sentenced in Brooklyn before 30 June 1983 had completed the program successfully, and 89 percent had done so in Manhattan.

Judges usually imposed jail sentences upon those brought back for violating the terms of their original sentence. To document how the courts responded when offenders failed to complete their community service obligations, we examined the court records of all persons who had been sentenced to the project in all three boroughs between 1 December 1980 and 30 June 1982 and had had their cases restored to the calendar for having failed to complete the seventy hours. Of the 785 persons sentenced to community service during that period, 106 (or 14 percent) had been terminated by the project and had had their cases restored to the calendar. Seventy-one of these persons had been found and brought back into court; the remaining 36 persons did not show up and could not be found. (Warrants were issued for their arrest, although many of these warrants will not be acted upon until the offender is arrested again for another crime.)

Table 2.1 shows how these cases were handled by the courts in the three boroughs. All eighteen of the Manhattan cases brought back to court had their conditional discharge sentences revoked and new jail terms imposed. The proportions were somewhat lower in Bronx (77 percent) and lower still in Brooklyn (68 percent). Those not sent to jail in the Bronx had their cases disposed in ways that exacted no further punishment from the offenders. In two instances, judges decided that the offenders had fulfilled

Table 2.1. *How Cases Were Handled by the Courts When Offenders Refused to Complete Community Service Orders*

	Bronx		Brooklyn		Manhattan		Three boroughs combined	
	No.	%	No.	%	No.	%	No.	%
Resentenced to jail	24	(77%)	15	(68%)	18	(100%)	57	(80%)
Discharged	2	(6)	2	(11)	—	—	4	(6)
Probation	—	—	1	(5)	—	—	1	(1)
Case dismissed	5	(16)	4	(18)	—	—	9	(13)
(Subtotal cases disposed)	31	(100%)	22	(100%)	18	(100%)	71	(100%)
Warrant ordered	12		10		13		35	
Total number persons ordered back to court	43		32		31		106	

SOURCE: Community Service Sentencing Project files.

NOTE: Included are all Bronx and Brooklyn participants sentenced to community service between 1 December 1980 and 30 June 1982 and then terminated by Vera Institute officials, restoring participants' cases to the court calendar. Manhattan figures refer to the period beginning 1 October 1981 (the date the project officially opened in that borough) through 30 June 1982. In some instances, these terminations resulted from rearrests.

enough of their service requirements to discharge their obligations. Five offenders had their cases dismissed—an odd turn of events, for a dismissal wipes out not only the sentence but the conviction as well. (In one of these instances, the community service sentence had been voided with a dismissal when the offender was rearrested and sentenced to jail on a new charge.)

In Brooklyn, two returned offenders were found to have fulfilled enough of their work obligations to earn a discharge. Four others had their cases dismissed. Three had not completed their community service orders, were rearrested on new charges, and the court disposed of both the new and old cases simultaneously. Two people received state prison terms for the new charges and the third was sent to jail. Judges may have intended these imprisonment sentences to cover the violation of the earlier community service order. Indeed, the subsequent sentences may have been stiffened because of the project violations.

Table 2.2 shows that the median jail sentence imposed for violating the community service order was eighty days in the Bronx, ninety days in Brooklyn, and ninety-six days in Manhattan. Sentences were clustered at the low end of the spectrum in the Bronx, with a larger proportion of longer terms imposed in the other two boroughs.

Conclusion

Community service sentences can be imposed in large numbers not only upon relatively well-to-do first offenders who possess valuable skills, but also upon those chronic property offenders who are generally not violent, but who nonetheless present the courts with difficult problems. This is the principal lesson of the Vera Institute's experience. When the institute began its experiment in the Bronx Criminal Court in 1978, this was not at all clear. The national trend during the preceding decade had been for the courts to use unpaid community service almost exclusively in instances where first offenders had committed not very serious crimes. The Vera Institute demonstration shows that the courts will sentence even chronic thieves with very long criminal records

Table 2.2. *Length of Jail Sentences Imposed on Offenders Resentenced for Having Failed to Fulfill Community Service Orders*

Length of sentence (days)	Bronx		Brooklyn		Manhattan		Three boroughs combined	
	No.	%	No.	%	No.	%	No.	%
0– 30	6	(27%)	1	(8%)	2	(12%)	9	(17%)
31– 60	3	(14)	1	(8)	1	(6)	6	(10)
61– 90	8	(36)	3	(23)	5	(29)	16	(31)
91–120	2	(9)	—	—	2	(12)	4	(8)
121–150	1	(5)	—	—	1	(6)	2	(4)
151–180	2	(9)	4	(31)	—	—	6	(12)
181–210	—	—	1	(8)	—	—	1	(2)
211–240	—	—	—	—	1	(6)	1	(2)
241–270	—	—	1	(8)	—	—	1	(2)
271–300	—	—	—	—	1	(6)	1	(2)
301–330	—	—	—	—	—	—	—	—
331–365	—	—	2	(16)	4	(24)	6	(12)
	22	(100%)	13	(100%)	17	(100%)	52	(100%)
Unknown	2		2		1		5	
Median sentence (days)	80		90		96		90	
Mean sentence (days)	82		183		171		136	

SOURCE: Community Service Sentencing Project files.

NOTE: Included are all Bronx and Brooklyn participants sentenced to community service between 1 December 1980 and 30 June 1982 and then terminated by Vera Institute officials, restoring participants' cases to the court calendar. Manhattan figures refer to the period beginning 1 October 1981 (the date the project officially opened in that borough) through 30 June 1982. In some instances, these terminations resulted from rearrests.

to labor in densely populated urban neighborhoods. One reason why the courts are willing to do this is that the sanction has been strictly enforced. Failure to perform as ordered has been reported, and errant offenders have been brought back into court for additional punishment. Another reason for the success of the experiment was that these offenders were not left on their own to work in the community, but were closely supervised by foremen employed by the institute. Whatever reluctance judges may have had about placing thieves in neighborhood organizations was much alleviated by the knowledge that these offenders were rarely out of the foreman's sight during working hours. This work crew model seems to have been well suited to handling very large numbers of convicted criminals in public works projects.

Beyond this success, however, there remain some important questions. First: are judges really using this sanction in lieu of jail sentences, as the institute's managers had hoped? This was one of the institute's central objectives, but in the early days of the project, managers were not sure that the courts had adopted the project with the same ends in mind.

Second: what is the impact of community service experience upon those so sentenced? Do they feel that they are performing "slave labor," and does the emphasis on punishment rather than rehabilitation embitter them and alienate them further? Or does it have a more beneficial effect, leading them to become more law-abiding? In short, does the imposition of the sentence have any impact on the offenders' subsequent criminality, and would a short jail term have produced better or worse results?

Third: do the various benefits of the community service sentence outweigh the costs? The sanction is certainly not cost-free. Having to organize offenders in small work crews that are supervised by paid foremen is considerably more expensive than ordering convicted white-collar offenders to produce something—an educational film on drug abuse, for example—under minimal supervision. And if these thieves continue to steal during their off-hours (they are permitted, after all, to live at home), these additional crimes must be considered real costs.

The following chapters address each of these questions in detail.

Chapter Three

A Jail Substitute or
Just Another "Walk"?

In establishing its community service project, the Vera Institute sought to provide the courts with a new criminal sentence to be used as an intermediate-level punishment. "We aimed to drive a wedge in the schedule of available punishments at that point between short jail sentences and all other non-incarcerative sanctions," explained Michael Smith, the Vera Institute's director. "From that point, we would try to expand by cutting deeper in both directions, getting more offenders who would have drawn short jail terms as well as those who would have received other lesser sentences."[1] The critical question was what this mix of offenders would look like. If at least half of the offenders sentenced to community service would otherwise have gone to jail, the project would be considered a success. The goal was to get the community service sentence accepted as a substantial punishment, and a fifty-fifty ratio would be taken as a sign that the project had made its mark. If more than half of the participants would have gone to jail, all the better. This would leave room for subsequent sliding without seriously damaging the reputation of the sentence.

Project planners sought to avoid having the community service sentence imposed only in circumstances where judges were not really considering jail. They didn't want the sentence to be yet another "walk"—another nonincarcerative sentence perceived by the courts, offenders, and the public as a lenient "break" rather than a punishment. Moreover, if community service were ordered only as an added condition of probation or in instances where offenders would otherwise have received a discharge, it would be difficult to justify the expenditures required of the project. Ulti-

52

mately, either the state or local government would have to pick up the tab for the administration of the sentence, if it was to find a permanent place in the repertoire of court-imposed sanctions, and this would be unlikely to occur should the sentence not prove to be "cost beneficial." The way the sentence was initially used by the courts was seen, consequently, as a matter of crucial importance. If the sentence were to be established in the lower range of nonincarcerative sanctions, planners feared it would be difficult if not impossible to "upscale," because judges would be reluctant to revise their initial definition of the sentence. Planners therefore reasoned that it was better to aim high and be forced back, if necessary, to a fifty-fifty split between jailbound offenders and those not headed for jail.

How successful was the project in getting offenders who otherwise would have gone to jail? Did planners aim the wedge too high or too low? Did they actually succeed in the hard task of designing and implementing a new criminal sanction that was accepted as a true alternative to incarceration, or has the community service project been simply another reform that has not lived up to its designers' intentions?

Answering this is much more difficult than it might seem at first glance, because the question presents one with a vexing methodological conundrum. How can one determine what the courts would have done in the absence of the innovation, if all we can see is what occurs after the innovation has been brought on the scene? One strategy would be to reconstruct the way sentences were imposed prior to the reform and then undertake a before-and-after analysis, comparing the practices that existed before the introduction of the reform with those observed afterwards. Unfortunately, such a strategy is enormously expensive and time-consuming, because the court records that exist for cases closed at some point in the past are scattered among several different agencies. Pulling together all the data that are needed to develop a rich picture of pre-reform sentencing patterns is extraordinarily difficult.

Why not just ask judges what they would have done had the community sentence option not been available? This question was put to a few dozen judges and their answers reveal the shortcomings of this approach.

These are not the most heinous cases. It would depend upon the recommendation of the DA and the strength of the case, but it would probably be between a fine, probation, or a small jail sentence. I can't pin it down. . . . You can't generalize.

More often than not, probably jail in some dimension. But it's hard to talk in a vacuum. Probably you'd be talking jail time of some sort. But somewhere down the line, the case may fall apart. Vera may then turn out to be inappropriate but if the guy had already accepted Vera, you'd never find out what would have happened.

What would have happened? Probably not much. I'd probably be adjourning them, because defense counsel would probably utilize the tactic of delay for this type of case, and eventually, many of these cases might be dissolved for lack of prosecution or all the other sundry reasons why cases fade away.[2]

Most judges were unable to give clear, consistent, and unqualified answers to the questions, not because they were unthinking individuals but rather because they simply were never faced with the circumstances posited in the "what if" query. Like most people, judges do not typically make their decisions by rank-ordering all their options and then picking the most preferred among them. If they did, their second best choice would be easily recognized. Instead, they generally weigh their various objectives and the constraints that impinge upon them and then make a decision. This usually ends the deliberative process. Figuring out what would have been a second best course of action is a waste of energy, especially because the mix of opportunities and constraints would have been very different had the community service sentencing project not been available to them. Given the heavy workloads in the criminal courts, most judges do not have the leisure time that would be required for such mental gymnastics.

Even when judges did give quick and clear replies, recounting what they would have done, there is good reason to wonder if they really would have done what they said, if the option had really not been available to them. In many instances, the project's court representatives had pressed them to declare what kind of sentence would be imposed if the participant failed to perform the community service as ordered. Most judges knew that the court representatives needed assurances that a jail sentence would otherwise be coming, and it is not unreasonable to expect that they tailored their replies so that the defendant would be accepted by the project. This does not mean that they actually would have imposed the jail sentence had the situation been different.

Perhaps the most compelling reason for not relying upon judges' reports of what they would have done, however, is that even they cannot predict the outcomes of sentencing deliberations with perfect certainty. Sentencing decisions result from the interplay of many different factors, not all of them in the judges' control: the strength of the evidence, the district attorney's ability to capitalize upon its strengths and hide its weaknesses, the skill and willingness of the defense attorney to engineer a disposition more favorable to the defendant, and the defendant's ability to hold out for a better deal. In short, sentencing decisions in almost all criminal court cases are negotiated ones.[3] They are not unilateral pronouncements from the bench. Both defense attorneys and prosecutors have inputs into the decisions, as do the defendants by virtue of withholding their guilty pleas. If the community service option were removed from the negotiation, the mix of constraints would differ and the negotiations would be conducted in a different context. Judges cannot easily predict what would happen in a changed world.

'Watch What We Do, Not What We Say.'

Rather than relying on judges' guesses about what they would do in imagined circumstances, a far more reliable method of assessing a reform's impact is to examine how judges actually acted. The optimal method of doing this is to set up an experiment.[4]

Experiments in the social and natural sciences permit the investigator to hold constant all factors but one. When that one factor is manipulated, changes in outcomes can be traced unambiguously to the presence or absence of this condition—in this instance, the community service option. Imagine, for example, that the investigator could convince the courts to submit all offenders sentenced to community service to a lottery-like selection procedure. This procedure would permit a random assignment of some offenders to community service, with others being sent back to court for re-sentencing. Faced with the unavailability of community service for these latter offenders, the courts would have to impose other sentences. By examining the sentencing decisions made in these returned cases, one could get a good measure of how persons sentenced to community service would have been handled if the sanction had not been available in the first place. This is because both groups—the "experimental" group of those sentenced to community service and the "control" group of those sentenced otherwise—would be very similar in their essential characteristics. They would have been sorted into one or the other group by random assignment rather than a more purposive selection. Moreover, both groups would have been subjected to the same courthouse processes right up to the final sentencing decision.

We were not able to impose upon the project and the courts an experimental selection and sentencing procedure. Interestingly enough, the main obstacle was not the objection to offenders being sentenced by lottery-like methods. Rather, the principal stumbling block was the project's need to establish and then maintain a relatively high caseload of offenders sentenced to community service. For the project to prove itself to the funding agencies that put up the initial seed money, it would have to demonstrate that the courts actually use it. Researchers were therefore not allowed to cut into the pool of eligible candidates, diverting some of them into a control group by blocking their admission to the project.

"Quasi-Experiments": Modeling Sentencing Decisions

The analytic strategy we adopted instead was a two-pronged one. The first part involved a statistical dissection of a large sample of actual sentencing decisions. The aim of this analysis was to uncover a pattern in judicial sentencing decisions; knowing what this pattern looked like would assist our estimating how persons sentenced to community service would have fared in the absence of the project. The second prong of this research strategy was to observe how the courts selected and sentenced some offenders to community service while rejecting others. Trained observers spent many months in court recording these transactions. These were augmented by interviews with several dozen attorneys, judges, prosecutors, and project court representatives and managers. Instead of relying upon any one set of data to determine how the community service project was being used by the courts, this research strategy amounted to a kind of triangulation: several different kinds of information were analyzed to see what kinds of conclusions they pointed to. Fortunately, the observations and interviews reinforced the estimates that the statistical analysis produced, which gave us confidence that our overall conclusions were essentially correct.

This combination of observational and statistical methods is not necessarily a crippled second best alternative to the traditional experimental design. To be sure, these after-the-fact statistical analyses yield somewhat less certain and more qualified estimates than experimental studies would have provided, but they have important advantages. Experimental studies focus on the final outcomes of a process—in this case, the final sentencing decision. They do not in themselves provide us with a way to examine systematically the factors that contribute to these results. The decision process itself is treated as an unexamined "black box" in most experimental studies, and attention is focused on what goes into the box and what comes out. Relying on interviews, observation, and after-the-fact statistical modeling as we did permits one to explore not only the results of the decision making processes, but also why and how cases were resolved as they were. A much fuller understanding of how the courts are affected by the introduction of the community service sentencing option can be developed by this approach.

The remainder of this chapter describes the assumptions and methods we used to determine how participants would have been sentenced in the absence of the Vera Institute community service project. Also shown here are the summary results of this investigation: the estimated proportion of each borough project's participants who would have gone to jail and our estimates of how long their jail sentences would have been. Explaining why the boroughs differed in their use of the sanction—which was uncovered by the second prong of our research strategy—is the subject of chapter 4.

Building Models to Predict In/Out Decisions

To obtain as accurate an indication as possible of how project participants would have been sentenced if they had not pleaded guilty to a community service order, we undertook a four-step analysis. First, we selected a large number of cases involving offenders and offenses that were very similar to those of the project participants. None of the offenders in this population had been given community service sentences. This population provided us with a baseline against which we could examine the participants. Second, we developed statistical models that described the disposition processes in a way that permitted relatively accurate predictions of how cases of the sort examined in this baseline population were disposed. Next, the models derived from this population were applied to participants' cases. This yielded for each participant an estimated probability of getting a jail sentence. Finally, we estimated the amount of time that participants would have spent in jail had they not been given community service sentences. These latter estimates were also based upon an analysis of the sentencing decisions in the comparison group, but we relied upon a method of extrapolation that was much simpler than the statistical modeling techniques.

The Baseline Population

Because we relied upon patterns discerned in the processing of one group of defendants to estimate what would have happened to defendants in another (that is, participants), the selection of defendants to be included in this first group was of critical importance. Instead of going to court records and collecting information on a number of apparently similar cases, we constructed a paper trail for defendants who had been found eligible for community service by the project's court representatives, but had then been rejected subsequently for one or another reason. Because they had passed the same initial eligibility tests that had been applied to participants, we were assured that these rejected defendants resembled participants more closely than would any other group selected from the general population of defendants arraigned in criminal court. For example, they all had more than one previous adult criminal conviction; they were charged with offenses that were considered acceptable for the community service project in each of the boroughs; their recent arrest histories showed no past crimes involving violence; and court records showed no indication of current drug or alcohol dependency. Moreover, the court representatives had used their knowledge of disposition patterns in the court to select into this group defendants who appeared most likely to receive a jail sentence if convicted. Because the policies and practices of judges, prosecutors, and defense attorneys can change over time, we examined rejected defendants whose cases were in court at the same time as our participant sample. Both groups were initially screened by project court representatives for eligibility between 1 October 1981 and 30 September 1982. A total of 867 eligible but rejected defendants were identified, and their cases were tracked by researchers up to the point of disposition. During the same time span, a total of 676 participants were sentenced to community service.

But how comparable was this group of rejected defendants? To be sure, rejected defendants differed from participants in one crucial respect: they had been explicitly dropped from further consideration for a variety of reasons. This does not seriously damage their usefulness for the analysis, however. Strict comparability is not required when one relies on statistical models for generating estimates. This is because the rejected group was used only to develop models that best captured the patterns involved in disposing cases. What is required for comparability is that participants would have been subjected to the same court processes as rejected defendants had they not been given community service sentences. They need not have shared exactly the same characteristics. For example, the participants as a group may have had fewer or more previous arrests than the rejected ones; what matters is that the number of prior arrests would have affected the disposition of the case in the same way even had the community service option not existed.

Rather than trying to model the patterned interactions that preceded all the different ways of resolving criminal cases in each borough, we limited our attention to examining two outcomes: whether a jail sentence was imposed, as contrasted to all other alternatives (including all other kinds of sentences, as well as a dismissal of the charges altogether), and, if a jail sentence was imposed, how long it was. Both of these outcomes were analyzed separately. The jail/no jail decision (the "in/out decision") was modeled using linear logistic regression techniques.[5] The sentence length decision was estimated using a simpler technique that will be described more fully below.

Preliminary analysis revealed distinctive sentencing practices in each of the borough courts, and no single model could be developed that accurately reflected the patterns found in all three courts. The analysis was therefore carried out on each borough's sentencing decisions separately, resulting in a model for each court.

Early examination also showed that sentencing patterns differed within each borough at different points in the disposition process. In some instances, offenders pleaded guilty at their first hearing (at arraignment, that is), while others waited to do so in a subsequent hearing. (Virtually all offenders convicted in these lower criminal courts plead guilty; during 1983, for example, only 0.5 percent of the offenders convicted in New York City criminal courts went to trial.[6]) The constraints that operated on defendants, prosecutors, and judges differed depending upon whether the plea was entered at arraignment or in a later hearing. For example, all the people in our pool of rejected defendants had been held in detention prior to arraignment, which put them all on equal footing when negotiating plea and sentence agreements. By the time subsequent hearings were held, however, some of these defendants had either been released on their own recognizance or had made bail, while others had remained in jail, and this difference had a significant impact on their ability to negotiate favorable sentences.

Because the factors associated with getting a jail sentence were found to differ somewhat at the various stages of adjudication, sentencing decisions imposed at arraignment were analyzed separately from those made in post-arraignment hearings. But because so few of the rejected defendants' cases were disposed at arraignment, statistical models could only be developed for sentences imposed in post-arraignment hearings. These models ultimately were used to estimate how many of the participants would have been sentenced to jail if they had not received the community service order, regardless of whether these participants had pleaded guilty at arraignment or in a later hearing. The reasons for using the models in this way, as well as the limitations of the estimates that resulted, are discussed at length in the Appendix.

Modeling the Sentencing Decision

The first step in modeling the in/out decision was to track all of the rejected defendants that were selected for the comparison group and to record when their cases had been disposed as well as what that disposition had been. Of the 867 defendants in the entire group, 641 had had their cases disposed by the time their court records were checked. (Of those who had not been disposed, 27 percent had failed to appear at their scheduled court hearing, thereby triggering the issuance of an arrest warrant; 4 percent had been transferred to the superior court for prosecution as felonies; the remainder were cases being continued on the court calendars primarily because the plea negotiations had been stretched out by one or another party.) A total of 564 defendants saw their cases reach disposition in the post-arraignment hearings, and it was this population that was used to model the disposition decisions.

Of the 564 defendants whose cases reached final disposition in post-arraignment hearings, 30 percent were sentenced to jail. The others either had their charges dismissed or were sentenced to a discharge, fine, probation, or a jail sentence with full credit given for time served in pretrial detention. There were some differences in these final dispositions among the three boroughs (see table 3.1), the reasons for which will be discussed more fully in the next chapter.

The next task was to identify the factors associated with receiving a jail sentence in this population of 564 rejected defendants. The files for these defendants were examined on a case-by-case

Table 3.1. *Criminal Court Disposition of Defendants in Baseline Population, by Borough*

Reached final disposition:	Bronx	Brooklyn	Manhattan
Dismissed/ACD	23%	31%	7%
Convicted & sentenced:			
Conditional discharge	16	20	20
Unconditional discharge	2	0	0
Fine or fine/jail alternative	32	9	1
Probation	4	8	5
"Time served"	4	5	4
Jail	19	25	63
Total disposed	100%	100%	100%
	(n = 317)	(n = 118)	(n = 129)

SOURCES: Disposition data from New York City Criminal Justice Agency.
NOTE: This table considers post-arraignment dispositions only. Fine or jail sentences require that the offender pay the specified fine or be jailed. Which of the two outcomes followed in each case was not recorded, although we expected that the majority paid the fines or, at least, were not sent to jail for failure to pay. "Time served" sentences are legally considered jail sentences, but the offender's time in pretrial detention is counted against the sentence, permitting the offender to walk out the door without having to serve more time.

basis and a number of characteristics were measured and recorded. Using a computer, we determined how strongly each of these characteristics was correlated with receiving a jail sentence, as opposed to all other dispositions. These correlations were also tested for their statistical significance. Table 3.2 summarizes these findings.[7]

In all three boroughs, whether or not a jail sentence was imposed was most strongly associated with a defendant's pretrial detention status at the time of sentencing and somewhat less strongly associated with a defendant's prior criminal record. The charges for which the defendants were arraigned made essentially no difference in the in/out sentencing decision, at least in the population of defendants examined here. (Charges at conviction were similarly not related to the in/out sentencing decisions in this popula-

Table 3.2. *The Relationship Between Receiving a Jail Sentence and Several Other Characteristics*

Characteristic	Strength of Association		
	Bronx	Brooklyn	Manhattan
In pretrial detention at time of sentencing	.45 ***	.40 ***	.43 ***
Number of prior arrests	.15 **	.39 ***	.17
Number of prior felony convictions	−.04	.04	.06
Number of prior misd. convictions	.14 **	.38 ***	.10
Number of total prior convictions	.11	.39 ***	.14
Days since last conviction and arraignment for instant offense	.12 *	−.02 *	−.10
Days between arraignment and disposition	−.04	−.05	−.23 **
Imprisoned for most recent prior conviction	.13 *	.15	.26 **
Ethnicity of offender is white/anglo	−.02	−.20 *	−.17
Offender married	−.05	−.07	.14
Age of offender	.04	−.14	−.02
Number of open cases still pending at time of screening	.13 *	.29 **	.11
Arraigned on:			
Class B felony	−.05	(none)	−.11
Class C felony	−.02	.22 *	(none)
Class D felony	−.03	−.11	(none)
Class E felony	.09	.10	.10
Class A misd.	−.01	−.05	.17
Class B misd.	−.05	.07	−.20*

NOTE: Rejected defendants whose cases reached disposition in post-arraignment hearings only.
* $p \leq .05$
** $p \leq .01$
*** $p \leq .001$

64   A Jail Substitute?

Table 3.3. *The Proportion of Rejected Defendants Who Received Jail Sentences, by Pretrial Detention Status and Borough Where Disposed*

Status at time of disposition	Proportion receiving jail sentences		
	Bronx	Brooklyn	Manhattan
Detained	48%	49%	79%
At liberty	8%	12%	34%

SOURCE: Computed from information provided by the New York City Criminal Justice Agency.

tion of defendants.) These findings are consistent with those found in studies of sentencing in other jurisdictions.

Table 3.3 shows the proportion of rejected defendants given jail sentences in the three borough courts, tabulated separately for persons held in detention at the time of sentencing and those who were at liberty either because they had posted bail or because they had been released on their own recognizance. In all boroughs, persons being held in jail at time of sentencing were much more often given jail sentences than others. This was not simply because detained defendants were the most likely candidates for jail sentences that could be fulfilled completely by counting the time already served in detention. "Time served" sentences were considered nonincarcerative sentences for our purposes, which eliminates this as a possible explanation.[8] The principal reasons why this pattern prevailed were that judges were more likely to require high bails of those they deemed most likely to get a jail sentence if convicted, and because defendants held in detention were in weaker positions from which to negotiate favorable sentences. To be sure, the relationship between pretrial detention status and sentencing decisions was more complex than can be accurately summed up in a short sentence, but our purpose at this point is merely to sketch out the general patterns we found without trying to explain them fully. A more extensive explanation of why these patterns occurred is the subject of the following chapter.

In all boroughs, offenders with more extensive and more serious prior criminal records were more often given jail sentences. There is no single indicator of a defendant's prior record that completely encompasses all aspects of his or her previous behavior, so we measured a number of different characteristics related to prior conduct and prior experience with the courts. Some differences between the boroughs were found in the characteristics associated with the in/out decision. For example, the Bronx and Brooklyn courts appeared to be responsive in the in/out decision to the sheer number of a defendant's prior arrests and convictions, especially misdemeanor convictions, which were far more plentiful in this population than felonies. In Manhattan, for some undiscovered reason, a weak and statistically insignificant association was found between the likelihood of imprisonment and the number of prior arrests or convictions, but what did matter was whether or not the sentence imposed for the most recent prior conviction was a prison or jail term. In this borough (and in the Bronx as well), those whose last sentence sent them to jail or prison were more often given jail sentences than others were in the cases we examined. In addition, the number of prior arrest cases still pending disposition ("open" cases) apparently had little impact on the sentence given in a current case in Manhattan, whereas in the Bronx and Brooklyn courts it was found that defendants with more open cases were more likely to receive jail terms in the current case than others were. (That previous cases were still open indicates either that the defendant had jumped bail or otherwise had failed to appear in court when required, or that defendants had been rearrested within a short time period, before their previous arrest case was closed.)

The lack of association between charges at arraignment and the likelihood of receiving a jail sentence is made evident in table 3.4, which shows the proportion of rejected defendants who were given jail sentences, classified by their highest charge at arraignment. Ignoring the very high or very low percentages in the charge classes in which there were only a few offenders, there was very little variation by level of charge in the Bronx and Brooklyn in the proportions of defendants going to jail. In Manhattan, almost all

Table 3.4. *Arraignment Charges and Sentencing Decisions: The Proportion of Offenders Receiving Jail Sentences, by Most Serious Charge at Arraignment and by Borough*

Statutory class of most serious charge at arraignment	Proportion sentenced to jail					
	Bronx		Brooklyn		Manhattan	
Felonies:						
Class B	0% (n = 4)		0% (n = 1)		0% (n = 2)	
C	14	(28)	100	(4)		(0)
D	18	(180)	27	(85)	0	(2)
E	21	(169)	29	(29)	100	(2)
Misdemeanors:						
Class A	17	(155)	23	(44)	63	(132)
B	0	(4)	50	(2)	0	(3)
Violations:	0	(2)	0	(0)	0	(0)

SOURCE: Computed from project files and from data provided by the New York City Criminal Justice Agency.

offenders were arraigned on Class-A misdemeanors, and there was, consequently, almost no variation at all in the severity of arraignment charges. When each of these cases was examined in greater detail, comparing the types of offenses committed (e.g., burglary, possession of stolen property, etc.), we still were unable to find any significant association between offenses and sentences. Within this relatively narrow band of offenses considered for community service, the decision to impose a jail sentence simply turned on other factors.

Having identified a number of different characteristics that were correlated with receiving a jail sentence in this population of defendants, the next step was to combine these characteristics into a set of statistical models that had some power to predict sentencing decisions. These models, which took the form of mathematical statements, were formulated by testing several "what if" propositions to find the one that best fit the observed pattern of actual dispositions. For example, what if the courts had imposed jail sentences more often upon defendants who had longer criminal records, more serious charges, more recent convictions, and who were older? Furthermore, what if the prior record was 5.7 times more important in this consideration than the level of the charge and 3.2 times more important than the length of time passed since the last conviction? Fortunately, a computer enables one to build accurate models relatively easily because one can quickly test many different assumptions about how the various factors interact. By a process of elimination, statistical models were built for the in/out decision in each borough pool of rejected defendants. The criteria used to choose the best model in each borough were parsimony (having the fewest number of predictive variables), accuracy (predicting correctly the highest proportion of dispositional outcomes), and whether the model made sense from a theoretical point of view—that is, whether the results squared with our understanding of how the courts work, or at least might conceivably work.

In Brooklyn, a single model was developed that correctly predicted 80 percent of the post-arraignment in/out decisions. (Eighty percent is a substantial improvement over what one would get by blind guessing or flipping a coin. Using a coin toss to predict the outcomes, the ratio of jailed/not jailed would be estimated at about fifty/fifty.) This model included five factors: the number of the prior arrests, the number of days between the current arrest and the most recent prior conviction, whether the defendant had received a jail sentence for that most recent prior conviction, whether the defendant was in pretrial detention at the time of disposition, and whether the defendant was white. In the Bronx, the following characteristics, taken in combination, were found to predict 87 percent of in/out decisions: the number of prior arrests, the time elapsed between the most recent prior conviction and arraignment in the current case, and pretrail detention status. The Manhattan model included the time elapsed between arraignment and disposition, whether jail had been imposed for the last conviction, and the offender's pretrial detention status at the time of dispostion. It correctly predicted 78 percent of the jail/no jail outcomes in the rejected defendants' pool.

Estimating the Jail-Substitution Rates

These models were then applied to the participant pool in order to estimate the proportion of participants in each borough who would have gone to jail had they not been sentenced to community service. The computer went through each participant's case, weighting each of the predictive variables in the way specified by the statistical model, and thereby produced for each participant an estimated likelihood that a jail sentence would have been imposed. (The models themselves are described in the Appendix.)

In the Bronx, we estimated that 20 percent of those participants screened for eligibility during the period 1 October 1981 to 30 September 1982, and whose cases were disposed in post-arraignment hearings, would have been sentenced to jail had they not gotten community service. (This does not include those who would have been given sentences of "time served" and then released immediately upon conviction.) In Brooklyn, the estimated proportion was 28 percent. In contrast, we determined that in Manhattan an estimated two-thirds of the participants would have gone to jail had the community service option not been used. Citywide, the combined estimated proportion would have been 45 percent.

These estimates were developed by examining the patterns of disposition in post-arraignment hearings and then applying them to participants whose cases had been disposed at post-arraignment. We then assumed that participants who had pleaded guilty at arraignment would also have gone to jail in similar proportions. (As noted above, there were too few rejected defendants whose cases had reached disposition at arraignment to model them separately.) The reasons for making this assumption and the possible shortcomings of the estimates that were developed on this basis are discussed in the Appendix.

Estimating Length of Jail Sentences

How long would these participants have been sentenced to jail had the community service alternative not been chosen? An unsuccessful attempt was made to answer this question by statistical modeling. Rejected defendants' cases were examined to identify the characteristics that were correlated with the length of the jail sentences imposed. Unfortunately, very few correlates were found. A statistical model of the sort constructed to predict the in/out decision could not be developed.

However, an estimate was developed from an analysis of the same population that was used to construct estimates of the proportion of participants who otherwise would have been jailed— rejected defendants whose cases had been disposed in post-arraignment hearings. During the period between 1 October 1981 and 30 September 1982, these rejected defendants were given sentences, that averaged 75 days in the Bronx, 70 days in Brooklyn, and 143 days in Manhattan. Most inmates did not serve these full sentences, because their sentences were shortened as a reward for good behavior while in jail. For every two days without a disciplinary citation, one day was cut from the court-imposed sentence. Moreover, time spent in pretrial detention was credited against the sentence, thereby shortening the time required to be served after the date of sentencing. Disciplinary records of jailed rejected defendants were not examined, and for the sake of analysis, we assumed that all inmates had been given full credit for good behavior, reducing their court imposed sentences by a third. (This yields a conservative estimate of time actually served, for some undetermined proportion of those sentenced to jail lost "good time" credits for misbehavior and thereby served a larger portion of their court-imposed sentence than was assumed here.) Furthermore, the estimated number of pretrial detention days served before sentencing was computed and subtracted from this definite sentence-minus-good-time figure. After these adjustments had been made, the estimated time rejected defendants spent in jail after sentencing averaged thirty-nine days in the Bronx, forty-three days in Brooklyn, and seventy-three days in Manhattan. We assumed that if participants had not been given community service sentences, those sent to jail instead—whether at arraignment or in subsequent hearings—would have received sentences of approximately the same length as did these defendants. Our grounds for assuming this are discussed more fully in the Appendix.

What Judges Did When Participants Failed: Contradictory Evidence?

As discussed in chapter 2, we discovered that judges usually imposed jail sentences when participants were brought back to court for having failed to complete their community service obligations. In Manhattan, 94 percent of those resentenced were sent to jail; in Brooklyn, 67 percent; and in the Bronx, 71 percent. (See table 2.1.) Does this resentencing conflict with our estimates that a much smaller proportion of participants in each borough would have been sentenced initially to jail in the absence of the project?

Our interviews revealed that judges and prosecutors were not reluctant to demand additional punishments for offenders who had failed to perform as ordered, and that these punishments were often stiffer than what offenders would have received in the first place had the community service option not been available. Asked how he would sentence somebody who had failed in the community service project and was returned to court, one judge replied:

I probably would add on some time to the sentence because the defendant didn't complete the project. It depends on the guy's record and the DA's recommendation. I think we may be giving them more time than they might have gotten had they taken straight time instead of Vera.[9]

As for prosecutors, one assistant district attorney in Brooklyn who had the power to veto or approve proposed candidates for community service relished this ability to enhance the penalty for failure.

I will be honest enough to tell you that there are many defendants whom I make my decision about on the basis of a gut feeling that they will not complete the program. And I got 'em if they screw up. It's almost like, with this fellow's record, I can give him the program because it really isn't a risk. In the back of my mind, I know that I'm going to get in fact more time than I would have gotten if I had tried the case.[10]

Whereas both this judge and the assistant district attorney measured their penalties in increased jail time, the same tendency probably operated with offenders who would not have been sentenced to jail in the first place, but who later failed. The imposition of a jail sentence after failing to complete the community service obligation does not, therefore, indicate whether a judge would have imposed a jail term in the initial sentencing decision.

Judges were also under pressure from project managers to jail failing participants, which was a constraint that did not operate when original sentencing decisions were made. Vera Institute project managers had an interest in seeing that non-completers were punished with jail sentences. Indeed, the single most potent weapon they wielded was the threat to send participants back to court and thereafter to jail. Project officials frequently made their interest in jail sentences known to the court. They needed to have their threats made credible, and judges may have acceded to their requests in order to empower them as enforcers of the sentences. Stiffer sentences may have been the result in instances of failure.

These resentencing decisions were therefore more useful as tools to rule out possibilities rather than to establish firm conclusions about how community service was used by judges. That is, if judges rarely jailed participants who were returned to court, we could quite reasonably assume that most would not have gone to jail in the first place. Because a majority of the participants returned by the Vera Institute project were sentenced to jail, this conclusion must be ruled out. What we are left with is the possibility that many defendants might have gone to jail in the first place had the community service option not been available, but precisely how many would have cannot be determined by examining these decisions.

Did the Bronx and Brooklyn Projects Improve their Aim?

The finding that the Bronx and Brooklyn projects were not displacing jail sentences at the desired rate was disappointing news to the institute's managers. Preliminary results of the statistical analyses reported in this chapter were shared with institute project managers in early 1983, and the citywide director, Judith Greene, initiated a shake-up of both personnel and procedures for screening potential participants. Greene had been the director of the

Manhattan unit since its inception and was promoted in late 1982 to the newly created position of citywide director. By midsummer, Greene had developed more restrictive criteria for screening cases in both the Brooklyn and Bronx units. These criteria were based largely upon statistical analyses that identified the characteristics associated with having received a jail sentence. In addition, changes were made in the way potential candidates were referred to court representatives for screening, so that a larger stream of jailbound defendants were brought into the project's reach. (These organizational modifications are described more fully at the end of chapter 4.)

To see whether these changes resulted in an improved jail-displacement rate, the same estimating procedures we have described were repeated, this time in examining the adjudicatory decisions made in cases disposed after these changes were instituted. The results were quite dramatic. The analysis of July–December 1983 decisions in the Bronx indicated that an estimated 52 percent of the participants given the community service sentence in that borough's court would otherwise have gone to jail for approximately sixty-seven days, on the average. This was a great improvement over the earlier rate, estimated to have been about 20 percent.

In Brooklyn, an analysis of decisions made between October 1983 and September 1984 indicated that approximately 57 percent of those sentenced to the project would have gone to jail otherwise. Had they gone to jail instead of having been ordered to perform community service, they would have received sentences averaging about sixty-five days.

In Brooklyn, these changes were accomplished without incurring a reduction in the numbers of persons sentenced to community service. Indeed, during the twelve months following the changes, there was a 17 percent increase in project intake over the levels reached during the previous twelve months. In the Bronx, intake declined about 20 percent during the year following the project's reorganization. This suggests that one reason the proportion of otherwise jailbound offenders increased in that borough was that the project defendants least likely to be jailed were eliminated from further consideration without being replaced, one for one, with defendants heading for jail. This occurred partly because project staff had a difficult time conforming to the new procedures. (Some resisted going after defendants they thought belonged in jail.) Personnel changes were instituted subsequently to remedy this problem. Intake began to rise afterwards.

In conclusion, the Vera Community Service Sentencing Project was successful in its efforts to be used by the courts as a substitute for jail. The two branches that opened first in the Bronx and Brooklyn courts initially fell short of the planners' and managers' ambitions, because they were used relatively infrequently in place of jail sentences. Experience and close analysis was a good teacher, however, and by the time the third branch of the project opened in Manhattan, some crucial lessons had been absorbed. Different procedures were established in that borough and these were successful in netting jailbound offenders. These lessons were refined further and applied later to the lagging Bronx and Brooklyn branches. That the performance of these two latter units could be so dramatically improved shows that reforms can be redirected even after they have become well established in the lower ranges of the penal schedule.

The reasons the Bronx and Brooklyn projects did so poorly in their early years and then were turned around, and why the Manhattan unit fared so well from the outset are explored in the following chapter.

Chapter Four

Gatekeepers and Advocates:
Why Courts Responded Differently to the Reform

Ever since the eighteenth-century French philosopher Marquis de Condorcet and his followers advanced the doctrines of progress and the "infinite perfectibility of mankind," Occidental man has been driven by the desire to improve society and its institutions. Not surprisingly, reformers have been almost unceasingly preoccupied with improving those key control institutions of societies— the courts and legal systems. But despite the extraordinary attention given to the technologies of transformation in other realms, remarkably little study has been made of how and why the courts respond to systematic efforts to change them. Perhaps this is the consequence of our intensely judgmental stance towards them: we want most to know if the courts are meeting the large demands we make on them, and if particular reforms succeed or fail. Thus, the forms of social inquiry now most popular—called "policy analysis" and "cost/benefit analysis"—are concerned almost exclusively with results. Unfortunately, what we lose in this preoccupation with results is an informed understanding of how and why the courts respond as they do to reform initiatives.

Evaluating the outcomes of particular attempts to change the courts is undoubtedly important, but of potentially greater usefulness is the development of more general knowledge of reform processes. Knowing how and why planned changes succeed or fail pays dividends, not only because comprehending the world more fully is intellectually rewarding, but also because such understanding enhances our ability to change institutions. From ad-

74

vances in scientific knowledge have come more powerful technologies of control.

Because general social scientific theories are built upon descriptions of specific events, and because there exist in the published literature very few detailed accounts of attempts to implement sentencing reforms, this chapter is devoted to an explanation of why the Vera Institute's community service sentencing project experienced such different fates in each of the three New York City boroughs. Why did the Bronx and Brooklyn courts fail to use the community service sentence as a frequent substitute for jail, when the Manhattan courts readily did so? And how did the institute manage, in the Bronx and Brooklyn courts, to steer the use of the sentence onto a different course after it had become firmly established as an alternative, not to a jail term, but largely to other nonincarcerative dispositions? In the sections that follow here, I seek to explain these outcomes by examining the dynamics of how ideas were translated into reform strategies, and how each of the different parties involved in plea and sentencing negotiations responded to the institute's intervention.

Judge-Centered and Prosecutor-Centered Selection Procedures

The most important single factor that determined the subsequent course of reform in each borough—and which explains many of the differences in the way in which the courts used the new sentencing option—was the way the authority for screening and sentencing decisions was allocated by project managers. In Manhattan, managers implemented a screening and selection procedure that placed judges in the drivers' seats. This resulted in a large number of jailbound offenders being ordered to perform community service. In the other two borough courts, screening and sentencing procedures were more prosecutor-centered, and the district attorneys' offices held the dominant position. In these courts, prosecutors used their power to restrict the sentencing of jailbound offenders to community service.

In the Bronx and Brooklyn, prosecutors acted as gatekeepers in the selection process, controlling the initial decisions regarding a defendant's eligibility for community service sentencing. In Manhattan, defense attorneys rather than prosecutors acted as the gatekeepers, deciding which cases to take to the judge for community service consideration. The structural differences in the two selection procedures are graphically represented in figure 4.1, which shows the sequence of decisions by which the various parties to plea negotiations signed off on a community service sentence in each borough.

In Bronx and Brooklyn, screening began when court representatives identified arrested defendants who met the necessary requirements for entry to community service. The district attorney's office was then consulted for its decision. Approval was given or the case was rejected. Once rejected, the case was considered "dead" from the court representative's point of view. Defense attorneys and judges were not told that the defendant had been considered and rejected, and they were not permitted at any later date to resuscitate the defendant's eligibility. Prosecutors were thereby given an effective veto power over all cases considered for community service.

Once a defendant in either of these two borough courts had received the prosecutors' approval, court representatives discussed the community service alternative with the defendant's attorney, usually a lawyer working for the Legal Aid Society (a government-supported agency responsible for representing indigent defendants). The defense attorney might order the case dropped from consideration, or the attorney might permit the court representative to talk it over with the defendant. The defendant was then told about the project, the requirements for work, and the policies for enforcing the sanction. The defendant could accept or reject the offer. At this point, the court representative made a final choice: did the defendant appear reliable enough to trust on the worksite? If so, and if all parties agreed to the sentence, the prosecutor and the defense attorney brought the case to the judge, who almost always ratified the settlement. (Of the 1,241 Bronx and Brooklyn defendants found eligible at screening during the two-year period between 1 October 1980 and 30 September 1982, only thirteen were denied community service sentences by judges.)

Figure 4.1. The Sequence of Decisions Leading to Community Service Sentences

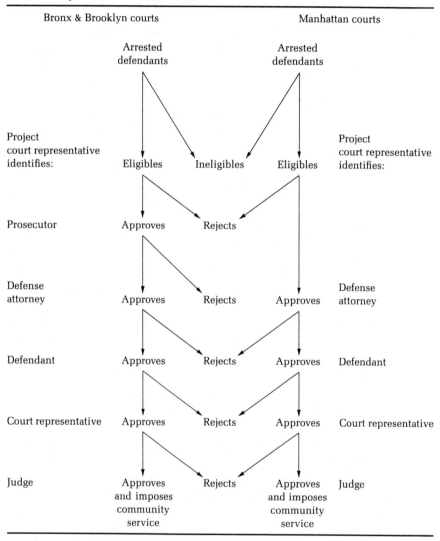

The prosecutor held no such power in the Manhattan court, and defense attorneys played the gatekeeping role there. Court representatives sorted through defense attorneys' case files in the courtroom before the cases were to be called, and they decided in consultation with defense attorneys whether the defendant should be considered for community service. If defendants met the project's screening requirements and defense attorneys agreed to consider recommending the sentence, defendants were approached. As in the other two boroughs, defendants had the right to accept or reject the offer. Court representatives were also empowered to reject defendants if they appeared too unreliable. If the court representative chose to accept the defendant, the defense attorney proposed community service in the plea bargaining conference with the judge. As a matter of established office policy, prosecutors always opposed community service and they sometimes prevailed. But judges made the ultimate decisions, so virtually all offenders ordered to perform community service in Manhattan were sentenced over the objections of prosecutors. (Prosecutors opposed the sentence because the district attorney's office had targeted chronic property offenders for aggressive prosecution, with the aim of jailing them. The Vera Institute project sought to provide judges with a nonincarcerative option for this same general defendant population, an objective that collided directly with what the prosecutors wanted. Rather than agreeing to negotiate the use of the sentence on a case-by-case basis, the district attorney's office promulgated a policy of firm opposition to the sentence in all instances.)

Because judges in the Bronx and Brooklyn courts almost always ratified the community service sentencing agreements that were reached before bringing these cases to the bench, it is fair to describe the selection procedures that existed in those two boroughs as prosecutor-centered. Prosecutors dominated the selection process to such an extent that they effectively controlled sentencing to community service. Defense attorneys may have chosen to take their defendants out of the running, and court representatives may have decided that the defendant presented too much of a risk to the project. Nonetheless, it was the prosecutor who had the strongest hand in deciding who got community service and who didn't.

The selection process in Manhattan was judge-centered. Real sentencing authority in matters of community service was always wielded by the judge. Defense attorneys operated only as gate-keepers, choosing when to recommend a defendant for community service, but it was up to the judge to make the effective final decision. Moreover, judges in this borough frequently took the initiative in asking court representatives to consider a defendant for community service, an event that was quite rare in the other two boroughs.

Bronx and Brooklyn: The Consequences of Prosecutorial Control

The design of the Bronx and Brooklyn selection procedures had two principal results for sentencing to community service. First, the volume of offenders approved and sentenced to the project was lower in the Bronx and Brooklyn courts than in Manhattan, partly because prosecutors knocked a sizable proportion of the proposed candidates out of the running. Secondly, prosecutors not only choked off the intake, but they also tended to eliminate exactly those offenders the project aimed to get: the defendants who were most likely to get short jail sentences.

That prosecutors restricted the flow of offenders into the project in the Bronx and Brooklyn is evident from an examination of what happened to defendants after they were declared eligible by court representatives. All defendants so designated between 1 October 1980 and 31 September 1982 were tracked to the point either of having been sentenced to community service or rejected. Table 4.1 shows how many of these were rejected at each stage of the selection process.

In the Bronx, 32 percent of all defendants found eligible at the initial screening were rejected by the district attorney's office. Brooklyn prosecutors rejected 17 percent of all eligible candidates. In contrast, only 8 percent of eligible defendants were rejected by defense attorneys in the Bronx, and 9 percent were rejected in Brooklyn. As noted above, judges in these two boroughs rarely overturned these agreements. This was very different from

Table 4.1. *The Proportion of Eligible Cases Rejected by Each
Party to the Negotiations in Each Borough*

	Bronx	Brooklyn	Manhattan
Total of screened eligibles	100%	100%	100%
Proportion rejected by:			
DA's office	32%	17%	0%
Probation officer	1%	3%	2%
Defense attorney	8%	9%	5%
Judge	0%	1%	15%
Defendant	3%	7%	2%
Court representative	16%	18%	20%
Proportion ultimately sentenced to community service:	38%	45%	56%

SOURCE: Project files.
NOTE: Includes all persons screened and found eligible between 1 October 1980
and 30 September 1982.

the pattern of selection decisions made in Manhattan courtrooms.
Prosecutors there were not able to veto any defendants, and judges
were the final arbiters, deciding against the sentence in 15 percent
of all eligible cases in this borough.

Prosecutorial vetoes thus contributed to a lower rate of intake
into the projects in these two boroughs. Whereas 56 percent of all
defendants found eligible in Manhattan were sentenced to community service, only 38 percent of defendants in the Bronx and
45 percent in Brooklyn were so sentenced. (In all three boroughs,
probation officers also rejected some defendants who were already
on probation and were going to be sent to jail for violating the
terms of that sentence.)

Prosecutors not only constricted the pipeline into community
service in the Bronx and Brooklyn courts, but they also filtered out
defendants who were more likely to get jail sentences. This is
clear from several pieces of information.

During the period from 1 October 1980 to 30 September 1982, court representatives were asked to record the reasons given whenever a case was rejected by any party to the negotiations. Tables 4.2 and 4.3 classify the rejected defendants in each borough by the leading reason reported and by the person who made the decision.[1]

Prosecutors in these two boroughs usually rejected defendants because they wanted them to receive jail sentences instead. Of the 323 Bronx defendants rejected by prosecutors during the two-year period of this study and for whom the court representatives recorded their reason for rejection, 41 percent were vetoed because the prosecutor sought a jail sentence instead. In another 3 percent of the cases, prosecutors wanted a "more severe" sentence, which should probably be interpreted as jail. Thirty-five percent of the prosecutors' vetoes were imposed because defendants' criminal records were too extensive, which again indicated that more jail terms were being sought. In total, about four out of five of the prosecutors' rejections were motivated by their desire to get a jail rather than a community service sentence for defendants.

The same general pattern was evident in Brooklyn. Although prosecutors in that borough rejected a smaller proportion of eligible defendants, their reasons were essentially the same. They wanted to "hit" them with harder sentences, usually by sending them to jail. Of the ninety-seven defendants rejected and for whom the reasons for the rejection are known, prosecutors turned down eighty-five either because a more severe sentence was preferred or because the defendants' criminal records were too serious.

Defendants rejected by prosecutors were clearly the most likely to get jail sentences upon conviction, of all the persons declared eligible for the project. They had longer criminal records than the defendants approved by prosecutors; they had been imprisoned more often for their most recent conviction; and they were more frequently held in pretrial detention awaiting resolution of their cases—characteristics found to have been correlated with a higher probability of getting a jail sentence.

However, one cannot conclude from these findings alone that prosecutors tended to approve only those defendants who would not otherwise have gone to jail. It seems possible at first glance to suppose that prosecutors might have been rejecting only those de-

Table 4.2. *Bronx Defendants Not Approved for Community Service Sentence: Reasons for Rejection, by Person Responsible for Decision*

Rejection reasons	Court rep.	DA's Office	Defense attorney	Judge	Defendant	Probation Officer	Unknown	Total
Has medical, drug, alcohol, or other behavioral problems (including "bad attitude")	51	4	1	—	2	—	8	66
Criminal record too light:								
Too few prior arrests/convictions	3	6	—	1	—	—	1	11
Criminal record "too extensive":	—	36	—	—	—	—	—	36
Record "too serious"	3	14	—	—	—	—	—	17
Too many recent arrests	3	18	—	—	—	—	—	21
Too many bench warrants	3	5	1	—	—	—	—	9
Had prior case(s) pending	4	39	1	—	2	5	4	55
Violated probation/parole	1	—	—	—	—	4	—	5

Seeks other disposition:								
More favorable (unspecified)	14	22	35	1	4	—	—	76
Dismissal	—	3	30	—	11	—	—	44
Discharge	—	1	—	—	—	—	—	1
Fine/restitution	2	24	10	—	3	—	—	39
Probation	—	3	—	1	—	—	—	4
More severe (unspecified)	—	11	—	—	—	1	—	12
Jail	—	133	—	—	2	2	1	138
Case "lost (i.e., defendant didn't appear; pled guilty to another case; case transferred, dismissed)	79	3	—	—	—	—	72	154
Miscellaneous other	14	1	5	2	11	2	4	39
Unknown reason	18	32	7	—	7	1	82	147
Total Bronx rejected defendants	195	355	90	5	42	15	172	874
	(22%)	(40%)	(10%)	(1%)	(5%)	(2%)	(20%)	(100%)

SOURCE: Project files.

Table 4.3. *Brooklyn Defendants Not Approved for Community Service Sentence: Reasons for Rejection, by Person Responsible for Decision*

Rejection reasons	Court rep.	DA's Office	Defense attorney	Judge	Defendant	Probation Officer	Unknown	Total
Has medical, drug, alcohol, or other behavioral problems (including "bad attitude")	36	1	1	—	—	—	7	45
Criminal record too light:								
Too few prior arrests/convictions	—	3	3	1	—	—	—	7
Criminal record "too extensive":								
Record "too serious"	1	7	—	2	—	—	—	10
Too many recent arrests	7	17	—	—	—	—	—	24
Too many bench warrants	3	2	—	—	—	—	—	5
Had prior case(s) pending	19	4	3	1	—	—	5	32
Violated probation/parole	1	—	—	1	—	12	—	14

Seeks other disposition:

More favorable (unspecified)	1	5	17	—	2	—	—	25
Dismissal	—	1	15	—	29	—	1	46
Discharge	—	—	2	—	—	—	—	2
Fine/restitution	—	1	2	—	—	—	—	3
Probation	—	—	1	—	1	—	—	2
More severe (unspecified)	1	10	—	—	—	1	—	12
Jail	—	45	1	3	—	1	1	51
Case "lost (i.e., defendant didn't appear; pled guilty to another case; case transferred, dismissed)	30	—	—	—	—	—	12	42
Miscellaneous other	3	1	4	—	7	—	6	21
Unknown reason	2	8	4	—	1	—	10	25
Total Brooklyn rejected defendants	105 (29%)	105 (29%)	53 (14%)	8 (2%)	40 (11%)	14 (4%)	42 (12%)	367 (100%)

SOURCE: Project files.

fendants who would have gone to jail for long periods of time, leaving in the pool those headed for sentences of ninety days or less. This was not happening, however, as the following evidence indicates.

In the Bronx and Brooklyn projects, court representatives used prosecutors' files to screen defendants, and one central piece of information they employed to identify prospective candidates for the project was the sentence being sought by the district attorney's office. Shortly after arrest, a specialized branch of the district attorney's office in each borough examined every felony case and decided how to track it for subsequent prosecution. (This unit is called the Felony Case Evaluation Unit in the Bronx and the Early Case Assessment Bureau in Brooklyn.) For a defendant to have been eligible for the institute's community service project, a court representative had to have seen that prosecutors were tracking his or her case for disposition as a misdemeanor. These tracking decisions usually included a sentence offer to be extended to defendants in subsequent pretrial hearings. These were noted, for example, as "A + 90," indicating that the felony charges could be dropped to a class-A misdemeanor with a recommendation to the judge of a ninety-day jail sentence. In the Bronx, court representatives usually didn't consider a defendant eligible for community service if the case was being tracked for a sentence longer than ninety days. Because Vera Institute planners intended the sentence to be used in instances where defendants would otherwise have been jailed for ninety days or less, the court representatives decided to ignore all cases for which prosecutors were asking sentences longer than this. Therefore, when Bronx prosecutors rejected defendants because they wanted jail sentences, they were not doing so because they sought sentences longer than ninety days. Such defendants were not even taken to the prosecutors for consideration.

In Brooklyn, project administrators observed that prosecutors did not always get the judge to impose the sentences they had recommended, so they instructed their court representatives to aim higher. Consequently, defendants were declared eligible by court representatives in this borough if the district attorney's files showed prosecutors planning to request jail sentences for as long as six or nine months. Given this fact, it does seem possible that prosecutors in this borough might have been rejecting defendants who were going to get longer jail sentences, leaving those headed for shorter jail time in the pool of approved defendants.

An examination of what actually happened to these rejected defendants tells a different story, however. We tracked to the point of final disposition in the criminal courts all defendants whose cases had been rejected by prosecutors because a jail sentence was being sought. In the Bronx, only 31 percent ultimately went to jail. In Brooklyn, 53 percent ultimately went to jail. (See table 4.4.) Most of these jail sentences were also for terms of less than ninety days. Table 4.5 shows that only 20 percent of the defendants rejected by the Bronx prosecutors received sentences longer than ninety days. In Brooklyn, only 33 percent got more than ninety days. These data reveal that prosecutors in these two boroughs worked to keep out of the community service project exactly those defendants who were most likely to receive jail sentences of ninety days or less, thereby frustrating the project planners' ambitions.

Planners' Assumptions and the Design of the Prosecutor-Centered Selection Process

Why were Bronx and Brooklyn prosecutors given such a key position in the selection process? The principal reason was that planners originally thought that this arrangement would produce most efficiently the desired results: the frequent substitution of community service sentences for jail terms. Unfortunately, planners overrated the prosecutors' ability to control sentencing, while at the same time, they underestimated the extent to which these decisions were produced by adversarial negotiations. This is quite clear from the early formulations of what the Vera Institute planners were up to.

By and large, planners subscribed to the notion that there exists in each jurisdiction a set of known and commonly shared rules which specify which penalties are to be applied to particular classes of offenses and offenders. In their conversations, they frequently invoked the conception of a "tariff" system, a schedule

Table 4.4. *Sentences Imposed on Bronx and Brooklyn*
Defendants Rejected for Community Service Because
Prosecutors Said They Wanted Jail Instead

Final disposition	Bronx	Brooklyn
Dismissed/ACD	25%	22%
Convicted & sentenced:		
Conditional discharge	13	10
Unconditional discharge	1	0
Fine	6	0
Fine or jail	13	10
Probation	6	0
"Time served"	5	6
Jail	31	53
Total disposed	100%	100%
	(n = 185)	(n = 51)

SOURCE: Rejection reasons obtained from project files; dispositions obtained from The New York City Criminal Justice Agency.

NOTE: Included here are all defendants screened and found eligible between 1 October 1980 and 30 September 1982, and subsequently rejected by the district attorney's office for the explicity stated reason of wanting jail or for reasons that could be construed as wanting jail (such as "too many recent arrests"). Excluded are defendants rejected because prosecutors wanted fines, probation, discharges, dismissals, or because defendants had too few prior arrests or other similar reasons indicating leniency.

"Fine or jail" sentences require that the offender pay the specified fine or be jailed. "Time served" sentences are legally considered jail terms, but the offender's time in pretrial detention is counted against the sentence, permitting the offender to walk out the door without having to serve more time.

that matched crimes and criminals to particular kinds of punishments.[2] Sentences were understood to be ranked by courthouse regulars as being exceedingly harsh at one end of the scale to mildly annoying (or no punishment at all) at the other. As described in chapter 2, a number of concerned officials thought that the existing tariff schedule had worrisome gaps in it, and the community service sentence had been advocated as a way of filling them. Available sanctions were thought to be ill-suited to the needs

Table 4.5. *Length of Jail Sentences Imposed on Bronx and Brooklyn Defendants Rejected by District Attorneys' Offices Because Prosecutors Sought Jail*

Length of sentence (in days)	Bronx	Brooklyn
1– 30	18%	17%
31– 60	34	25
61– 90	26	25
91–120	10	8
121 +	10	25
	100%	100%
	(n = 61)	(n = 24)
Average number days	82	109
Median number days	60	90

SOURCES: Reasons for rejection obtained from project files; length of sentences imposed were obtained from New York City Criminal Justice Agency files.
NOTE: Includes only eligible defendants screened between 1 October 1981 and 30 September 1982 and subsequently rejected because prosecutors reportedly sought jail sentences.

of the courts when faced with a variety of offenses that were relatively petty but still in need of punishment. As the project managers put it, they hoped to drive a "wedge" into that tariff schedule, aimed at the "seam" between short jail sentences and the other nonincarcerative alternatives (fines, probation, and discharges).

Although the use of the tariff terminology may have been somewhat new (in this country at least), the idea was not. Much of the writing on plea bargaining has promoted a similar conception of sentencing. For example, Abraham Blumberg, in his seminal work, *Criminal Justice*, argued that the adversarial trial system had effectively disappeared in America and that the courts had become plea bargaining bureaucracies.[3] He wrote that prosecutors, judges, and defense attorneys follow informal standards to process cases; that judges rubber stamp these consensual decisions in passing sentence; that the task of the defense attorney is to "con" defendants into pleading guilty to terms fixed by courthouse regulars.

This notion of the courthouse-as-bureaucracy gained extraordinarily wide currency in both the popular imagination and in scholarly journals,[3] and it is not surprising that Vera Institute planners thought in much the same terms.

Central to this conception is the image of sentencing as a classification task. The job of the bureaucratic personnel in the courts—the attorneys and the judges—is to figure out which rules apply to specific defendants, and whether this or that type of sentence "fits" or is "appropriate." The basic framework for these decisions is established in the state's written penal laws. But these statutory prescriptions are usually too broadly written to guide the sentencing of particular flesh-and-blood individuals. The courts have therefore developed, according to this understanding, their own more elaborate sets of informal rules to facilitate the case-by-case decision making.

In a report on the early phases of the Bronx project, those who planned and managed the effort revealed their conception of sentencing-as-classification:

> The Criminal Court caseload tends to consist of a few frequently recurring offense types—what David Sudnow refers to as "normal crimes. . . ." Prosecutors and defense attorneys seem to learn the types of dispositions that the other side expects in these routine cases. One gets a sense that, over time, precedents get established that suggest what disposition will be viewed as an acceptable outcome of plea negotiation for each type of incident. These norms are what Arthur Rosett and Donald Cressey have termed "going rates."[4]

The task of reform, according to this conception, is to change the classification rules—the consensual definitions of what kinds of punishments are "appropriate" for specified types of offenses—given existing standards of justice.

> To the extent that plea negotiations take place within such a framework, efforts to introduce a new disposition as an alternative to jail will face substantial difficulties until the parties mutually identify it as appropriate for cases where the going rate has been jail. And this necessary adjustment to the set of "going rates" must be worked out over time, in individual cases, no matter how vigorously any one policy-maker or program may argue for the principle that the new disposition ought to substitute for short jail terms.[5]

Despite the need for consensus in changing the norms, the planners saw the prosecutor as being the key figure in the sentencing process.

Ordinarly, the sentence imposed is the sentence recommended by the ADA, who will have reached an agreement with the defense attorney that a sentence to be recommended is a fair basis for disposition of the case upon guilty plea.[6]

This suggested an obvious strategy for changing sentencing practices: convince prosecutors to change office policies regarding sentencing recommendations. This was exactly the reform strategy that was adopted in the Bronx. Because the Vera Institute had good relations with the Bronx district attorney, planners approached him with the idea. They argued that the new sentencing alternative would be an appropriate one for a specified "band" of offenders and that the use of this new sanction would be a sound public policy. The district attorney agreed that his assistants would consider community service sentences in cases where defendants would otherwise be given short jail terms ("short" being defined as ninety days or less). The project's court representatives were instructed to identify all defendants tracked by prosecutors for dispositions in the criminal court and for whom the district attorney's files indicated that a jail sentence of ninety days or less would be offered. This seemed the logical way to intervene in the classification process, locating the "target group" of defendants, as they were commonly described, and thereby facilitating their being switched from the jail track to the community service track.

It would be a mistake to see the early planning and design stages of the project as having been driven only by a devotion to theory. Planners were pragmatists, and the design of the selection procedures was constrained by many different practical concerns, the most pressing of which was to get a community service sentencing project off the ground and accepted by the courts. The design of the selection process was therefore a kind of negotiated outcome, the result of planners' ideas intersecting with the demands of getting a project up and running.

Prosecutors were consequently given a central role in the process not simply because planners saw them as key figures in the process of classification and tracking of defendants for sentencing, but also because the district attorney in the Bronx was initially more enthusiastic about the project than was the judiciary. The administrative judge in the Bronx Criminal Court was initially reluctant to embrace the proposal because he thought that there were already too many "diversion" programs in the Bronx. After some hesitation he agreed to the project's presence. (Still, he resisted imposing community service as a sentence in and of itself. He preferred for reasons of administrative ease to suspend the imposition of sentence, ordering the offender to perform the required work, and then imposing an unconditional discharge at its successful completion. Planners objected to this because they wanted the new sanction to be a full-blown sentence, with full legal standing, rather than simply a coercive instrument of the courts that existed in a kind of legal netherworld.)

The decision to work closely with the district attorney resulted also from the discovery that the organized defense bar, represented by the Legal Aid Society, was hesitant to lend its support to the project. The society's management feared that the sentence would be used to upgrade punishments, extending more severe controls over people who were then being given discharges or light sentences not involving jail. Indeed, the director of the society's branch in that borough argued that the function of the community service project would be to "drive out" the pretrial diversion project, another Vera Institute project that existed to channel defendants out of the courts altogether. Whereas defendants formerly going into the Court Employment Project (the diversion program) had had their charges dropped, they would now get a conviction and a community service sentence, if the new Vera Institute proposal was adopted by the courts. Vera Institute planners did not intend this outcome to result from the introduction of their community service project, but the society's managers feared that the district attorney's office would seduce the project, turning it to serve its own interests, which were, in the eyes of defense attorneys, repressive.

The district attorney's support for the community service concept in the face of judicial and defense reluctance thereby helped to shape some of the early decisions about how to design a selection procedure. The district attorney agreed to let project court representatives use his office's confidential case files to identify potentially eligible community service participants. Because of this opening, it seemed both logical and efficient to set up a selection process whereby court representatives would begin their round of approvals by consulting prosecutors first. Court representatives couldn't take the prosecutors' files to the defense attorney, and it was easier to walk them over to the assistant district attorney in charge. Only those who were approved would be discussed with the defense bar. The agreement to use the district attorney's files thus made other design choices easier.

Planners also thought that prosecutors were the key decision makers in plea negotiations and that their recommendations effectively controlled sentencing determinations.[7] They believed that most judges in the Bronx would not buck the prosecutors' requests in sentencing matters. The important point regarding the community service sentence was, therefore, first to get the approval of the district attorney's office. Once that was obtained, the other parties were expected to fall into line.

The selection process thereby evolved from a fortunate conjunction of what the planners wanted and what they thought they could obtain. They didn't simply bumble into the courts, following the path of least resistance, and fall into the district attorney's lap. They recognized, quite rightly, that the prosecutor in New York courts, as in other courts across the land, is the key actor in the criminal process. This perception was linked to the then-prevailing conception of plea bargaining as a bureaucratic sorting-out process, and the result was a sentencing procedure keyed to the prosecutor's classification decisions regarding sentencing.

Underestimating the Adversarial
Character of Sentencing

Unfortunately, the assumptions about plea bargaining and sentencing that underpinned the design of the prosecutor-centered selection process gave too much importance to the prosecutors' classification and sentence recommendation powers. Courts are not bureaucracies, because they lack the essential characteristics of bureaucratic organizations. It is more accurate to see them as arenas for handling cases and settling disputes. People who meet in these arenas are often members of bureaucratic organizations (the district attorney's office, for example), but the court itself is not so constructed.[8] Like all collections of people who work closely together and frequently with one another, the "work group" of the courthouse, as some have called this collection of defense attorneys, prosecutors, and judges, develop a common culture, a set of informal norms that structure sentencing decisions. But the mistake of many theorists has been to think that these informal rules—or tariffs—prescribe the outcomes of sentencing negotiations.

The norms that structure the courthouse work group interactions are really of two distinct kinds: those that define the procedures to be followed and those that establish the range of acceptable sentences.[9] The former are the "game rules," and the latter are what might be called "penal norms," because they prescribe certain kinds of punishments for particular classes of offenses and offenders. Put another way: penal norms, both those formally codified in written law and those informally agreed upon in the courtroom, match appropriate sentencing outcomes to types of offenses and offenders. (This is the tariff schedule.) In contrast, the procedural norms—the game rules—prescribe only how sentencing decisions will be made. Sentencing decisions can therefore be tightly structured by rules of procedure, but loosely constrained as to what the outcomes will be. In this circumstance, the outcome is determined not by the application of a clear-cut substantive rule, but by the application of power—one party's ability to drive home a settlement that is more favorable to him, despite the high costs incurred by opponents.

In the relatively rare instances where defendants are convicted at trial, sentencing outcomes are determined unilaterally by judges and are constrained primarily by penal norms.[10] The charges for which defendants are convicted define the defendants' legal culpabilities and place them within a range of permitted sanctions. Judges have some room to weigh various considerations, applying their own interpretations of the state's penal objectives, but the conviction charge effectively pigeonholes the defendant, fixing him or her in a range of legally authorized punishments, while closing others. In these circumstances, sentencing is very much a classification exercise. Judges determine what an appropriate penalty shall be according to the norms prevailing in statutes and in the court.

Ninety-nine percent of all convictions in the lower criminal courts in New York City are gotten by guilty pleas, however, and almost all of these pleas are the result of plea bargaining.[11] These plea bargains typically involve negotiating not only what the charges will be, but the sentence as well. As a Brooklyn prosecutor said:

> No defense counsel worth his salt is just gonna take the plea and leave the question of sentence in the realm of the gods. He's gonna deal with it up front. Some of them don't care so much for the title that's on the crime as much as the time that's on the crime.[12]

Negotiating both the title and the time that's on the crime is adversarial, with the defense attorney jockeying to get the most favorable results for his client, while the prosecutor generally aims to achieve the result that fits his notions of justice and his law enforcement goals. Even though the judge ultimately imposes the sentence, what the sentence will be is determined by negotiation, rather than by the judge in a unilateral fashion. All parties have some leverage to define the terms of trade and thereby the sentence. For example, defendants can refuse to plead guilty and delay the settlement, thereby increasing the burden on the courts. Prosecutors can threaten to take the defendant to trial and win a conviction on the top count, and judges can threaten to sentence harshly in such circumstances. There exist a variety of different strategies each party can pursue to shape the desired sentencing outcome.

This is the important point that was not fully appreciated by the Vera Institute planners: sentences are not the outcomes of a classification exercise, where the schedule of "going rates" prescribes a penalty that is considered appropriate and just by all parties to the negotiation. Rather, they are the outcomes of adversarial competitions, battles in which all parties seek to optimize their own individual and organizational objectives at the lowest possible cost to themselves. The sentence that is ultimately determined upon depends to a great extent upon the strength of the prosecutor relative to the defense attorney. Whether one party to the competition has a strong or weak strategic position depends upon the nature of the evidence, the ability to threaten and win at trial, the skill of the attorney in being able to capitalize upon the case's evidentiary strengths and weaknesses, and the ability of the prosecutor or defendant to maneuver in ways that will increase the chances of getting what they want. In other words, sentencing outcomes negotiated in plea bargaining are determined in large part by skill, power, and differences in power, and not strictly by the application of penal norms.

Tariff schedules do exist and they are informally subscribed to by people who work in the courts. But they only establish the range of acceptable outcomes, the floor and the ceiling on the punishment scale. They determine that persons charged with negligent homicide should not be given a ten dollar fine, for example, or that a first offender who committed a burglary of a store at night should not be given fifteen years in state prison. Precisely where the sentence actually falls within the broad range of permitted punishments depends upon which party to the bargaining is better able to get his or her way. Each has a different set of interests that impels him or her; each has access to different resources (time, case investigators, good witnesses, etc.) that determine their advantage over other parties. These constitute constraints on each party, define their strategic position in bargaining, and thereby contribute to the kind of sentencing agreement that is ultimately hammered out.

That sentences are negotiated in the Bronx and Brookyn courts instead of being imposed unilaterally by judges (or controlled by prosecutors) came clear from interviews with attorneys in those courts. As two prosecutors in the Bronx described it:

Let's say I ask for a sentence of three months, and defense counsel asks for no jail. The attorney for each side makes his arguments. This is part of the plea bargaining process. The outcome is usually a compromise. Somebody has to come down. Usually the judge makes it happen. It is in effect a twisting of the arm of the DA—and now you have two against one. It can go the other way, too. It is very hard to argue your position when you have a judge saying that the case is not worth jail.

An offer of 30 to 60 days means that I'm going to argue for jail. It doesn't necessarily mean that I'm going to get it. Every offer I made was higher than what I anticipated the disposition to be in the case. By asking for 30 or 60 days, this means that we might get 30. If I offer 30 or 60, the defense attorney would probably walk over to me and ask, "What do you think about this?" At that point you would probably go down. In fact, I expect to go down.[13]

In many instances, the judge plays an active role in hammering out the plea and sentence agreement. In the words of a Bronx prosecutor:

After the defense counsel and my side had discussed the offer, we would then approach the bench with either myself or one of my assistants conveying the offer. Rarely, if ever, would we discuss the merits of the case or the defendant's record at the bench conference. We would each convey our offer. The judge would say to the defense counsel, "What are you looking for?" and the defense counsel would say something in return. The judge would offer either what you, the DA, had to offer or something lower, and the defense attorney would go and convey the offer to his client. The judge would say, "What is this case worth to you?" partly so that he wouldn't undercut you too much, or else he would say that this case is a piece of shit. We know that we are about to get a disposition rammed down our throat.[14]

That Bronx prosecutors cannot dictate what the sentences will be is evident in a comparison between prosecutors' recommendations and the sentences ultimately imposed. We were interested in finding out what happened when prosecutors rejected defendants because they sought jail rather than community service sentences, so we tracked a group of such defendants to the point when their cases were closed. This group included all ninety-five defendants who had been found to be eligible for community service in the Bronx between 1 October 1980 and 30 September 1981 and had then been rejected by prosecutors. Of these ninety-five, we were able to locate the prosecutors' final recommendation to the judge prior to sentencing and the sentence itself in only fifty-five cases. (Many of the other forty defendants had jumped bail and had not had their cases reach disposition by the time of data collection.) In fifteen of the fifty-five cases, prosecutors wound up recommending sentences other than jail, even though they had earlier rejected these defendants for community service because they wanted jail. (See table 4.6.) As one would expect, most of these (thirteen) did not go to jail. But in the thirty-seven instances in which prosecutors did ask for jail, judges imposed imprisonment terms only 57 percent of the time. Thus, prosecutors could not in fact pick who went to jail and who didn't.

Roughly the same pattern existed in the Brooklyn Criminal Court. The relationship between prosecutors' offers and sentences imposed was not examined in the same statistical fashion in this borough, but our observations and interviews indicated that the same general practices prevailed. Prosecutors did not control sentencing decisions. Rather, sentencing outcomes were negotiated. Asked whether defense attorneys conferred first with prosecutors to reach a settlement before taking the case to the judge, a high-level prosecutor responsible for overseeing the Brooklyn district attorney's criminal court operations replied:

Some judges prefer that, but there are very few of them in this court because, left to our own devices, we're too adversarial. Generally judges direct it, force it, tell what their opinions are, think we're too soft, too hard—it varies from judge to judge. But most times, when things are going smoothly, when the judge hasn't felt hurt in any way, he normally calls both parties up. They walk up and he says, "What's this case about? What do you want? What do you offer?" It's a tri-partite involvement. Sometimes, though, he acts as a total dictator, saying "You're totally wrong." I've seen that very few times, though.

Asked how often the judge imposes a sentence different than that which the prosecutors' recommended in that borough, he responded:

I would say that, in fairness, it would be in the realm of 50 percent of the time. Because, by nature and by strength of the case, it's our job as prosecutors, I think, that we tend to be a little more conservative than the defense, of course, and the judges, while they are fair, they are also under great pressures—calendar control pressures. They have to force us to be reasonable and to move off the mark, and they do the same thing with the defense, or this whole place would come to a standing, screeching halt.[15]

Table 4.6. Prosecutors' Sentencing Recommendations and Judicial Decisions in the Bronx

		Prosecutor's final recommendations			
		Jail	Non-jail sentence	No recommendation	
Sentence imposed by judge	Jail	21 (57%)	2 (13%)	1 (33%)	24
	Non-jail	16 (43%)	13 (87%)	2 (67%)	31
		37 (100%)	15 (100%)	3 (100%)	55

SOURCE: Bronx District Attorney's Office and New York City Criminal Justice Agency.

In short, prosecutors cannot dictate sentences in Brooklyn either. They are only one party to the decision, albeit a party with a strong hand, but others have some leverage in establishing the terms of trade in the plea and sentence negotiations.

Changing Tariff Schedules and Game Rules

Because sentencing decisions in the lower criminal courts are typically negotiated ones, attempts to change the way they are made must accomplish two things if they are to succeed. First, key decision makers must agree to follow new substantive rules. That is, sentencing reforms seek to modify the norms prescribing the kinds of sanctions appropriate for different classes of offenses and offenders. Sometimes they involve changes in the statutory law (more specifically, in the substantive penal law), but they almost always also require a transformation of the unwritten and informal norms—the rules of thumb—which judges and other engaged parties use to guide decisions regarding sentences to be imposed upon criminal offenders. Second, a reform that is to be successful must also change the game rules of negotiation in a way that facilitates the implementation of these new substantive rules.

In the case of the institute's community service reform, institute managers sought to promulgate a new substantive rule: that community service orders constitute an appropriate substitute for jail sentences of ninety days or less in crimes not involving violence against persons. Furthermore, the sentence was to be considered well-suited also to instances in which the offender was not quite on the verge of going to jail, but was close to it. In all three boroughs, the reformers promoted the identical rule. What differed among them, however, was the way in which procedures were changed by the introduction of a new screening and selection process. The "game rules" were changed in different ways in different boroughs. In the Bronx and Brooklyn courts, the changed procedures strengthened the hands of the prosecutors in their negotiations with defense attorneys and judges, and these prosecutors did not really accept the redefinition of the tariff schedule. In Manhattan, the prosecutors' resistance to such a redefinition was nearly neutralized by the way the judges were involved. Moreover, the selection procedures dovetailed with plea bargaining practices in that court in such a way as to increase the likelihood of judges imposing community service in lieu of short jail sentences.

Why Bronx and Brooklyn Prosecutors Rejected Defendants for Community Service

Prosecutors in the Bronx and Brooklyn Courts frequently blocked consideration of community service because they didn't think it was an appropriate sanction. That is, they refused to change their standards of what constituted acceptable sentences. To be sure, the district attorneys in both boroughs formally agreed to let the Vera Institute do what it proposed to do: seek community service sentences in instances where defendants would otherwise receive jail terms of ninety days or less. But even though this suggestion was adopted as an office policy, many of the prosecutors charged with approving individual defendants for the project found the policy difficult to implement. As one Bronx prosecutor said:

Let me tell you my outlook. I always had problems with Vera. It's an alternative to jail, right? But if I felt someone should go to jail or if the case warranted that this person should be incarcerated, then, to me, he *should* be incarcerated. If I felt that someone should not be incarcerated, then working for someone [i.e., performing community service] is fine, but that is not the point of Vera. . . . I could see Vera as an alternative to other types of sentencing such as a conditional discharge, a condition being that you complete Vera. In my view, anyone who did an act where jail is appropriate, to be told that instead you will be doing work for the community—it is apples and oranges. . . . If he is to do community service work, the decision should not have been made for him to go to jail in the first place.[16]

Many prosecutors never accepted the idea that a seventy-hour unpaid labor assignment had the same "weight" as a jail sentence. They saw it as less punishing, and many refused to go along with what they perceived to be a scaling down of penalties.

I'm looking for punishment and I don't really think the program [i.e., the Vera project] is punishment.
I think he has to do heavy time. We're asking for 90 days.[17]

Another commonly-given reason for rejecting the community service option was that prosecutors in these two boroughs thought it was less effective than jail in reducing crime. They often expressed the belief that community service was yet another "rehabilitative program," and they felt it appropriate only for younger offenders with less extensive records. Older offenders or people with longer criminal histories were seen to need stronger medicine to make them go straight.

I don't feel that career criminals will benefit from Vera. One of the purposes of putting someone in Vera is a sincere belief that he'll benefit and not be back before court. This guy's record indicates he wouldn't be such a person. [This defendant, arrested for burglary, had seven prior arrests, three convictions, one of them for a felony. The prosecutor was offering a plea to a class-A misdemeanor and 90 days in jail.]

I wouldn't approve anybody who is out of their teens. By that point, they should know how to get their own job. I look at Vera as a way of growing a kid up—maturing him. If a kid is committing a crime once he is out of his teens, there is nothing to rehabilitate. . . . If he's out of his teens, he should know by himself that this lawbreaking is not the way to go.

A number of times I've given refusals because, while it's within the guidelines that we have, the frequency has been such or the background is such that I don't think that any social service would help, and I think that it would be giving him one more laugh at the criminal justice system. "I beat it again." If that comes through by the frequency or the type of crime, I'll normally withhold my agreement for the program.[18]

Many Bronx and Brooklyn prosecutors saw the community service project not as a functional equivalent of jail but as the last stop before jail. That is, it is a few rungs down from jail on the crime-control and punishment ladder. Each time a person is convicted, he should be hung from the next highest rung. First convictions for minor crimes earn discharges or fines. The next round may be a probation sentence, perhaps a heavier fine, perhaps a short stay in jail. For each "bite of the apple," as one prosecutor put it, the punishment should be heavier. Community service, in this view, is a useful addition to the arsenal of punishments and is best used as a "last chance."

If the defendant has done a number of years in jail, he's not going to get anything out of Vera. . . . What are they going to think of two weeks work?

On the other hand, if it is a seventeen-year-old kid, who had a couple of arrests, all for petty stuff—let's say he's gotten fines in the past or a conditional discharge—maybe working for two weeks will straighten him out.

I look at cases and consider people I would be asking for thirty to sixty days because their number was up. They'd already received an ACD, a violation, a fine, and hadn't learned anything from that. It was time to ask for time, but the crime wasn't that serious—there wasn't any physical injury involved.

My own feeling is that people should be gotten early, first or second time in the system, before they have become jaded by contact with the system. I think you're aiming too late to have an impact on the basis of community service.

Shoot for the areas where the defendant needs something more than just a fine. There's the possibility that something a little stronger will bring him around, if it is not a persistent kind of conduct. One last shot.[19]

Weak Cases and Reduced Leverage

Bronx and Brooklyn prosecutors did recommend community service in some instances where they thought that the defendants really deserved jail, but often these were instances in which they were not likely to get a jail sentence anyway. In other words: they may have wanted jail, but they lacked sufficient leverage to ensure this outcome. Asked what difference the existence of the Vera Institute project made in the way cases were prosecuted, one Bronx assistant district attorney responded:

I guess the difference would be in the plea bargaining arrangement. It sometimes made it easier to get a disposition in a borderline situation between getting a jail sentence and not getting one. The situation would be where I thought there would be difficulty in getting [a] jail sentence, and for purposes of getting a plea, Vera was an alternative. You would want to get jail time on many cases, but you know your likelihood of getting it isn't great in some instances, so Vera is a good alternative in those cases.[20]

Defense attorneys saw this happening. A Legal Aid Society attorney in Brooklyn answered in this way when asked how community service sentences were being used in that borough:

The cases that trouble me are cases where the defendant's got a record; if he's convicted he'd probably get substantial time; where there is a real question as to guilt and where there's a very good defense case. Those are the kinds of cases that the program tends to be offered, which is one of my problems with it.[21]

If prosecutors try to take weak cases to trial, they run the risk of losing. (Fifty-four percent of all trials in New York City Criminal Courts during 1981 resulted in acquittals.[22]) Getting a plea to community service amounts to getting "half a loaf," which is better than none at all. At least the defendant is convicted, and if he fails to fulfill the court-imposed requirements, jail will almost certainly be imposed. Indeed, the chief prosecuting attorney in the Brooklyn Criminal Court said that using community service strengthened his chances of getting jail sentences in instances in which he would not otherwise have gotten as stiff a plea as he would have liked.

Prosecutors' leverage in getting a jail sentence depends not only on the strength of the case, but also on whether the defendant is already in jail, awaiting the outcome of the case. As one prosecutor put it:

If a guy is out, it's tough [to get a plea to a jail sentence]. Many times a judge will say, "You're not going to get him to plead guilty to a jail sentence." My response is that I'm not going to let a defendant get away with a sentence that is inappropriate, because a judge in arraignments made a mistake [by letting a defendant out on low bail or on his/her own recognizance]. Many times, you don't have a choice, however. The reality of the situation is that the guy isn't going to plead guilty, so the alternative is a trial. By the time the case goes to trial, a complainant may be fed up. So you get what you can get. Then you're faced with a situation where probation may be better than having a case dismissed. It's tough to get a plea to a jail sentence.[23]

A sentence to community service is also better than having a case dismissed, at least from the prosecutor's point of view. Asked if he would approve of community service if the defendant was being held in pretrial detention, a Bronx prosecutor said:

I would be less inclined to offer it if someone is in jail, because it is a lot easier for me to get the 30 days if the person is in. If the person is out, it is very rare for someone to plead guilty and then go to jail.[24]

Not surprisingly, a large proportion of Bronx and Brooklyn defendants sentenced to community service in 1982 were not being held in pretrial detention at the time of their convictions. In the Bronx, 47 percent of those participants screened during the twelve-month period between 1 October 1981 and 30 September 1982 were in detention at the time of being sentenced to the project. Sixty-four percent of the Brooklyn participants found eligible for the project during this period were being held in detention at the time of pleading guilty. In the statistical analysis of disposition outcomes described in chapter 3, the defendant's detention status was found to be a powerful predictor of whether a jail sentence would ultimately be imposed. By approving defendants who were at liberty, prosecutors in the Bronx and Brooklyn were channelling into the project those least likely to plead guilty to a jail term, even though they may have thought that a stretch behind bars was well-deserved.

There is yet another indication that prosecutors in these boroughs were dumping into the community service project their "garbage cases," as the weaker cases are called in the argot of the courts. When the preliminary findings of this evaluation were communicated to the managers of the project, a decision was made to restructure the way defendants were selected for community service in the Brooklyn and Bronx courts. Before this point in time, court representatives had sifted through the prosecutors' case files that were being brought into the courts in order to locate defendants eligible for community service. Alerted to the strong relationship between detention status and sentencing, Judith Greene, now the citywide project director, ordered a test. Court representatives were asked to conduct their searches for eligible defendants using the court calendars, not the prosecutors' case files. These court calendars list the defendants' detention status as well as their charges. Court representatives recorded the names of detained defendants and then went to the prosecutors' case files to see if these defendants could be found. Many of these case folders were not there. It turned out that defendants in detention were often marked by the district attorney's office for sustained attention and full prosecution. As the director of the Brooklyn project later told me, "these missing case files were for defendants that the district attorney's office was real serious about jailing."[25] The folders were being held by prosecutors at their desks instead of being placed in the general file bins. By relying on the stacks of files in the bins, the court representatives were unwittingly being restricted to cases that had already been deemed ready for quick disposition, to be induced by "easier" plea offers.

In summary, Bronx and Brooklyn prosecutors used their dominant position in the selection process to frustrate the project's attempt to change the norms governing sentencing decisions. They resisted approving the new sanction in instances where they would previously have sought short jail sentences, and they effectively blocked other parties from using the sentence in the same way. They generally approved defendants who would otherwise have received lesser sentences, not requiring a stay in jail, either because their cases were not grave enough to demand one, according to prevailing standards of justice, or because prosecutors lacked the leverage needed to extract a guilty plea with a jail sentence. The upshot was an overall stiffening of penalties, with the community service order being imposed most often as a substitute for lesser penalties.

Why Prosecutors
Sometimes Cooperated

Not every participant approved and sentenced to community service in these two boroughs would have escaped jail in the absence of the project, however. Using the statistical modeling techniques described in the last chapter, we estimated that about a fifth of the Bronx participants would have received jail sentences, as would about a quarter of the Brooklyn participants. Why did prosecutors approve these persons for the project while steering others away from community service in the direction of jail?

Part of the answer to that question is that the district attorneys in these two boroughs did, after all, agree to recommend the sanction in cases where jail sentences of ninety days or less would have been deemed appropriate otherwise. For a variety of reasons, they accepted the argument that such a policy would be valuable and worthwhile. Their assistants, who were charged with implementing the policy, more often than not used the sanction for defendants who were not really headed for jail, but in some instances they approved a particular jailbound individual for the project simply because they felt some willingness to honor the agreement. They may also have seen it as trading: they used their approvals in most cases to extract a more punitive settlement for defendants who otherwise would have gotten less severe dispositions, but they may have thrown the project's court representatives some "red meat" once in a while. Bargaining and trading is the name of the game in the criminal courts, and dispositions are the coin of the realm. Prosecutors built up cordial relationships with the project's officials, and some value was placed on working with them. Court representatives were frequently rejected in their pursuit of a defendant, and prosecutors may have felt some compunction to give in occasionally. These sentiments may have been felt more keenly at the higher supervisory levels in the prosecutors' office, where broader policy concerns—and concerns about the office's reputation—were more pressing. (In Brooklyn, all approvals were made at the supervisor's level, and court representatives in the Bronx not infrequently took to the supervising attorneys cases that the lower-level assistant district attorneys had refused to pass on.)

Prosecutors may also have agreed to substitute community service for jail because they knew that the risks of putting offenders in the Vera Institute project were quite low. Attendance and behavior on the worksite was strictly enforced, and they knew that people who didn't perform as expected would be brought back to court for resentencing. They would then get their jail sentences in these cases.

Impact of Selection Procedures on Court Representatives' Screening Decisions

Because project planners overrated prosecutors' abilities to control sentencing decisions in the Brooklyn and the Bronx courts, court representatives in these boroughs systematically overlooked many offenders who were getting short jail terms and would have been eligible for community service. This happened because the screening decision focused too narrowly upon prosecutors' sentence offers rather than on what judges actually decided. The prosecutors' plea offers played a key role in the earliest screening decisions. As we have described, court representatives in the Bronx and Brooklyn began their screening efforts by looking in the case files to see what kind of sentence recommendation the prosecutor was planning to offer the defendant. Unfortunately, these were poor indicators of the sentences that would be imposed further down the line. Even though prosecutors might have wanted a jail sentence in the early stages, they often had to scale down their demands in subsequent hearings. Judges also refused in many instances to impose a jail sentence, even though prosecutors asked for one, as we have discussed and as was shown in table 4.4.

In the Bronx, court representatives also overlooked many defendants who were getting short jail sentences and should have been considered eligible for the project simply because they treated the prosecutors' sentence offers as if they were the sentencing decisions themselves, instead of as the bargaining chips they really were. They often passed over cases in which the prosecutors' file indicated that a sentence longer than ninety days was being offered. Even though these longer sentences were offered by prosecutors in the end, judges frequently imposed sentences in the "target range," which is to say, between one and ninety days. To get some estimate of how many such cases there were in the Bronx, a random sample of 135 people was drawn from all offenders given jail sentences by the Bronx Criminal Court between 18 November and 17 December 1981. None were charged with crimes that would have made them ineligible for community service, and all had one or more prior convictions—an entry requirement for the project. Fifty-six of them had received jail sentences of ninety days or less. In twenty-six (or 46 percent) of these fifty-six cases, the prosecutor's last offer to the defendant was for a jail term of four months or more. Judges had therefore undercut these offers, imposing shorter sentences than were requested. These defendants would not have been considered eligible by the Bronx court representatives. These court representatives were therefore overlooking half of all the offenders who ultimately received sentences in the target range of ninety days or less.

Cautious and Aggressive Screening Decisions

Bronx and Brooklyn court representatives were also excessively conservative in their selection of eligible candidates, because they gauged their decisions to what they thought prosecutors were willing to accept. Manhattan court representatives, in contrast, were much more willing to accept defendants who had very long criminal records, if they met the basic minimum entry requirements for the project. Whereas the Bronx and Brooklyn court representatives frequently passed over defendants whose cases were "too serious," Manhattan court representatives were not inhibited by such a self-imposed ceiling. This reflected different management stances in the boroughs, but also different organizational imperatives. Prosecutors were given the gatekeeping role in the Bronx and Brooklyn, and the court representatives made their accommodations to this exercise of veto power.

That Bronx and Brooklyn court representatives were more cautious in screening decisions than their colleagues in Manhattan is evident from an examination of the defendants found eligible in each of the boroughs. Because project officials in all three boroughs focused their attention on defendants charged with roughly similar property crimes, the most important feature distinguishing the seriousness of certain cases was the defendants' criminal records. People with more prior convictions were more likely to get jail sentences, and court representatives in each borough learned what the market would bear with regard to community service possibilities. Bronx defendants declared eligible by court representatives for community service between 1 October 1981 and 30 September 1982 had an average of 2.9 prior criminal convictions before their arrest in the current case. The corresponding figure for the Brooklyn defendants eligible during the same period was 2.5 prior convictions. Manhattan defendants declared eligible during the same period had much longer records; they had an average of 6.9 prior criminal convictions.

This does not reveal the whole story, however, for there were also some borough differences in the kinds of offenders brought into court. As a group, the defendants arraigned in Manhattan—

whether or not they were declared eligible—had longer criminal records than defendants in the other two boroughs. But even when this difference is taken into account, the Manhattan court representatives were still more aggressive in their screening decisions, targeting their efforts on those defendants most likely to get jail sentences because of their long criminal records.

This can be shown in a comparison of defendants declared eligible for the project with the larger population of arraigned defendants in each borough. We could not, for lack of adequate documentation, determine exactly how the pool of eligibles chosen by the court representatives compared with the total population of potentially eligible defendants in the criminal courts. However, a special sample drawn by the New York Criminal Justice Agency provides a means of developing a reasonably good indication. This sample included all persons arraigned in each of the three boroughs during two weeks of October 1980. Using this file, we eliminated all defendants who would not have met the essential minimum requirements for community service: having at least one prior criminal conviction and being arraigned for certain types of offenses (primarily nonviolent property crimes). By applying these rules, we were able to construct a pool of defendants who could have been considered eligible for the Vera Institute project. We cannot, of course, be absolutely certain that the caseload during these two weeks was exactly similar to the one that the court representatives examined throughout 1981–1982, but it is likely that the differences were not terribly great.

The average number of prior criminal convictions for this two-week population of arraigned defendants in the Bronx was 3.8. Because the average number of prior convictions was lower for those defendants who were declared eligible (2.9), we can reasonably conclude that court representatives were not considering defendants with longer records, choosing instead to limit their attention to those defendants having fewer prior convictions. The same pattern was evident in Brooklyn. The total potentially eligible defendant population during the two-week period in October 1980 had an average of 4.5 prior convictions. The defendants declared eligible by the project during the 1981–1982 period had an average of 2.5 prior convictions. Again, court representatives apparently restricted themselves to the lower end of the defendant spectrum.

In Manhattan, the average number of prior convictions was almost identical for both groups (7.1 prior convictions for the two-week sample and 6.9 for all screened eligibles). This shows that court representatives in this borough were not hindered by a self-imposed ceiling on their choices. Persons with as many as sixty-one prior arrests and thirty-four prior convictions were declared eligible and sentenced to the Vera Community Service Project, a possibility that was unheard of in either of the other two boroughs.

Court representatives in the Bronx and Brooklyn stayed away from defendants with long criminal records for an understandable reason: they thought that the odds of getting a prosecutor's approval were too long to bother with. This was obvious from the answers we got when we asked them why they had thrown aside case files on defendants who appeared to meet the minimum entry requirements.

Forget it; I'm not even going to look at this case. The defendant has thirty-three arrests. They'll never give it to us.

If you take somebody with twenty-eight priors to the DAs, they look at you like you're crazy and say "You don't really think this guy is acceptable, do you?"

When [the files show that the DA's office is asking for an A misdemeanor and six months in jail], they're not even going to deal with me. They'll laugh me right out of court.[26]

Bronx and Brooklyn prosecutors set an upward limit on the kinds of defendants that they would approve for community service, and court representatives learned quickly what that limit was. Court representatives sometimes tested the rule, trying to get the prosecutor to budge, but they chose to pursue a more cautious course for the sake of efficiency. Why bother to spend the time logging in defendants who had little chance of being approved? The work was already very demanding, and one's caseload could be made more manageable by staying within the bounds of what the prosecutor had already defined as acceptable.

Manhattan court representatives worked under similar pressures; they had a flood of potentially eligible defendants each day and they had to choose which ones to pursue. But they lacked the upward limit imposed by the prosecutors' office. The only limit they considered was what the judge would and would not accept. Many judges imposed the community service sentence upon defendants who had very long records, and this meant that court representatives could try even if the odds looked long. Court representatives in the other two boroughs could not adopt this approach because they were tailoring their screening decisions to the prosecutors' offers that were made in plea bargaining sessions. This was, as we have seen, one long step away from the actual sentencing decisions themselves.

Where Were the Defense Attorneys in Brooklyn and Bronx?

Why didn't defense attorneys in the Bronx and Brooklyn block community service in cases where defendants could have gotten less severe dispositions? The screening process was designed so that a defense attorney's approval would act as a failsafe, ensuring that defendants who were not likely to get jail would be steered away from community service and toward other nonincarcerative outcomes. But only one in eight or nine defendants approved by Bronx and Brooklyn prosecutors were rejected by defense attorneys. Our estimates show that most of the defendants whose sentences to community service were not blocked by defense counsels would not have gotten jail sentences. Why did this failsafe break down?

Interviews with defense attorneys revealed that they sometimes agreed to a community service sentence because they thought it was an appropriate alternative to another nonincarcerative sanction. That is, they did not agree that it should always be used as an alternative to jail. Some saw the project as offering some assistance in finding a defendant a job, and some thought that it would be useful to the offenders. A Bronx attorney said:

I've operated on the assumption that were someone to complete Vera with an interest in the job, that if they were interested in employment, that someone would actually follow through on it. I do not see it as merely a way of avoiding jail.[27]

One saw it as a useful alternative to a fine.

Sometimes it could be a situation in which we have a fine but the client is indigent, so cannot pay. In that kind of case, I think, community service would be appropriate.[28]

Another defense attorney said:

Judges give fines in the Bronx without regard to the defendant's ability to pay. Some people are better off doing two weeks in Vera than ending up in jail for failure to pay a fine, or, worse yet, ending up paying a fine when they don't have enough to eat.[29]

Some saw that the sentence was being used as an alternative to lesser sanctions by the courts and concluded that, indeed, it should be used in this way. Asked what kinds of cases were being considered appropriate for community service, one Legal Aid Society attorney in the Bronx responded:

If any, the best kinds are people who don't work, are young, committed relatively minor crimes, and can't pay a fine. Judges use the Vera project as an alternative to a fine. Bench conferences give me that impression.[30]

Defense attorneys cannot be faulted for agreeing to using community service in this fashion, because the project administrators themselves have said that the sanction may legitimately be used in place of other lesser sentences. Project planners did not set their sights on a single and narrowly defined goal. They did not say that community service should be imposed only as an alternative to a short jail sentence. Rather, they articulated their mission as trying to develop a new option that would float somewhere between short jail terms and other nonincarcerative sentences on the scale of severity. Although they chose to emphasize retributionist principles, they also suggested that community service may be useful as a rehabilitative tool. This indicated that the sanction could be used in an approved manner in lieu of all other sentences. What was seen to matter most to planners and project administrators was the mix: they hoped that it would be about fifty/fifty, used at least half of the time in cases in which the defendant would otherwise have gone to jail.

Planners may have hoped that defense attorneys would perform the role of failsafe in the selection process, but their duty in this regard was never defined to them in a clear fashion. It would have been different had the project administrators asked them to assure that all proposed community service participants would otherwise have gone to jail. But what they were really asked to do was not be a failsafe but rather to be a regulator, working to keep the mix of jailbound and other offenders at the fifty/fifty mark. To perform this role well, defense attorneys would have had to have been kept well-informed by the project managers, so that they would have known what their colleagues were doing and what the particular mix in the project intake looked like from week to week. This didn't happen. (One problem was that project administrators themselves did not have any way of assessing what the mix of sentenced offenders looked like. In the Bronx and Brooklyn units, they mistakenly thought that most would have gone to jail otherwise. They thought so because they had no independent method of gauging other possible outcomes, except for what the district attorneys' files indicated.)

For the first few years of the project, community service administrators in the Bronx and Brooklyn made few attempts to enlist the cooperation of the defense bar. Court representatives could do their work without involving them, except for getting their approval of this or that defendant. All screening decisions were made using information held in the district attorneys' files and the second sorting decision was made by prosecutors. ("I see the project as being an offshoot of the DA's office," said one defense attorney.)[31] Legal Aid attorneys had very vague ideas about why some offenders were brought to them for community service consideration, while others weren't. ("What lottery did you pick this guy out of?")[32] When asked if they knew which kinds of offenders were considered appropriate by the Vera Institute for community service, most defense attorneys gave answers that either coincided only peripherally with the actual standards used by the court representatives or were quite off the mark. It is fair to attribute this lack of consensus both to project administrators' failure to interest and involve defense attorneys in the project and to the pronounced antipathy felt by the organized bar toward the project in these two boroughs because of its close alliance with prosecutors.

One important reason attorneys gave for pleading their clients to community service was that they could not guarantee a better outcome if the offer was passed up, even if the chances of getting jail were minimal. Plea bargaining is inherently risky, and the outcomes are not subject to a defense attorney's control. Prosecutors hold the upper hand. ("The DAs set the stage for the case," says one Legal Aid attorney.) They define the risks to which the defendant is exposed by setting the charges. They often make the opening offer in the negotiations. The defense attorney is in a subordinate position, having to respond to the situation defined by the prosecutor and having to negotiate with the prosecutor and sometimes with the judge to dismiss the charges or, failing that, to settle for the least punitive punishment. Defense attorneys have some leverage that enables them to win more favorable terms than the prosecutor is offering, but that leverage is often extremely limited. The prosecutor's offer of a community service sentence is hard to resist, simply because community service is a definite "out," a sentence not requiring imprisonment. The defense attorney may have thought another less punitive outcome could have been obtained, but no attorney can ever guarantee that to his client.

You never know what's going to happen if you don't take what's being offered at that point. I am hoping for conditional discharge. They're offering me thirty days and we've turned it down once. Now they offer me the Brooklyn Community Service Sentencing Project and my client takes it. It's impossible for me to say whether he would have gotten the thirty days or a straight conditional discharge or whether he could have gone to trial and beaten it or whether he would have lost.[33]

The alternative to counseling the client to accept the offer is to continue bargaining, working hard to strike a more favorable settlement. One strategy is to "jerk the case around," getting as many adjournments as possible, threatening to file motions on legal technicalities ("I'd paper them to death."[34]), and threatening to go to trial.

I'd try to draw [the cases] out a little longer, try to wear the DA and the judge out. If a guy is in jail, you would cop to small time. If a guy is out, you string the case along for a long time until you get a violation and a fine. In the out cases [when defendants are not in pretrial detention, that is], I tend to string them out until I can figure out some sort of non-jail disposition.[35]

This strategy of delay is risky, however.

People who commit petty larcenies are the most unreliable in terms of coming back to court. There's always the danger that they'll bench warrant and come back to court [that is, they will fail to appear, and a bench warrant will be filed, leading to more severe punishment]. The chance that the client will bench warrant is the trade-off to prolonging a case in the hopes that you can ultimately wear down the opposition.[36]

Some defendants will therefore choose to plead guilty to a community service sentence, not only to get a guaranteed "out," but also to avoid the bother of having to come back into court. "Jerking the case around" is the prime defense maneuver employed to wear down the opposition, but the defendant is also getting jerked around in the process. Some prefer to end it by copping out to community service.

If I think the Vera program is inappropriate because they're not going to go to jail anyway, I leave it up to my client: "You have a choice of beating the case but you'll have to come to court three or four times, or you can do community service." Most defendants say "Vera" when faced with this choice.[37]

Accepting a prosecutor's offer of community service achieves two purposes. It reduces the risk of getting hit with something worse if the negotiations turn out badly, and it cuts the defense attorney's workload. Once a plea is taken, the case is closed, and the attorney can devote his or her attention to other defendants. In the words of one attorney:

Community service is a good "out" for defense counsel—truly a way to keep clients out of jail. They might not have gone to jail if defense counsel was willing to carry on with the case. I don't think you'll find that many defense counsels are willing to spend that amount of time on a misdemeanor case.[38]

Weakening the Defense Attorney's Hand?

Bronx and Brooklyn defense attorneys, in their interviews with the research staff, frequently voiced the opinion that the introduction of the community service sentence in their courts strengthened the prosecutors' hands in bargaining. The end result, in their view, was that it had become more difficult to get other lesser sentences (ones not entailing a jail term). Some attorneys felt that the prosecutors were asking for short jail terms more often after the community service option became available simply to increase the odds that a community service offer would be taken. They feared that if the offers were rejected, the judge would be more inclined to impose a jail sentence, because the prosecutor would be pushed into the position of carrying out the alternative—a recommendation of jail.

> When you have a grey-area case, where a judge may sentence somebody to a short period of incarceration but also may go for a fine, if we were approached first by the court representatives, we could tell them that we could get the guy a fine without involving community service. But when Vera approaches the DA first . . . the DA takes the position that the defendant will get jail if we don't work out the Vera sentence. At the bench conference, the DA will be telling the judge that he wants 30–60 days if the defendant doesn't take Vera. And I'm saying, "Look, this is worth a $50 fine." [39]

No data were collected that would enable us to explore this question systematically, but it is probably safe to say that the introduction of the community service sentence in these two borough courts did not result in a large-scale shift of offenders from the non-jail track onto the jail sentencing track. Instead, the more important shift was the displacement of other nonincarcerative sentences by the use of community service. This happened because prosecutors were able to define the terms of the proposed trade by offering early the community service sentence and because defense attorneys and their clients acceded to the offer. Defense attorneys complained not only that it was hard to find good arguments against the offer, but also that one also looked unreasonable turning it down.

> A recommendation for jail, especially short jail, is an easy target. My client isn't going to get rehabilitated there; he's going to get sexually assaulted; come out more scarred and alienated than when he went in. But a community service sentence is harder to argue against if the DA offers it. It seems so reasonable. If the DA didn't offer community service, I could convince the judge in most instances that a fine would be better in these cases than jail. But once the community service offer is made, you can't argue against it in favor of a fine. And if you turn it down, you are seen as being unreasonable and risk the jail sentence. [40]

Attorneys complained further that the choice of taking a plea to community service was especially tough if the offer was made at arraignments. Court representatives followed a policy of not permitting eligible defendants to be considered twice. This offer came around only once.

> Here in Brooklyn, it's being offered at arraignment or on the first adjournment date, and it's a "take it or leave it" situation. So I'm advising somebody blind because I don't know the case yet. . . . The combination of the project working only by DA referral and being done so early in the case, but also on a take it or leave it basis—it won't be reoffered—this makes it easy to abuse this. . . . It's a way for the DA's office to clear shitty cases with convictions without defense counsel knowing the worth of the case. Two cases I had were bad prosecution cases, which I think would either have been dismissed or resulted in violations or won by us at trial. But the clients weren't willing to take the risk.[41]

It was this aspect of the community service sentence—the control over the timing of the offer—that gave prosecutors more of an edge against defense attorneys. All other sentences can be considered at any stage in the plea negotiations, and no others require the formal approval of the prosecutor. It is no surprise that prosecutors will generally approve the offer, if the timing of it enhances their leverage in plea bargaining. If any party to the negotiation had been able to open up consideration of community service, and if the prosecutor had not been given the power to veto eligibility, the defense attorney's hand would have been strengthened relative to the prosecutor's in the selection process. Whether this would have led to a heavier use of the sentence in instances in which jail would have been imposed is not clear, however. This would have depended in large part on how defense attorneys and judges chose to use the sentencing option.

The Success of the Manhattan Project

The introduction of the Vera Community Service Sentencing Project into the Manhattan Criminal Court yielded very different results than it did in the Bronx and Brooklyn. Whereas most of the offenders sentenced to community service in the latter two boroughs during the 1981–1982 period would not have gotten jail in the absence of the project, about two-thirds of the Manhattan participants would otherwise have been put behind bars, according to the estimates described in chapter 3. Because planners had hoped to draw half of the participants from the jailbound track, the Manhattan branch exceeded expectations and was considered a resounding success, except for the persistant opposition of the district attorney's office.

No single factor was responsible for bringing about this high jail displacement rate, but the screening and selection procedures that were developed in this borough go a long way toward explaining this outcome. Prosecutors were not given an opportunity to veto community service in instances where they were jockeying for jail sentences, and judges were more actively involved in sentencing negotiations. This had several important consequences for the way the court representatives did their work.

Because prosecutors didn't have the power to veto proposed defendants, court representatives were encouraged to orient their screening decisions to the actual sentencing practices of the judges, rather than to what the prosecutor was planning to recommend to the judge. As we have discussed, Bronx and Brooklyn court representatives gauged their screening decisions according to what they thought prosecutors would or would not approve, which was not always consistent with the judges' sentencing decisions. In Manhattan, paying attention to the judges' decisions helped court representatives to hone their sense of what the market for community service sentences was in each courtroom. They were better able to pick out the defendants who were actually going to get jail sentences. Without the prosecutor standing at the gate, they were permitted a clearer view of the practices that they were trying to affect: judicial sentencing decisions.

Not only were they able to predict sentencing outcomes better, but court representatives in this borough were also not inhibited by the prospect of the prosecutor's veto. In the other two boroughs, prosecutors routinely vetoed out of community service those whom they wanted to send to jail, and the court representatives learned quickly what the rule was, what the limits were, and they tended not to push them too often. In Manhattan, the court representatives worried only about a defendant's meeting the basic minimum entry requirements, and there was no real and fixed upper limit to what the judge would consider. Moreoever, defense attorneys were professionally motivated to obtain the most favorable and least damaging dispositions for their clients, and they were ready to propose community service at that moment in sentencing negotiations when all else except jail seemed to be off the menu. Because both were trying to keep defendants out of jail, there was a natural alliance between defense attorneys and court representatives. They worked together in a way that facilitated community service dispositions in instances where jail would have been ordered.

Finally, the design of the selection procedures in Manhattan permitted the court representative to become a more vigorous advocate for the community service project than in the other two boroughs. Because they were permitted to deal directly with judges, instead of speaking through prosecutors, they developed their own relationships with judges. They were there not only to answer questions about the institute project, its program, and its enforcement practices, but they were also able to answer questions about the suitability of specific defendants. Court representatives often had done at least as thorough a job of investigating a defendant's background and case as had the defense attorneys, and this gave them some credibility with the bench. This kind of work was much less likely to be done in the other two boroughs, because the prosecutors controlled the offering of community service.

Of course, neither procedures nor court representatives actually sentence defendants. Judges do that. The selection procedures and court representatives in Manhattan only facilitated the judges' consideration of community service and the sentencing of defendants to the Vera Institute project. Judges were the ultimate decision makers, and they were the ones who had to accept the policy of ordering defendants to do unpaid labor instead of sending them to jail. The following section explores why judges did modify their sentencing practices to bring about this substitution of sanctions. Before turning to this question, however, it will be helpful to explain why the Manhattan unit adopted screening and selection procedures that differed from those developed earlier in its Bronx and Brooklyn predecessors.

Redesigning Selection Procedures in Manhattan

Planners did not go into the Manhattan court with a new theory of how to reform sentencing and then devise a strategy to implement it. Rather, there was once again an interaction between the exigencies of getting a project established and planners' improved understanding of how sentences are determined.

Planners entered into negotiations with the district attorney's office in Manhattan with the intention of setting up exactly the same kind of selection and sentencing routines that were established in both the Bronx and Brooklyn courts. But officials in this office balked at the proposal that they recommend community service in cases in which judges were likely to impose jail terms of ninety days or less. There was some willingness expressed to approve community service in cases where prosecutors were asking for no more than ninety days, but planners had by then become aware that prosecutors do not always get the sentences they want— at least not in this borough. The district attorney's office then agreed to cooperate in a small research effort to look at the match between prosecutors' recommendations and judges' sentencing decisions. I was asked to analyze decisions made in cases of all offenders sentenced to jail by the Manhattan Criminal Court during twenty-five days in June 1981. The list was pared down to defendants as similar as possible to those who would be in the "target group" of the proposed community service project. This included people jailed for ninety days or less, charged at arraignment with crimes that would not have made them ineligible for community service, and having one or more prior criminal convictions. The names of these offenders were given to the district attorney's office, and it provided for each case the sentence that the prosecutor had recommended to the judge, if any recommendation had been made.

The results revealed a considerable gap betweeen what prosecutors had asked for and what judges had imposed. In 49 percent of the cases in which offenders had received jail sentences of ninety days or less, the district attorney's office had asked for longer terms. When prosecutors had asked for "substantial time," defined as jail sentences between six and nine months long, 57 percent of the offenders had been given sentences of ninety days or less. Had court representatives limited themselves only to those defendants for whom prosecutors were recommending sentences of ninety days or less, the pool of eligible and jailbound defendants would have been sharply constricted. The district attorney's office would not agree to recommend or acquiesce in community service sentences when its prosecutors were asking for more than three months of jail time, and the Vera Institute planners consequently decided to have court representatives deal directly with judges and defense attorneys. The result of this conflict has been a pattern of strenuous and persistent opposition from the prosecutors in Manhattan to the use of the sentence in precisely those cases where the court now employs it: for offenders with long records who are headed for jail.

Once the district attorney's office closed its doors, project planners were forced to develop new and different selection procedures than the ones they had initially favored. Not only did prosecutors refuse to recommend the community service sentence, but they also forbade court representatives from looking in their case files when searching for prospective participants. This meant that the court representatives would have to look elsewhere, so they enlisted the cooperation of defense attorneys. The Legal Aid Society in that borough agreed to open its files to court representatives, and this established a close working relationship between defense attorneys and court representatives. Defense attorneys were given the opportunity to act as gatekeepers, deciding which cases to take to the judge for community service sentencing. Court representatives were permitted to deal more directly with judges than was customary in the other boroughs, and they ultimately became stronger advocates for the sentence than did court representatives in the Bronx and Brooklyn. This affected their screening practices in ways that aided their being able to identify more accurately offenders who would otherwise have gone to jail. Thus, the Manhattan procedures for intervening in sentencing evolved partly by conscious design and also as a response to unforeseen exigencies. Once established, however, they dovetailed with plea and sentence bargaining practices in a manner that produced the desired results more efficiently than did procedures in the other two boroughs.

Why Manhattan Judges Substituted Community Service for Jail

Judges were very quick, on the whole, to embrace the new sanction. Many began sentencing offenders to community service by the dozens as soon as the project's doors opened. As described in chapter 2, the intake of the Manhattan unit quickly reached a very high level, much faster than the Brooklyn and Bronx units had done in their start-up phases. This was due partly to the fact that the pool of potentially eligible defendants was larger in Manhattan than in the other two boroughs, but it also undoubtedly stemmed from the enthusiastic response given the project by many judges.

Why were Manhattan judges so willing, as a group, to impose the sentence in instances in which they were ready to send the offender to jail? The answer seems to be that judges are always faced with the tough dilemma of responding appropriately to law-breakers, with very limited resources at hand, and they welcome the expansion of their relatively small repertoire of alternatives. Community service was seen as an appropriate penal response in many instances in which jail sentences had been relied upon for lack of any better alternative. At least as important was the effect that the community service option had on the judges' abilities to move cases. The press of defendants charged with relatively minor crimes in New York City is staggering, with over one hundred and eighty thousand persons arraigned in the lower courts each year.[42] If a defendant will plead guilty to a community service sentence, the case can be closed immediately, and the judge can chalk up one more disposition. This yields two benefits: judges are rated on their disposition rates, and speed is highly valued by court administrators. Second, this strategy of triage preserves strained court resources for dealing with the more difficult cases. Some judges apparently believed that these gains outweighed whatever benefits were sacrificed by not sending these defendants to jail.

Working in the criminal court is a dispiriting task, one that breeds a sense of futility. Judges are asked to control crime, but defendants have a myriad of personal and social problems that affect their ability to "go straight." An extraordinarily high proportion of lower court defendants are heavy abusers of drugs and alcohol. Most are unlettered, unskilled, and unemployed; many have very complicated and unstable living arrangements; and the lot of most is misery and struggle. What kind of criminal sanction is "appropriate" when an unemployed and unskilled mother of three children steals kitchen appliances from department stores to make money? When a middle-aged addict steals repetitively to support his habit or his children? When a young truant snatches pocketbooks from women getting off buses? Judges impose sanctions upon hundreds of thousands of these petty criminals with the expectation that many—if not most—will appear before them again in the not-too-distant future. The best they can hope for is that their decisions make some slight differences in the offenders' lives. Jail certainly doesn't promise magic. Seeing so many defendants who have gone there several times before, judges have seen living evidence that a stretch in jail does not cure criminality. The city's Probation Department is overburdened and underfinanced, having suffered substantial budget cuts for several years in a row, and many judges express disbelief that probation can rehabilitate criminals effectively. Most thieves who come into the court for petty crimes are poor, and judges worry about their ability to pay fines without having to resort to more stealing to raise the money. Having yet another penal instrument—a community service order—at their disposal broadens their resources to respond to these difficult cases.

When asked why they imposed community service sentences instead of jail terms, some judges reported simply that the sanction was sufficiently punishing. ("It's a tough sentence. It would be against the Constitution if it weren't a sentence.")[43] But most revealed a much more complicated kind of reasoning, which indicated their concern for balancing a number of different considerations. One judge's response is worth quoting at length to show the flavor of this deliberation:

The people you're getting [in the Vera project] are mostly people who've committed larcenies, who have long records, whose crimes result from blocked futures. They're jail-bound because their crimes are not victimless. Consumers have to pay for the crimes because of the add-on costs in the stores which suffer the thefts; these petty thefts are *not* victimless. There must be some punishment imposed on chronic thieves, because the merchants of this city cannot be expected to tolerate this kind of activity as a cost of doing business here, and the city depends upon the existence of these stores. . . .

When this project was first called to my attention, I was hopeful that it would reduce the recidivisim rate. The project director later told me that you found the recidivism rate slightly lower, but not a lot lower than Rikers [Island jail sentences]. So what I'm left with is an alternative punishment that has some of the good effects but not the bad effects of Rikers. . . .

It comes the closest to the notion of a reparation. You hurt somebody, you make up for it in some way. Now you're back in good graces. Jail is not reparation. You put somebody in jail, you have to sustain them in there. Community service is also less cruel than jail. . . . What Vera gives us is a credible opportunity to be a human being and not a bastard. . . .

Most of our problems in New York where I'd consider community service sentencing are problems of social stratification. The permanent underclass comes here to court on property crimes. The dilemma lies in the fact that these crimes may be related to economic conditions, but it is unacceptable to convey the message that because someone is poor, they can go into a department store and take something. . . .[44]

Another Manhattan judge uses the sentence primarily to punish, and he feels that the courts need a sanction that is somewhat less punitive than jail.

It's punishment. There's something unpleasant about having to do unpleasant work. It's also a kind of mild incapacitation. Jail is not appropriate for everyone. It's not cost-effective. There's something inherently brutalizing about jail, and to avoid doing that is a worthy experiment. We're talking about minor offenses. It's important from my point of view that we're talking about petty crimes. . . . As long as public confidence in the system is not demonstrably affected by the use of alternative sentencing, then we're saving money. It may be that a humane society is required to have an additional level of punishment short of jail.[45]

Another Manhattan judge put it this way:

In cases where you have somebody who has a long history of shoplifting and can be classed as making a life in crime, I put these people in the program on the theory that their past sentences haven't succeeded in getting them out of the crime thing at all. The project offers the possibility that something may happen as a result of this sentence. It's probably worth the gamble, because if he's arrested again, there's time enough to place him in a $26,000-a-year facility. There already is not room enough for all those persons who are committing violent crimes, much less these people.

Another element, which I'm afraid to say is always on my mind, is that we have a city with vast numbers of poor people in it. These people have kids who don't have a lot of pocket money, and they live in a city that gives off a hedonistic aroma. Department stores display huge amounts of merchandise and they have few people on duty, so it's a self-service operation. They are offering a huge temptation, and they turn around and ask us to be constables, imposing draconian punishments. The only resources I have are facilities which are very expensive and nowhere near what facilities should be. Vera comes along and its a godsend. It offers a sanction for the minor depredations without using the limited resources of jail.[46]

Several judges reported that they impose community service sentences partly because they want offenders to receive rehabilitative services. The Vera Community Service Sentencing Projects in all three boroughs provide a variety of social services to those participants who request them, including attempts to find people paid employment once they have completed their sentences. It offers judges a combination of punishing work and assistance in finding paid work. According to one Manhattan judge:

One of the main reasons I use your program is to break the cycle, to keep that guy from other people's property as long as possible. . . . I want to break the cycle, institute the work ethic and find someone a job. I really think that should be stressed—trying to find people work. I like to think that people who have jobs aren't going to risk being arrested.[47]

Another oft-mentioned reason why judges are willing to take the gamble is that the project promises to enforce vigorously the community service order. Offenders who don't show up for work are brought back to court. If possible, project officials will themselves bring into court those participants who don't complete their sentences. In other instances, project officials work closely with the warrant squad to apprehend them. Participants who violate the terms of the sentence are frequently brought back to court and given stiff punishments—usually jail sentences of substantial length. (See tables 2.1 and 2.2 in chapter 2.) Project officials keep running tallies of these resentencing decisions and use them to buttress their credibility as responsible enforcers.

Substituting Community Service for Lesser Sentences

By and large, Manhattan judges appear to have accepted the policy that community service is an appropriate sanction in cases where short jail terms would have been considered appropriate before the availability of the institute project. But not all people placed in the project would have gone to jail if the project had not existed. We estimated that about a third of the participants entering the Manhattan project during its first year would have otherwise avoided jail. (See chapter 3 for a description of our estimating procedures.) Why did judges apparently contravene this new norm in a third of their sentencing decisions?

From the responses given in interviews when asked this question, it seems that judges imposed community service in these instances for the same reason that prosecutors in the other two boroughs often approved defendants who would not have gotten jail terms. Some defendants had good chances of avoiding jail, not because judges and prosecutors believed that jail was not appropriate, but because the courts lacked the leverage to get a plea to jail time. Because sentences are typically negotiated, judges cannot simply make a unilateral decision as to what kind of sanction best fits the offense and the offender from a penological point of view. The demands of getting a guilty plea of any sort, as well as clearing the court calendar as expeditiously as possible, also weigh on the judges, and defendants who show greater ability to frustrate these objectives can strike a more favorable settlement for themselves. Most Manhattan judges we interviewed knew that the project only accepted offenders who deserved short jail terms. But some were willing to impose the sentence on persons they thought deserved jail, but who could not be induced to plead guilty to a jail term. As one judge said:

As I understand the project, it's an alternative to jail in a perfect situation. The standard is, does this merit jail, whether or not the system can effectuate jail. The system has a very weak capacity to effectuate jail in a case where somebody is out [on bail or released on their own recognizance.][48]

Another judge amplified this:

There may well be a realistic factor that mitigates toward a community service project when the person is out, because it is extremely difficult to say to someone who's out, "Go back in." It's easier to sell the project to someone who's out. If someone is in, I don't think I'd forego the use of the project if I thought it was appropriate. If a guy is out, it's a more palatable resolution of case, because you couldn't really offer a jail alternative that he would accept. Maybe in a case you might think is worth sixty days but is somewhat iffy, it's easier to lapse into giving him the program. If he's in, you might think this is *more* of a sixty-day case and you offer the sixty days with a chance of it being accepted.[49]

Defense attorneys in Manhattan did not block community service in these cases for much the same reason that attorneys in the other boroughs did not: if the attorney has a client who risks a substantial jail sentence if convicted at trial, that risk can be eliminated with a plea to community service. (Of course, the offender may ultimately get jailed for refusing to perform the work.) As one defense attorney in Manhattan explained:

Somebody who's out of jail, who's facing jail after conviction or facing probation—the court reps don't like me using the project for these guys, but I try to get them into Vera. In those instances, where someone is facing jail perhaps only after conviction after trial, that individual would normally have several pending cases. Given that we're dealing with shoplifters, the People's case is usually very strong. If you pressed the system enough to the point of trial on every one of these cases, you could be exposing your defendant to jail time to cover not only the one conviction but all the other open matters. So the project is an alternative to jail because I think things in criminal court have changed. The judges are a lot tougher. I think that at an early stage in the proceedings, judges are disposed to sentence someone to Vera as a plea bargain, but in the later stages he may incarcerate that same person.[50]

Defense attorneys don't plead guilty; their clients do. Attorneys pose alternatives, and the alternative to passing up a community service offer is fighting the case with a less-than-perfect chance of "beating" a jail sentence. Clients in these situations will often choose to cop out.

Can a Reform be Redirected Once its Course is Set?

Within several months of opening, the community service units in the Bronx and Brooklyn courts became steadily fixed on a course that turned out to be different from the one the institute planners had charted for them. Institutional alliances were firmly established with the district attorneys' office, and defendants sentenced to the project were of a roughly similar class: mostly people who would not have received jail sentences in the absence of the project. In Manhattan, the project did better. Court representatives worked closely with defense attorneys and judges, and the project achieved its established goal of having community service used as a substitute for short jail sentences in at least half of the cases.

Once faced with evidence that the Bronx and Brooklyn projects were off course (evidence developed by my research), the project's citywide manager decided to engineer a correction. During the spring and summer of 1983, a number of procedural and personnel changes were made which resulted in a shift in the kinds of offenders sentenced to community service in these two boroughs. Judging from my statistical analysis of subsequent sentencing decisions (described at the end of chapter 3), it appears that the projects succeeded in moving "up market" in the courts, raising the proportion of participants who would have gone to jail otherwise. At the same time, the Manhattan project suffered a slight decline in intake during the fall of 1983. Although the ratio of jail-bound to non-jailbound offenders did not appear to change significantly in Manhattan, the absolute number of people sentenced by judges to the project dropped.

Exploring these shifts—both the intentional interventions undertaken by management and the unintended downturn in Manhattan and the attempts to arrest it—is instructive because it helps to clarify which factors were most critical in determining the success of the reform aimed at substituting community service for jail sentences. It also shows which levers can be moved to change the course of a reform after it has become established and routinized.

Brooklyn: Moving Away From the Prosecutors

The institute's management decided to modify the selection procedures in the Brooklyn court to limit the prosecutors' ability to block jailbound defendants and to involve judges and defense attorneys more actively in screening decisions. The program's city-wide manager, Judith Greene, who had been director of the Manhattan unit before being promoted to manage the citywide program, chose to move Brooklyn toward the "Manhattan model" of selection and sentencing. In late February 1983, judges and defense attorneys were invited to refer to the project defendants whom they thought would otherwise go to jail. Although court representatives would continue to search for eligible defendants on their own, they also agreed to consider defendants referred to the project by others—a new step in opening up the process and involving parties other than the prosecutors in the early selection stages. The district attorney's office was also informed that court representatives would not permit prosecutors to veto these cases that were referred to them by others; judges would have the final say. This was a half-step transformation of the selection routines, because court representatives would continue to give prosecutors the right of first veto in cases found by their own screening efforts.

The routines in Brooklyn were changed at the same time in an effort to get the court representatives there to be more aggressive. Even though prosecutors would retain veto power over some cases, the court representatives were asked to dive deeper into the pool of persons headed for jail. Up to this point, court representatives followed standards that had been promulgated by Vera Institute management and some that had been set by prosecutors. As described, the project management's basic requirements set the floor: first offenders were not to be considered, because they were least likely to get jail. Prosecutors established what amounted to a ceiling: defendants having a long string of prior convictions were routinely passed over, because prosecutors would not approve of them. Court representatives had confined themselves to defendants falling somewhere between these two outer boundaries.

To make the court representatives more productive of jailbound cases, the program manager looked first to the statistical tests that had been performed on sentencing decisions in 1982. This research had identified several factors that were predictive of going to jail. The distribution of these characteristics and a comparison of persons not sentenced to jail with those who were jailed suggested refinements of the screening requirements. To be screened into the eligible pool after March 1983, Brooklyn defendants had to be in pretrial detention. Furthermore, whites were to be excluded. In addition, to be considered eligible they had to have at least two of the three following characteristics: seven or more prior arrests, fewer than eighteen months since their last conviction, and a sentence to imprisonment for their most recent conviction. Although some persons having these characteristics might not in fact be jailbound, the program's manager rightly believed that these new requirements would yield a higher proportion of offenders headed for short jail sentences.

A good deal of resistance to these changes was encountered. The court representatives had internalized the previously established norms and could not bring themselves in good conscience to declare these more serious cases eligible for community service. Faced with this new task, they left the job. A court representative from Manhattan was installed as the senior representative, and she trained new recruits.

Prosecutors also balked at the new procedures, which bypassed their veto authority. Right away, two cases referred to the project by the Legal Aid Society's attorneys were taken to the judges and sentenced to the project without prosecutors' approval, but it was not until the third case was brought before a judge that the issue came to a head. Project managers were summoned to a meeting of high-level administrators in the district attorney's office.

At this time, the project managers disclosed the research findings showing that no more than 28 percent of the offenders approved for community service sentences in 1982 would have gone to jail in the absence of the program. Informed that the project was not living up to its stated goal—a goal that the district attorney was committed to—these supervising prosecutors agreed to permit changes that would bring the project closer to its target. They accepted the policy change that defendants referred to the project by judges and defense attorneys would not have to gain the approval of the prosecutor before the community service option could be put before the judges, but they wanted to retain their role as gate-keepers in cases identified by court representatives. The *quid pro quo* for retaining this power was that they would have to loosen their reins and approve for the project more jailbound offenders brought to them by the project's court representatives. Court representatives were now going after more serious cases, and prosecutors began approving many of them.

The Brooklyn district attorney's office was willing to accept such a change for two reasons. First, the office was committed to developing innovative approaches to case management and sentencing. Elizabeth Holtzman, formerly a liberal Democratic congresswoman, had recently won the job of DA in a campaign in which her principal opponent had been a long-time assistant to the previous district attorney and was the candidate of the local Democratic Party organization. She ran on a reform platform, and she instituted a number of policy changes during her first year (1982). She and her top-level managers embraced the concept of community service and were willing to depart from the more restrictive standards that had been established by her predecessor. Second, administrators in the Brooklyn district attorney's office seem to have realized that the community service project could operate without their office having any control whatsoever over the sentencing decisions. The Manhattan courts are right across the East River and the workings of the community service project there were well known. From the prosecutor's perspective, the alternative to letting the project displace jail sentences more frequently was to lose control altogether.

The effects of the changes in screening procedures and approval policies in Brooklyn can be seen in the kinds of participants sentenced to the Brooklyn project during the months of July, August, and September 1983. These offenders had an average of ten prior arrests and seven prior convictions. This compared to the average of five prior arrests and three prior convictions for participants sentenced between October 1981 and September 1982. Most importantly, a larger percentage of those sentenced to community service after June 1983 had been in pretrial detention at the time of sentencing: 72 percent as opposed to 63 percent in the earlier period. Less time had passed since their last scrape with the law: an average of ten months had elapsed between their most recent prior conviction and their arraignment on the current charges, compared with an average of twenty-two months for participants sentenced to the project in the earlier period. Fifty-three percent of them had served time for the most recent prior conviction, compared to 42 percent in 1981–1982.

This shift in the type of participant sentenced to community service in Brooklyn suggested that the project's drift into the range of lesser sanctions had been arrested by procedural and policy changes. Statistical analysis confirmed this. As described at the end of chapter 3, our statistical models indicated that an estimated 57 percent of those sentenced to community service during a twelve-month period following the project's reorganization would have gone to jail in the absence of the option. This was rightly counted as a success story.

Bronx: Changes in Screening

Similar changes were instituted in the Bronx in May 1983. New and tougher eligibility criteria were established, again drawing upon preliminary research results that had been shared with management. To be declared eligible after 1 May 1983, defendants had to be in pretrial detention and had to have at least two of the three following characteristics: a prison or jail sentence for the most recent prior conviction, eight or more prior arrests, or four or more prior convictions. Court representatives ceased using the district attorney's files when searching for eligible candidates and followed the Manhattan practice of using court calendars. This ensured that court representatives did not systematically overlook defendants who met eligibility criteria.

Bronx prosecutors agreed to approve defendants who met these tighter criteria. The same two reasons that moved the Brooklyn prosecutors seemed to motivate the Bronx prosecutor's decision to accept the changed entry requirements. First, the district attorney had, after all, agreed to substitute community service for short jail sentences in at least half of the cases referred to the project. When key administrators in the office were shown that the procedures followed through 1982 had failed to produce this result, they agreed to change procedures.

Second, the district attorney's office also wanted to avoid losing all control over the selection and sentencing of offenders to community service. Prosecutors could see that the judges had grown comfortable with the project and believed that many would be willing to sentence offenders to it without the prosecutors' prior approval, as was the custom in Manhattan. If judges were to take that course, it would open up the possibility of community service in the Bronx being used almost exclusively in lieu of short jail sentences, which would contravene one of the district attorney's policy objectives regarding the project: that the sanction be used as an alternative to nonincarcerative sentences in half of the cases. Rather than risk losing this alternative, the office agreed to ease up on its restrictive practices in granting approvals for sentencing to community service.

The new Bronx screening criteria, together with the active participation of the Bronx prosecutors in finding and offering up jail-bound cases, resulted in different kinds of offenders being sentenced to the project than had been the case through 1982. During the months of July, August, and September of 1983, participants sentenced to the Bronx project had an average of twelve prior arrests and eight prior convictions, compared to six prior arrests and four prior convictions for participants sentenced during the October 1981–September 1982 period. Eighty-two percent were being held in detention at the time of sentencing compared to 43 percent during the earlier twelve months. Sixty percent had gone to jail or prison upon their most recent prior conviction, compared to 43 percent previously. All these telltale signs pointed in the right direction. Whereas no more than 20 percent of the 1982 offenders would have gone to jail in the absence of the project, a substantially larger proportion—approximately 53 percent—of these more recent participants would have been imprisoned, according to our statistical estimating procedures. This was a dramatic turnaround.

Manhattan: New and More Restrictive Judges

The results of the adjustments in screening criteria in the Bronx and Brooklyn indicate that some prosecutors, if approached in the right way, at the right time, with the right evidence, can be persuaded to lighten their hands on the gate to alternate sentencing. Judicial acceptance is also necessary, of course. How far judges will go in Brooklyn and the Bronx has never really been tested, because prosecutors have been the ones to set the upper limits on what will get to the bench. Prosecutors have raised the upper boundary in both boroughs, and judges continue to ratify the plea agreements that have been hammered out between assistant district attorneys and the defendants' lawyers. However, because of the way prosecutors in Manhattan are bypassed, judges' standards regarding the use of the community service sanction are more determinative of the upper limit there. However, a recent turn of events shows how those standards can change and thereby restrict the number of people sentenced to the Vera Institute project in lieu of jail.

In mid-1983, a number of newly appointed judges were assigned to Manhattan's Criminal Court. No changes were made in screening criteria; court representatives followed the same ones that had been instituted in that unit's early days. However, many of these new judges were less receptive to the use of the community service sentence as an alternative to jail than were the judges who had welcomed the project when it opened its doors. Some of these judges had previously served as prosecutors in the Manhattan district attorney's office before having received their judicial robes, and they seem to have brought that office's resistance to community service with them into their new positions.

This more restrictive stance affected the court representatives' screening decisions. As in the other two boroughs, court representatives responded to resistance by censoring themselves, declining to consider cases that met the offical entry requirements but were perceived as being too serious to be accepted by the new judges. One of the Manhattan court representatives repeated almost word for word something that one of his colleagues in the Bronx had said two years earlier: "I don't want to get laughed out of the courtroom."

The result of these two changes was a decline in the number of offenders sentenced to the project, although the proportion of participants who would have gone to jail otherwise appears to have remained relatively stable, judging from the profiles of the participant population. Instead of keeping the intake at previous levels by bringing in softer cases for sentencing, the court representatives simply incurred more judicial rejections.

This drop in intake was a short-lived phenomenon. Once court representatives were discovered to be censoring themselves, a renewed effort was made to supervise their screening decisions more closely, so that they would not become overly cautious. The new judges also became more comfortable with the project and more frequently substituted it for short jail sentences. Judges work under different constraints than do prosecutors, and the pressures of having to move their caseloads to speedy dispositions may have encouraged a greater receptiveness in them to community service than the ex-prosecutors among them had felt while working on the other side of the bench.

This points to the importance of having to work continually on modifying the norms that govern sentencing decisions. If all parties to the plea negotiations do not accept norm changes (as Manhattan prosecutors do not), the informal standards that structure decision making in the court do not become shared by all. Prolonged resistance of the sort that the district attorney's office has kept up makes the environment quite unstable. In the normal course of events in plea bargaining, judges generally come down somewhere between prosecutors and defense attorneys. When these two parties are very far apart, there is considerable pressure on judges to choose sides or to find other ways to resolve the conflict. When the Manhattan unit first opened, much effort was expended teaching judges about the project, its enforcement practices, and the services it could deliver to offenders. Persuaded that the sanction was indeed appropriate as a substitute for short jail sentences in many cases, judges were willing to impose the sanction over the prosecutors' strong objections. Similar efforts will probably have to be made with new judges coming onto the bench.

Conclusion

Initiatives to change the way courts sentence criminals usually come from the world beyond the courthouse steps. They result from the actions of legislators, mayors, governors, presidents, journalists, editorialists, and private public-interest organizations such as the Vera Institute of Justice. Coming as they do from the outside, these attempts to reform the courts are not usually greeted with enthusiasm all around, for they generally aim to disturb the way courthouse regulars do their work. To the extent that existing work routines are organized, resistance to change is organized resistance.

Even when powerful outsiders such as the legislators rewrite the rules governing sentencing decisions, it is difficult to secure compliance with these new rules because of the way the courts are structured and sentencing decisions are made. Courts are not bureaucratic organizations, with a top-down ladder of command, and this makes it impossible to order the troops to change direction by barking new orders. Instead, the organization of the court is continually being negotiated. The basic parameters are fixed, to be sure, but negotiations are occurring constantly at different levels. Opposing attorneys and judges negotiate the disposition of each case, which involves a sentence to be imposed, if a conviction is obtained. Above the case-specific negotiations are more general struggles between different sides over a variety of issues and policies. The social organization of many institutions is the ongoing product of continual negotiations, but this aspect of organization is perhaps even more pronounced in the courts, because they were designed as arenas for adversarial competition.

The fate of any attempt to change the rules governing sentencing decisions therefore depends upon how the different players in the courts renegotiate their working agreements with regard to sentencing decisions. The choice of allies is important to that outcome. Leverage, skill, and finesse become crucial factors.

The alliances that were forged in the early stages of each borough's project were enormously influential in shaping the way the community service sentence was ultimately used in the courts. By placing the prosecutor in the gatekeeper's role in the Bronx and

Brooklyn courts, the district attorneys' offices quickly managed to capture the new sentencing option and harness it to their own agenda, which called for stiffening the penalties given to persons who were not quite jailable but deserving of a punishment more severe than was previously imposed. In Manhattan, the closer alliance of the court representatives with defense attorneys furthered more effectively the policy objectives of the institute. Even though prosecutors may agree to request a substitution of community service for jail, an alliance between them and a jail-diverting project borders on being an unnatural one. Prosecutors are under too many pressures that push them in directions opposed to nonincarcerative reforms. Defense attorneys, on the other hand, see their role as keeping their clients out of jail whenever possible. They are more natural partners for such reform initiatives.

This is not to say that prosecutors will always obstruct such innovations or that defense attorneys will always protect and advocate them. Prosecutors in the Bronx and Brooklyn courts did change their position and now recommend substituting community service for jail almost as frequently as the Vera Institute managers desire. And in Manhattan, where defense attorneys have greater control over the imposition of the sentence, about a third of those being sentenced to community service would not be going to jail in the absence of the program. What happened in the Bronx and Brooklyn courts was that prosecutors were pulled back from their more normal inclinations because they didn't want to lose something that they valued: the ability to have the sentence used in half the instances as a substitute for lesser nonincarcerative sentences. The Manhattan experience indicated clearly that judges would use community service without the support of prosecutors, and this enhanced the institute's bargaining power.

Because of the negotiated character of criminal case dispositions, if reformers want to change existing practices, it helps if they become players. Instead of passing a law, promulgating a new standard, or defining a new rule in some other fashion and then expecting the courts to implement these changes automatically, the Vera Institute placed reform catalysts—"change agents"—in the courtrooms for eight hours a day, five days a week. A new role was defined, and the court representatives of the project became active partners in the plea bargaining negotiations. They were most successful when they understood fully the extent to which sentencing decisions as well as guilty pleas were negotiated, but the general point remains: sentencing reforms are perhaps most likely to succeed if advocates for those reforms are given an institutionalized place in the ongoing activities of the courts.

Finally, the Vera Institute experience shows that reforms can be redirected, even after they have settled down onto a relatively fixed course. Such corrections are easier to make when some sort of feedback loop exists to provide managers with information about how the reform is faring. Self-criticism sessions have been designed to do this in some settings. However, in the courts, where the solidarity of the workgroup is relatively low and dissension is chronic, the more effective mechanism is an ongoing evaluation of the sort that produced the findings in this and the previous chapter.

Subsequent chapters turn to an examination of how the community service sentencing project affected, not the courts, but those other consumers of the reform: the criminal offenders given the sentence.

Chapter Five

How Offenders View
the Community Service Sentence

Asked why he imposes community service sentences upon criminal offenders, one judge replied:

I am trying to say to the defendant—not literally, but in essence—"You are not getting away scot-free. You are being punished. However, we're hoping that you learn from this experience that something has happened to you as a result of your arrest and conviction. Next time, it's jail."

He wonders if offenders get the message, however.

Do the defendants view the community service as a joke, thinking, "I got away with something!"? Or do they think, "This is a real drag."? I don't know how they view it.[1]

The use of unpaid community service is a relatively new sanction in the New York City courts, and the way offenders perceive the sentence is undoubtedly of much interest to those who impose it. Although some judges order it as a punishment, it must be asked whether offenders see it as such, or is it viewed merely as "getting over," putting one over on the courts and law enforcement officials? Do offenders see it as restitution for the crimes they committed, or is the link between their victims' suffering and the community service work too tenuous to be perceived? If offenders do not see it as making restitution, how do they define the sanction's purpose? However they see its aims, do they think it is a fair penalty for their crimes, or do they feel unjustly treated? Are they further embittered and alienated by the order to work without pay? Would they have preferred to receive other kinds of sentences, and 140 if so, which ones? To answer these questions, interviews were conducted with eighty-one persons sentenced to the Vera Community Service Sentencing Projects by the Manhattan, Bronx, and Brooklyn courts.

What follows are the responses of offenders to these questions and our exploratory attempts to tease some general themes out of these answers. As with any collection of people this large, considerable variation was found from one person to another in their perceptions, opinions, values, and abilities to articulate their thoughts well. Rather than trying to explicate the exact nature of this variation in all its precise detail, this chapter examines only a few different questions and focuses upon the principal lines of reasoning that were revealed in defendants' answers. This report should be seen as an opportunity to let offenders talk to us, rather than as an undertaking of the grander exercise of describing their world view.

The channels through which they spoke were interviews with a Hispanic man in his early thirties who is "street smart" and an accomplished ethnographic observer and interviewer. For two years prior to conducting these interviews, he had worked with the Vera Institute's research project on crime and employment, and had interviewed many high risk ghetto youths involved in crime. He took notes during the interviews and then reconstructed the full responses shortly afterwards. All interviews followed a structured list of questions. Participants were guaranteed anonymity. The fact that he was a man and a Hispanic undoubtedly influenced to some extent the answers elicited from participants. Ideally, we would have matched the ethnicity and gender of subjects with interviewers, but such a luxury could not be afforded. Because this interviewer had been trained to present a neutral persona and had been closely supervised by a professional anthropologist during his previous two years of working at the institute, I suspect that the bias his presence created in the interviews was relatively minimal.

Before exploring the participants, it is helpful to know something about them and their social milieu. All were serving their court-imposed community service sentences during the months of late June, July, August, and early September 1982. Although they were not asked to describe themselves and their backgrounds for lack of sufficient time, we know that this group constituted half of all participants sentenced to community service during that period. Participants were chosen in a random manner for interviews, and their composition as a group was probably representative of all defendants sentenced between 1 July–30 September 1982. Table 5.1 shows the demographic characteristics of these July–September participants as well as their criminal records.

Participants in the project were typically Hispanic or black men in their mid-twenties who were single with few or no dependants. Fewer than a quarter of them reported their principal source of income during the month previous to sentencing as having been a legitimate job. About a third were recipients of public assistance in one form or another, either directly or through somebody in the family or household. The remainder reported having had either no income during the month or having gotten it from "other sources," which probably included criminal activity. (The tallies of "other sources" and "no income" are probably somewhat confused among the three boroughs, because it is not clear how project employees asked the questions in the intake interviews from which these data were drawn. It is possible that income from criminal activities was counted sometimes in one category and sometimes in the other.)

Participants were well acquainted with the courts and with the criminal justice system. They averaged between five prior arrests (in Brooklyn) and thirteen prior arrests (in Manhattan) before having been arrested in the cases that led to their community service sentences. For half of them, no more than ten or fourteen months (depending upon the borough) had passed since their last conviction, before they had been arrested again. For their last convictions, about three-fifths had received prison sentences. Just prior to being considered for community service, almost all of these offenders had been arraigned for nonviolent property offenses. A substantial proportion in Brooklyn and the Bronx were charged with burglary or offenses related to burglary (usually for stealing from a commercial building). The majority of the Manhattan participants were charged with petit larceny, most often as a result of shoplifting.

Table 5.1. *Characteristics of Participants Sentenced Between 1 July and 30 September 1982*

Demographic characteristics	Bronx	Brooklyn	Manhattan
Average age	26	23	28
Proportion male	95%	97%	86%
Ethnicity			
Black	28%	62%	58%
Hispanic	68%	31%	40%
White/anglo	4%	7%	2%
Marital status			
Single	50%	65%	72%
Married	28%	7%	10%
"Common-law"	22%	28%	18%
Number Dependents			
None	66%	82%	81%
One	3%	—	—
Two	13%	7%	8%
Three or more	18%	11%	11%
Reported source of income last month			
Legit. employment	21%	25%	11%
Public assistance	37%	39%	31%
Other	13%	11%	49%
No income	29%	25%	9%
Crime-related characteristics			
Average no. prior arrests	7	5	13
Median no. months since last arrest	14	14	10
Proportion receiving jail sentence for most recent prior conviction	57%	56%	60%

(continued on next page)

Table 5.1 (continued)

Type of offense charged at arraignment in current case	Bronx	Brooklyn	Manhattan
Burglary	23%	35%	—
Possession burglar's tools	4%	10%	5%
Trespass	2%	3%	5%
Possession stolen property	21%	10%	11%
Petit larceny	20%	7%	64%
Grand larceny	9%	28%	4%
Robbery	5%	—	—
Forgery/possession of forged instrument	6%	—	2%
Pickpocketing	—	—	3%
Theft of services	—	—	1%
Car theft	2%	3%	1%
Obstructing govt. administration	2%	—	—
Unlawful assembly	—	—	1%
"Con game"	—	—	1%
Drug sale/possession	5%	3%	—
Total number participants:	56	29	110

SOURCE: Project screening records and intake interviews.
NOTE: Proportion receiving jail sentence for last conviction includes anybody getting imprisonment terms in any combination of sentences, including "time served."

Do Offenders See Community Service as Restitution?

It is not uncommon to hear the belief expressed that community service has a reformative influence on criminal offenders. As one program director in California put it, "It's so healing in a criminal offense. . . . It helps people get in touch with their inner woundedness. . . . Community Service is very holistic, very healthy."[2] Some have tried to give this kind of thinking a more sophisticated footing, drawing on what social psychologists call "equity theory." The argument in its simplified form runs like this: All people, criminal and law-abiding alike, who have been socialized into human culture have internalized a norm of fairness, although that norm is more primitively developed in some than in others. A "fair" exchange is defined as one in which people get back what they deserve for their efforts. (What constitutes a fair and deserved balance between costs and rewards is a convention that is established and shared by a substantial proportion of those living in a common culture.) When people participate in an inequitable relationship, they experience distress. People feeling such distress will initiate actions to relieve it. This process restores psychological equilibrium and may promote greater social and psychological maturity.[3]

When applied to criminal victimization, this line of theorizing suggests a number of interesting questions. Do exploiters really feel distress and do they really seek to restore a fair balance? Is community service seen as a way of making restitution, or is the relationship between offenders' unpaid labor and the suffering of victims too tenuous to be discerned? And does making restitution, either directly or indirectly by means of community service, actually produce a long-term change in behavior and attitudes, beyond simply applying salve to consciences?

Interviews with project participants revealed that most of them did not see their work as restitution, other than a vague "paying back one's debt to society," which could also characterize any other kind of punishment, including a jail or prison sentence. Many did not even think that their crimes had involved victims. The expectation of changing offenders' attitudes toward crime by way of their making restitution therefore rests on questionable assumptions. To be sure, the experience of having served the sentence may have produced some desired changes in attitudes, social maturity, and civic responsibility, but our conversations with participants did not give much support to the idea that such changes resulted from the therapeutic effects of paying back victims in such an indirect and obscure way.

In our early interviews, we were surprised to hear most participants declare that there had been no victims to their crimes. We consequently decided to explore their conceptions of the term "victim." In about 55 percent of the instances in which we asked for their definitions of the term, we found that participants gave quite restrictive meanings. For example, victims to them are persons confronted directly by the offender in the course of the crime. This confrontation typically involves physical injury or attack.

A person who gets hurts after an incident like mugging, stabbing, fighting—stuff like that.

Someone who got hurt during a crime.

Someone who gets hurt in a robbery, homicide, molesting, or an assault.

A person who has been raped, robbed, or beaten up. Someone who has gotten perpetrated—you know, the victim of a crime.

A victim is if I hurt someone or do something to them.

A victim means to me, did I hurt anyone or did I take anything from anyone physically?

Someone who suffers at the hands of somebody else. Like if I throw a flower pot out of the window and it hits someone, that's a victim.[4]

A smaller proportion, about 45 percent of those asked, gave more generous definitions that encompassed a wider variety of victimizing acts.

Somebody whose rights have been violated. Something that has been done to somebody that's unjust.

Somebody who gets something taken away from them, like property, merchandise, or freedom.

The person that the crime was done to.

Someone or thing that has suffered some kind of injustice.[5]

Even by these broader definitions of victimization, many participants did not see their acts as having involved victims, simply because their offenses were crimes of theft. Stealing from a store is not stealing from a person. Committing a burglary from someone's home does not involve a victim, because nobody was there at the moment of entry.

I was only shoplifting. I didn't hurt nobody or knock them down.

There was no person or thing that suffered injustice. Gimbel's [a department store] is a name, not a person that you can call a victim. Also, Gimbels writes off their losses and collects insurance. Stealing from Gimbel's ain't like stealing from an old lady.

I took some magazines from a store, not from anybody's person.

The owner wasn't there.

There was nobody around.

Nobody got hurt by the crime so there's no victim. (Offender forged a signature on someone else's check.)

The stuff was stolen from the factory when the guy wasn't around. There was no person involved.

No victim, because there was nobody around and I was just taking the battery from the car.

I don't know who the owner of Macy's [a large department store] is. As far as I am concerned, Macy's is a corporation with a lot of money. Macy's ain't a person, so it ain't a victim.

This is a department store, a business. These companies have insurance and they're covered for their losses. I didn't steal from nobody, and I haven't beaten nobody over the head.

I wasn't the one that took the stuff. I know there was a victim but I didn't have no contact with him. I just had the stolen property because I bought it on the street. (Offender was convicted of possessing stolen property.)

No victim, because I don't be pulling knives on people or stealing from their apartments. I don't steal from poor people. I steal from people who have a little extra and I take the little shit. I'm not a violent guy. (The offender, who stole a radio from a store, defined "victim" as "If you leave a person out in the cold by taking everything he's got instead of one thing, that's a victim.")

I just got caught with the tire from a van. The tire came from a van, not a person. I didn't even know who the van belonged to.

I never got out of the store with anything, so what did he lose? (Offender was apprehended as he left the store with $50 worth of meat.)[6]

A few others said that there hadn't been a victim because there hadn't been a crime. Even though they had pleaded guilty, they still maintained that they were innocent of the crime for which they had been charged.

I wasn't stealing anything. I just happened to be in a store where I wasn't wanted. (Offender was a shoplifter who had been enjoined by the courts from entering the department store, and was charged with criminal trespass for coming in again.)

I didn't commit the crime.

I had a screwdriver and a pair of pliers in my bag but I wasn't trying to steal no car. (Offender was charged with possession of burglar's tools.)

I didn't steal the bicycle tire.[7]

Others, about 16 percent of those interviewed, agreed that there had been a victim in their crimes, but that *they* had been the victims.

I was the victim because the cop hit me several times. (Offender stole a van.)

I was the motherfucking victim because I was in a rented station wagon that was overdue and I didn't know that shit. I was the victim because I was robbed of my freedom. (Participant was convicted of car theft.)

I was the victim because it seems that I got the ten days of hard labor out of the deal and all the person lost was the buttons off his radio. (Offender stole a radio that was recovered in a damaged condition.)

I was the victim because the security guards beat me up.

I was the victim because I was wearing some black patent leather shoes and four guys wanted to take them from me. I beat them up and we were all arrested. (Offender was charged with criminal trespass and assault.)

I was the victim because I was the one who got put in bandages. I was kidnapped off the street by the police and put a ransom on [i.e., he was held in jail and had to pay bail to get out]. I didn't steal nothing.

I was the victim because I was charged with a lot of shit I didn't do.[8]

Only 20 percent of those asked reported unequivocally that their crimes had involved victims other than themselves. Where stores were involved, the participants were sometimes a little unclear as to who precisely had suffered the loss. Most saw the owner of the store as the victim. One person who had stolen from a jewelry store showed a somewhat more creative turn of mind:

I robbed a jewelry store so there was a victim. The people I stole from weren't the owners, they was just workers. It was really no loss to them, but it was important to them because it their job that they was protecting. They have to protect the stuff.[9]

By and large, most participants did not see the more indirect consequences of their thefts. It is true that many stores cover their losses, but this is done by raising the cost of goods to consumers.

Seeing the customers as the ultimate victims of their crimes involves too long a connection for most offenders to follow. Or, at least, offenders found it easy to rationalize away their crimes as having done little damage. Only a few dollars and cents are added to prices, and consumers are not likely to attribute higher prices to their specific acts of theft. Offenders were also found in many cases to minimize the importance of what they had stolen to the owners. As one participant convicted of car theft remarked, "the owner of the car was the victim even though it was a new car and she had insurance for it, so she wasn't really a victim. It was probably just an inconvenience for the time she didn't have the car."[10]

Because of the combination of offenders not seeing their crimes as having had victims and the absence of direct repayment to those victims, it is not surprising that most offenders did not see their community service work as making restitution. Asked for whom they were performing the service, the majority of the offenders answered, "the city," "the Vera Institute," "the neighborhood," or the "community." (The fact that they have been put under the supervision of the Vera *Community* Service Sentencing Project was not apparently lost on them.)

For the city because I came from the criminal court and the court's a part of the City.

For the city, you know, for Uncle Sam, the president, Mayor Koch.

I guess it's the borough president of the Harlem community.

I guess the city. Nobody ever told me who this work is for.

For the poor people who can't live in better places. (Offender was assigned to clean out apartment buildings to prepare for renovation and leasing to low-income tenants.)

For the neighborhood and the city because they own these buildings. The city is saving money from us.

For the system. For the city because the city had a vote in creating this project. The system accepted this project because of all the overcrowding in the jails. Now the community is benefiting because we are cleaning up the neighborhood for the people.

For the court, for the judge, and for the lawyer.[11]

In conclusion: offenders saw themselves as having been sentenced to community service because they broke the law (or, at least, because they were convicted of having broken the law, even though some continued to deny their guilt). Community service was not viewed by offenders as a form of restitution. Victims were not being paid back. Performing community service did not redress the inequitable "exchange" between criminals and victims. Theorists may hypothesize that psychological benefits accrue from offenders paying back victims, but performing unpaid labor in this community service program did not provide the opportunity to test this notion.

Why Am I Here?

If participants did not see their work as making restitution, what did they see as the purpose of their required attendance in the Vera Community Service Sentencing Project?

To learn how participants viewed the Vera Institute's community service sentence, they were asked an open-ended question: "What do you think the project is supposed to be doing with you people?" Having framed the question in this way, we were fishing more for their perceptions of the project's and the sanction's purpose than for the reasons for which they thought the courts had imposed the sentence. We were interested in whether they volunteered that the project was supposed to be punishing them, to be serving as a vehicle for making restitution, rehabilitating them, finding them jobs, or something else entirely unexpected.

Participants answered by looking first at what the project actually does and then deciding that this was what it was supposed to do. A few saw it as "paying back the community." Others saw it as no more than an obligation to work and stay out of trouble.

Basically, all I can see is that the project is here to make us work and do the seventy hours. I haven't seen the project do anything more for us.

The project is supposed to make your ass be here for seventy hours and if you aren't, then turn your ass into the court.

All the project is supposed to be doing is enforcing the ten days of work or I'll be in trouble.

It's suppose to make us do ten days of hard work and not get paid for it. It's supposed to be making us to do this work for the court. It's supposed to keep us out of trouble while we are here.

It's giving us a chance to work our sentence off and keep us off the streets until we get a job.[12]

Others saw the project as a job training effort, teaching both vocational skills and more general work habits.

The project is supposed to be helping us by showing us how to get up early and come to work.

It's supposed to keep me out of trouble and teach people how to do some work. There are people who never worked before and the project is suppose to teach us what normal people do to support themselves.

I guess it's rehabilitation. I use to shuffle and get over. Here I got to work or go back to jail. The project has helped me and I believe I can do anything that I want to do and as good as anybody else. It's supposed to help you learn how to get up in the morning, do some work, and get paid.

It's supposed to rehabilitate a person in a drug-free way. Again the idea of working and trying to get us into a motion. The project propels you into a work movement that you need in order to keep a job.

I guess it's suppose to get us in the right working habit. That's all I can gather from it.

I assume that it will give you some kind of orientation and job training so that you can get a job.[13]

Several reported that the project was also supposed to find people work after giving them "the work habit." This was not surprising because in each borough project there is a full-time support services coordinator who seeks employment for those who request it.

The project is supposed to be trying to help you by keeping you out of trouble and at the same time try to hook you up with some kind of job so you can better yourself.

I think that what the project does is first of all get you out of a jam. Secondly it provides a basis for bettering yourself through work, through orientation, and through referrals. The project helps you get off the streets so that you won't be getting in trouble.[14]

Others were somewhat less literal, seeing the sanction as carrying a lesson. It may be that they drew these conclusions spontaneously, although it is also possible that they were absorbing the messages given to them by the supervisors on the worksite, several of whom take every opportunity to preach the virtues of law-abiding behavior and civic responsibility.

Teaching us that stealing is not a way of life. It's supposed to teach you how to be responsible by coming on time and keeping your word.

The project is teaching us and giving us an opportunity to realize that we were doing wrong and a chance to change. Here in the project we have a chance to learn some responsibility and to live like other people in the society.

The project is supposed to make people face reality. Reality is doing something for yourself, not taking anything from someone, nor harming anyone, and doing something for society. This is a chance to help your people in a poor community so that they have a better place to live.

It's supposed to be showing the people not to be going out to steal to make their money. That there is plenty of ways of making money without stealing. The shit is, learn from the white man 'cause the white man is doing the right thing. That's why the white man has all the money. We are dumb doing the stealing and always being in trouble. I guess that's what the project is supposed to do.

I think it's supposed to show us some kind of responsibility plus show us we could do things we probably thought we couldn't do.

It's supposed to motivate us and give us self-pride. It's supposed to give us something to look forward to if you apply yourself. If a person takes advantage of the project to better himself, that's good. If he doesn't, he will end up saying this was just another program.[15]

The lack of perfect consensus in these responses reflects the fact that the Vera Community Service Sentencing Project does indeed have multiple goals. Although project managers and planners made no great promises about inculcating work habits and new law-abiding ways of living, supervisors on the work sites often preach that work pays and that working is better than stealing. Participants are put to work doing the kinds of labor that would bring a wage in the free market, and some do indeed learn rudimentary skills during their seventy-hour term. (As one participant said, "The project is supposed to be teaching us how to work, such as doing painting; for example, I have never used a paintbrush in my life, and I have learned here how to paint.") The project also operates as a broker of social services. At the time of negotiating the plea agreement in the courts, the project's court representatives frequently tell defendants that they will have employment referrals and other social services made available to them, and the support services coordinators in each borough do indeed refer participants to various agencies for employment and other services. The project also works to punish and to partially incapacitate offenders, keeping them out of trouble during the daytime with close surveillance. It is not surprising, therefore, that participants saw that the project was supposed to do all of these different things, and not just punish them.

Is Community Service Punishment?

To ask if a two-week stint of unpaid labor is punishing may seem as absurd as asking if water is wet. Many people may actually enjoy working for its own sake ("work is its own reward"), but it is not unreasonable to suspect that being ordered by a criminal court judge to labor at manual tasks for no pay is viewed as a punishment. The belief of the institute planners that they were designing a punishment rather than a rehabilitation project did not by itself endow this sanction with its punitive aspect. Unpaid labor performed under threat of jail already bears the marks of punishment. And judges assume that the two weeks of labor are punishing. As one judge put it, "it would be unconstitutional if it weren't a sentence" because it would fall under the Constitution's ban on involuntary servitude. Although many judges say that they impose it for reasons other than to punish, these other reasons are often subsidiary to the main intent: crimes must be punished to deter other would-be offenders, to deter those who are caught and sentenced from falling into errant ways again, and for the sake of retribution.

But is community service seen as punishment by those who are ordered to perform it? This question was raised when an interviewer came back from one of his first extended discussions with a participant and reported that the participant expressed pride that he went "off to work" in the morning, and came back weary in the evening from the "job," ready to be treated by his wife as one who has fulfilled his manly duty of working all day. He seemed proud to be laboring, even though it was for no money at all. Participants in subsequent interviews sometimes expressed similar sentiments: their self-esteem was improved by having a "job." As one thirty-eight year old man put it:

I don't think it is a punishment because when I come to the site in the morning I see things differently. I feel good riding the subway in the morning knowing that I'm going to work. You then say to yourself, "If I did these ten days with no problem, then I can do it on a regular job." [16]

Because of the positive value attached to work in this culture and the common belief that not having work is a mark of personal failure worthy of shame, it is not surprising to hear that labor is viewed as its own reward in many instances, even if it comes from a criminal sentence. Confronted with these reports, we decided to explore more systematically whether participants viewed the sanction as punishment.

When asked, "Do you think that this work is punishment?" a surprisingly large number—indeed, the majority of those interviewed—responded that it is not. Several of these responses were qualified and ambivalent ("sort of but not really"), and we did not force them to give an unqualified yes or no. Although there is some looseness in our tallies as a consequence of this ambivalence in some responses, we found that about three-fifths of those interviewed declared that the labor was not punishing.

What is interesting in these responses is the kind of thinking that they reveal. When faced with the question, participants often thought first about what punishment meant to them, thereby establishing their standards of comparison, and then assessed the community service sentence against those standards. Because most of these participants had been to jail before, jail had been enshrined as the archtypal punishment. Community service is not jail, and therefore it is not punishment.[17] This syllogistic thinking occurred frequently, and it was the most commonly given explanation of why community service was not considered punishing. The reasons why jail was seen as punitive was made evident in many of the responses.

There's no emotional comparison between this and jail. Out here you can talk to people and tell them about your problems. In jail, they don't want to hear your shit. You have to protect your macho image. In jail, you keep your little spot and protect it, that's it! In jail, everybody bullshits about being a pimp, being this shit, being that shit, and saying how bad they were. In jail, too, everybody is a lawyer. You tell them about your case and right away they tell you what to do to beat the case, how to appeal, and what you have to do. They know what's best for you—a lot of bullshit. Out here, you can sit down and watch a girl pass by and say something sweet. In jail, you just sit and watch the homos. Out here you're free after five to do what you please.

No, it's no punishment because if you had to do time on Rikers Island, you would have to work like this anyway. And here we have our freedom and you can accomplish something out of it. To me, jail is punishment because you're locked up and you get frustrated. In jail you can't eat what you want, you can't make telephone calls, and you can't see the ladies. That's punishment.

It's not punishment, because when you're in jail, you automatically have to work and if you don't you lose your good time [i.e., time off for good behavior]. Punishment is being locked up and not getting what you want or doing what you want.

If it was punishment, the court system would give up on you and put you behind bars. The fact that we are in the project shows that the system thinks that we can better ourselves and gives us a second chance. Punishment to me is being in jail with no chance at all.

You committed yourself to work for your freedom, and it ain't no punishment. We asked to be here, so it was our choice. Punishment would be if we went to jail.

You're free out here to do what you want. You don't have anyone on your back telling you to do this or that as long as you do your work.[18]

Jail is punishment because it severely restricts freedom, because it is a very coercive environment, and because jailers show little or no interest in the welfare of those locked up. Community service is not like jail and therefore it is not punishment. It restricts your freedom no more than a regular job ("it's just a job except that you don't get paid"); participants were free to choose the guilty plea and the sentence rather than risk a jail sentence; and the project managers show an active interest in helping the offenders "better themselves" and their circumstances. A thirty-five-year-old offender with a long history of prior convictions said with perhaps a little exaggeration:

> No, it definitely is a form of reward. I can hardly say it's punishment. The people here appreciate what the project is doing for them. Here in the project you actually feel as though you paid for the crime you did. The fact that you have your freedom and have been given an opportunity to work for the community is a reward and not a punishment. I don't think everyone who commits a crime should be punished. This type of atmosphere instills a good feeling in people.[19]

There is a certain irony in this. The Vera Institute planners designed and marketed the community service sanction as a punishment that could serve as an alternative to jail. Indeed, because they wanted it used as an alternative to a jail sentence, they felt that the project would have to provide what the courts were thought to want: punishment. In many participants' eyes, however, the sanction was not seen as punishing, precisely because it saved them from going to jail. (At least, they thought it saved them from going to jail. In many instances, a jail sentence would not have been imposed, as discussed in chapter 4.) Compared to jail, the project is a "piece of cake" and a "break."

> The project is something I asked God to give me a shot at.

> We would be in jail, so this ain't no punishment. This is a favor they did for us.[20]

The project could be designed so that it is more punitive, but the planners decided against this. Although the labor was meant to be punishing, it was also designed to do something else: to serve as a visible means of paying back the community. Project managers in the three boroughs sometimes reject certain proposed tasks for the participants because they are simply too nasty, too demeaning, and without any feature that could be perceived as reparative.

Many of the other offenders who thought that the project was not punishing seemed to be comparing the work not with jail, but with other kinds of work experiences. Punishment, according to this yardstick, is conceived of as extraordinarily difficult work, "hard labor," "slavery," and so forth. Because the work demands of the Community Service Sentencing Projects compared favorably to what participants imagined in their worst fantasies, the project's work requirements were not really punishing.

This ain't punishment, because we have our freedom—no slavery or bossing around. Punishment would be doing harder work than people can do.

We're not really doing hard labor and nobody is busting our chops.

Punishment to me is working hard and being forced to do things a man can't do.

For me, punishment is doing hard labor that I can't handle. This is light stuff.

It's too easy to be punishment. If it was punishment, we would be doing thirty days hard labor and not getting paid.[21]

Rather than being seen as punishment, the work was seen as "easy," "like a regular job," "we work like other normal people," or "like exercise."

If pressed, many of these participants probably would have agreed that the work was really something they would prefer not to do. Nonetheless, it is interesting to discover that many of them did not rank this form of punishment high in the hierarchy of possible sanctions. Some tried to find another way of classifying the sanction that was less than "punishment," but more than nothing.

Working here is like paying off a fine.

This is more like a scolding. Punishment is for me doing ten hours a day of hard labor and having rough guys over us. Here no one has a whip and we do the work nice and easy.

It's like when your parents punish you so you won't be bad. I think it's punishment, but not a real serious one.[22]

Slightly more than a third of those interviewed looked at their circumstances and decided that the work indeed constituted a punishment. The most commonly given reason was the lack of pay. This was followed by participants complaining that the work was too hard and the project too coercive.

I think it is punishment because I get up early in the morning and I be coming down here from Dykman Street in the Bronx every day. Like right now I could have been hanging out late with a girl, but instead I have to be going to bed early so I can get up early. Besides that, I have to be working all day for free.

In a way, the project is a punishment because you have to be here and you have to do the ten days. Especially when you know you have to put your whole heart's effort working nine to five, not making a dime and just having enough carfare to get home.

I thought painting would be easy because I do that on my own. Now, this here shit is involuntary labor. . . . Sometimes they come down too hard on us, and that ain't necessary. Most of us are older guys and don't like to be treated like this.

Of course I see the project as punishment because it's like doing time. This is like a chain gang. The only thing is that I have a special privilege of going home at night. I'm losing all the way around 'cause I lost my job.

This shit here is torture 'cause I don't like this kind of work. I think they give this kind of work to young people because they know we don't like this kind of work.

I think it's punishment. Truly, because some of the work we've done is unsanitary and we have no say. So in a way the project is punishment like jail. We are doing a sentence like if we were in jail. Like for instance, they have made us clean up human feces in the vacant lots and I don't like doing that. Some people answer back, but it doesn't pay to complain because if you don't do it, they send you back to jail.[23]

Do Participants See the Sentence as Fair?

Criminal sanctions are not imposed primarily with an eye to what offenders think is right and wrong, but, other things being equal, it is better if those sentenced feel they are being treated fairly by the courts. Punishment seen as unjustly harsh may create enormous resentment and hostility, further alienating the offender from the law-abiding community. One of the attractive features of the community service sanction, at least in the minds of its advocates, is that it seems an inherently fair response to law breaking. Working to enhance life in the community is, it is hoped, a more direct method of making amends for a crime than "paying one's

debt to society" in a jail cell. As we have discussed, many defendants apparently saw their work as making amends only in a rather
abstract fashion and not as a restitution that even indirectly paid
back the victims of their crimes. The notion of reciprocity and reparation apparently eluded many of them. The perception of inher-
ent fairness may have in this way eluded them as well. Nonetheless, criminal offenders may have used other standards for
assessing the fairness of the project.

To explore the ways participants felt they were being treated,
fifty-nine of them were asked, "Do you think that this work is a fair
penalty for the crime you were convicted of?" Only seven answered No. Five of the seven felt that it was unfair because they
were innocent of the crime and shouldn't have been punished at
all. Even though they had pleaded guilty to the charges and accepted the community service sentence, these five felt cheated.
Rather than risking a trial and a stiff sentence if convicted, they
had agreed to plead guilty even though they claimed they were innocent. "In my case, it ain't fair because I wasn't doing anything
wrong. I was messed up because I have a record and they were
going to fuck me over."[24]

Three felt that the sentence was unfair because it was too demanding and that a lighter sentence would have been more just.

I should get ten dollars a day, at least. Besides, I think I could have walked
on this misdemeanor charge. I could have paid a fine or gotten off lightly.

I should have paid a fine instead of this, or gone to jail.

I should have sat in jail instead of busting my ass here. I didn't commit no
crime so I really shouldn't be here.[25]

Fifty-two of the fifty-nine participants interviewed agreed that
the work was a fair penalty for their crimes, but their explanations
often revealed an interesting train of logic. Although the question
was framed to explore participants' thoughts about how their punishment fit their crimes, only nineteen of them tried to weigh the
gravity of their actions against the severity of the penalty. About
two-thirds of those who referred to their crimes thought community service was fair because their crimes were relatively insignificant. Six even thought it was fair because they were innocent, and
jail would have been unfair under these circumstances.

Going to jail for what I did would have been very unfair, so this is fairer to me.

The crime I did was really nothing because I was only charged with attempt. It's better than doing time.

Yeah, for what I allegedly did, it's a fair penalty. I really didn't do anything.

I didn't do something really bad. I was just shoplifting in Bloomingdale's, so this work is equal. If I had done something wrong, do you think they would have given me the program?

Yes, because I only took a small amount of something.

Yeah, because I was only convicted of shoplifting. It's fair because I was convicted and I did do the crime.

It's fair considering the record I have, although I have paid for the things I did in the past.[26]

Rather than evaluating the balance between what they did and their sentences, most participants assessed the fairness of the community service sentence by comparing it to other punishments they could have received. In all cases, they saw a jail term as the likely alternative, and community service compared favorably with it.

To do all that torture in jail? I'd rather be here in the program. I'm not saying that this is fair, but it's better than being in jail.

It kept me out of jail and that can't be beat.

This is fair because it means freedom.

It's better to be here than in jail. It's really half-and-half. Half fair because it's doing me a favor of keeping me out of jail, being that I have a record, and half unfair because I didn't do anything.

It's fair because you're not locked up with all those hard-ass niggers who are serious criminals.

Because I had a choice of going to Rikers Island or being here, and I thought this was fairest.

You have to be crazy to turn down ten days of community work in the streets to do six months in jail. To me, just being out here free is fair.[27]

Nine of the fifty-two participants explained that it was fair because the project permitted them to pay back the community. Six thought it was fair because they had been given a choice and they had agreed to it. In a small proportion of the responses, participants gave a number of miscellaneous other reasons, including the admission that they needed "some form of repression to stop me from doing these things," or because the project "treats me OK," or because the project is giving them the chance to learn something useful.

Would Participants Prefer Other Sentences?

Because participants so often based their assessments of community service upon comparisons with other possible punishments they could have received, we decided to explore the way they ranked the sentence in their hierarchy of preferences. Assuming that all would have preferred no obligation at all, we didn't bother to ask whether an unconditional discharge would have been preferred. Instead, we asked if in retrospect they would have preferred a jail sentence, a term of probation, or a fine of a certain amount.

Only six of the sixty-three participants who were asked this question said they would have preferred a jail sentence. Three would have taken five days in lieu of the seventy-hour community service work, and another three would have taken thirty days. (They knew that they would have served only twenty of the thirty days, if they hadn't had their "good time" stripped away for misbehavior.) These people were unhappy with the nature of the labor that was required of them.

Fifty-nine participants were asked whether they would have preferred a probation sentence, either a one- or three-year term. Two said that they would have chosen a year on probation, and another two answered "one to three years on probation."

A much larger proportion of those questioned would have taken a fine over the community service obligation. Of the fifty-seven participants who answered the question, twenty-seven, or 47 percent, reported that they would rather have paid a fine. This was followed with a question about the maximum amount of the fine they

Table 5.2. *Size Fines That Participants Would Have Preferred to the Community Service Sentence*

Maximum fine	Number of participants
$500	2
250	2
200	3
150	4
100	11
50	4
25	1
	27

SOURCE: Interviews with participants.

would have preferred to have paid. The distribution of answers is shown in table 5.2.

Of those who said that they would have preferred a fine, 41 percent were working at the time of arrest and would therefore have had a source of steady income. One of those, who said that anything up to a five hundred dollar fine would have been preferable, was working as a building superintendant, and he knew that the courts would have given him some time to pay it off. However, most answered that they couldn't have paid a fine. ("I ain't got no damn money to be givin' to nobody!")[28] Others said that they would have taken the project instead of a fine because they got something out of doing the work. "I wouldn't have paid no fine. It's like I said, I wanted something to do and this is giving me something."[29]

Conclusion

Those who designed the Vera Institute project sought to create a sanction that would be seen as being of intermediate severity, less punishing than jail and more punishing than other nonincarcerative sentences. They seem to have been successful, by and large, at least from the participants' point of view. Almost none of them would have preferred a jail sentence; probation was also seen as less preferable and probably more punitive. Many would have preferred a fine, although the amount of the fine was obviously an important issue. If our interviewer had probed more, I suspect that we would have uncovered a complex weighing of how much offenders valued the time that would be forgone by doing community service, how much money they had had at the time of sentencing and, consequently, their ability to raise money for a fine, and the demands of the unpaid labor itself. It is probably safe to conclude that a community service sentence was seen generally as less desirable than a fine of an amount that may not have been considered a realistic option (that is, a few dollars that could have been paid quite easily). Certainly an unconditional discharge was seen as the most desired outcome and less punitive than community service.

The interviews revealed that jail held a central place in their thinking. The threat and possibility of jail colored their evaluations of community service and was the punishment against which the community service sentence was most often measured. The project's unpaid labor was not seen as punishing by most because punishment was defined as "jail." Court-ordered community service was seen as fair because it is not jail, and jail would have been "not fair." Lurking behind this comparison may be some more abstract notion of distributive justice, but many participants probably saw the issues very concretely in terms of what could have happened to them, rather than what was fair and just from a more general perspective.

Finally, community service was not seen as a means of making restitution, at least not to the offenders' victims. Rather, it was seen more concretely and literally as doing work, simply because it was ordered by the courts as a penalty.

The way that offenders saw the community service sentence is certainly interesting for its own sake, but it is also important because it is so closely related to another important question about the impact of the new sanction: did the community service order have any impact on subsequent criminal behavior? The following chapter explores this question.

Chapter Six

The Effects of Community Service
on Subsequent Criminality

In the minds of many, perhaps the most serious question about using community service in lieu of jail is whether it provides less protection for the public from criminals than other sentences. Theorists may quarrel about what judges should be aiming at when imposing sanctions, but it is fair to say that the man on the street and most policy makers feel no ambivalence: judges should both punish criminals and do something to prevent crime. These two objectives are not thought to be contradictory. Indeed, most citizens believe that criminality is reduced because criminals are punished. It is therefore eminently reasonable to wonder whether the courts' use of community service sentences has resulted in more crime than would have occurred if other sanctions had been imposed.

Advocates for community service frequently express their belief that the sentence produces beneficial results of crime prevention, largely because criminal offenders are thought to be rehabilitated by it. The logic underlying this argument was summarized by Joe Hudson and his associates in their *National Assessment of Adult Restitution Programs*, a report funded by the National Institute of Justice:

> Restitution may be more rehabilitative than other correctional measures because it is rationally related to the amount of damages done, is a specific sanction which allows the offender to clearly know when requirements are completed, requires the offender's active involvement, provides a socially appropriate and concrete way of expressing guilt, and creates a situation in which an offender is likely to elicit a positive response from other persons.[1]

164

Critics may rightly suspect, however, that these as-yet-unproven benefits are offset by a weakened deterrent power of the law and by a diminished capacity for incapacitating offenders, especially if the sanction is used as an alternative to imprisonment.[2]

At present, the field is dominated by assertions and hypotheses, rather than facts. Very few researchers have even attempted to examine the impact of the sanction on subsequent criminality. Reports of recidivism are not uncommon, but in themselves they tell us nothing about the sanction's impact. Recidivism data about offenders given other kinds of sanctions are needed if we are to draw any meaningful conclusions. To date, only one study of community service's impact on recidivism has been published anywhere in the world that shows any methodological rigor at all: the British government's analysis of reconvictions sustained by community service offenders in Great Britain. The authors found that 44 percent of all persons ordered to perform community service were convicted of a subsequent offense within twelve months of sentencing. For the sake of comparison, reconvictions were counted among another group of offenders who had been considered for community service but were later rejected for one reason or another. Among these latter individuals, 33 percent were reconvicted within a year of being at risk (either after having been sentenced to a nonincarcerative sanction or after having been released from imprisonment). The authors found that the two groups were not quite comparable, however, and they shrank from drawing any strong conclusions.[3] By and large, it is fair to say that we know almost nothing about the crime-control effects of the community service sentence.[4]

This chapter explores the criminality of participants after having been sentenced to community service to assess whether the use of the sentence had either beneficial or adverse effects on public safety. Before discussing in detail the assumptions made and methods used in this assessment, it will be helpful first to summarize our major findings.

The Main Findings

Within one hundred and eighty days of being sentenced to community service, 43 percent of the participants in a three-borough sample had been arrested again and charged with crimes, most of which were nonviolent offenses involving theft or crimes against the public order. Given that participants as a group had had lengthy records of similar arrests before having been sentenced to the institute's project, it is not surprising that they continued their lawbreaking afterward as well.

There is no evidence that jail sentences would have deterred participants from committing subsequent crimes any better. Even if all participants had been sent to jail instead, the available data suggest that there would have been no discernable difference in the likelihood of those offenders being rearrested within a relatively short time.

Nor was there any indication that community service and jail differed in their rehabilitative powers. The data show that community service participants did no better than persons who had been released from jail, at least insofar as their rearrest patterns indicated.

The use of the community service sentence did result in an increase in the number of crimes committed, however. This was due not to a weakened deterrent capability, but to the fact that jail sentences would have incapacitated offenders for various periods of time, thereby eliminating the opportunities for committing crimes in the larger community. The magnitude of this increase depended upon how often community service sentences were used in lieu of jail and upon how long these jail sentences would have been. Using the estimates described in chapter 3, we determined that the use of the sentence varied considerably from one borough to the next during the period we examined most closely: 1 October 1981 to 30 September 1982. The Manhattan courts were far more likely to use the project in instances in which the offender would otherwise have been sent to jail, and those jail sentences would have been longer than in the other two boroughs.

Based on these estimates and numerous qualifying assump-

tions, we estimated that about 35 percent of the Manhattan participants' rearrests during the one hundred and eighty days after
having received the sentence would have been averted if the courts
had not ordered the community service sentence and had relied
instead on other sanctions that would have been imposed in its absence. Similarly, about 10 percent of the Brooklyn participants' rearrests and 7 percent of the Bronx participants' rearrests would
have been averted.

Extrapolating these borough-specific estimates to the intake patterns that existed during the period between 1 October 1981 and
30 September 1982, we calculated that about 33 percent of participants' rearrests citywide would have been averted if all those participants who were otherwise bound for jail had actually been put
behind bars.

These incapacitation effects were short-lived. If one were to
consider crimes committed over a period of time longer than one
hundred and eighty days, the percentage of them that would have
been averted by a short jail sentence would have been smaller.

The Extent of Recidivism

The most accurate measure of subsequent criminality would be
a tally of all illegal acts committed by the participants after the
date of sentence. Such a perfect measure could not be taken, however, because crimes that went undetected could not be counted,
and criminals not apprehended could not be identified as recidivists. For our purposes, we counted events that led to an arrest
as indicators of criminality. In doing so, we underestimated the
true extent of subsequent law breaking, because offenders usually
commit several crimes before getting caught. The exact ratio of
crimes to arrests is difficult to establish for this population, but it
may be greater than ten to one for persons specializing in property
crimes.[5] Using rearrests biases our estimates of criminality in the
other direction as well: some arrests do not lead to convictions,
perhaps because no crimes were actually committed. This bias is a
small one, however, and probably does not come close to correct-

ing the underestimation resulting from participants not having been apprehended for many of their crimes.

Arrest records were compiled for 494 persons sentenced by the New York City courts to Vera's Community Service Sentencing Project. This group included all persons sentenced to the Bronx project between 8 January 1981 and 2 March 1982; all persons so sentenced by the Brooklyn courts between 7 January 1981 and 5 March 1982; and all those sentenced to Vera Institute project in Manhattan between 16 September 1981 and 5 March 1982. These periods were chosen because at the time of data collection (September 1982), at least six months had passed since all these participants had been sentenced to the project. All participants having fewer than six months elapsed since their dates of sentence were ignored.

Table 6.1 shows the proportion of persons rearrested within one hundred and eighty days of having been admitted to the Vera Community Service Sentencing Projects. Thirty-nine percent of the offenders sentenced to the Bronx Project were rearrested within one hundred and eighty days of sentence. The proportion in Brooklyn was 42 percent, and in Manhattan, slightly higher at 51 percent. In all three of the boroughs combined, a total of 43 percent of those tracked were rearrested within one hundred and eighty days of sentence.

Participants continued to be rearrested beyond the one-hundred-and-eighty-day period. Court records were later checked for Manhattan participants and this revealed that by the end of the twelve months, the proportion rearrested at least one time had grown to 69 percent. Similar studies were not done in the other two boroughs for reasons of economy, but it is reasonable to expect that a similar deterioration occurred there as well.

By focusing on the first rearrest, we get an indication of what happens to individuals who are sentenced to community service. A better measure of subsequent criminality, however, is the total number of rearrests incurred by project participants during the period. Some participants were arrested more than once during this period; indeed, one person was arrested seven times during the one hundred and eighty days. Of the Brooklyn participants, 12 percent were arrested two or more times; 14 percent of all Manhat-

Table 6.1. *Proportion of Community Service Participants Rearrested within 180 Days of Sentencing*

Days between sentence to community service and first rearrest	Bronx			Brooklyn			Manhattan		
	Participants rearrested	%	Cum. %	Participants rearrested	%	Cum. %	Participants rearrested	%	Cum. %
0– 30	18	9%	9%	8	6%	6%	16	11%	11%
31– 60	22	11	20	16	11	17	15	11	22
61– 90	14	7	27	6	4	21	15	11	33
91–120	12	6	33	9	6	27	9	6	39
121–150	6	3	36	8	6	33	12	8	47
151–180	7	3	39	13	9	42	6	4	51
Not rearrested within 180 days	126	62	101%	86	59	101%	70	49	100%
Total in sample	205	101%		146	101%		143	100%	

SOURCES: Dates of sentencing from project files; rearrest dates from New York City Criminal Justice Agency.

NOTE: Included here were all offenders sentenced to the Bronx project between 8 January 1981 and 2 March 1982, to the Brooklyn project between 7 January 1981 and 5 March 1982, and to the Manhattan project between 16 September 1981 and 5 March 1982. Rearrest data were obtained only for persons apprehended within New York City; a few persons may have been arrested outside the city limits and would not have been counted here as rearrests. Note that only the time to first rearrest is computed here. Some offenders were arrested more than one time after being sentenced.

tan and Bronx participants sustained multiple arrests during this period. Of the 494 participants we tracked after having been sentenced to community service, 212 were rearrested within six months, but they were rearrested a total of 310 times during that half-year period. (See table 6.2.) In summary: the offenders sentenced to the Vera Community Service Sentencing Project were arrested an average of 0.6 times during the six months after having entered the Project.

There were some differences among the three boroughs both in the proportion of the project offenders who were rearrested and in the total number of rearrests. As table 6.1 shows, 51 percent of Manhattan's participants were rearrested within six months of sentence, compared with 42 percent in Brooklyn and 39 percent in the Bronx. Offenders sentenced to the Manhattan project were also rearrested more often during the six-month follow-up period. The 143 Manhattan offenders we tracked were rearrested a total of 106 times, or an average of 0.7 times per participant. This compared with 0.6 rearrests per participant in both the Bronx and Brooklyn. These differences were not the result of variations in the way community service was administered in each borough. Rather, they reflected the fact that Manhattan participants on the whole had been more actively involved in crime before they were sentenced to community service and then continued to be so afterwards.

Rearrested participants were most often charged with property and theft-related crimes. This is no surprise, because participants in all three boroughs had relatively long arrest records, principally for property crimes. Table 6.3 lists all of the 310 rearrest cases in the three boroughs, sorting them according to the most serious type of offense charged at arraignment. Seventy-five percent of the cases involved nonviolent theft of property. Nine percent were crimes against persons, most often robberies. The remaining 16 percent were miscelleaneous nonviolent crimes against the public order, including weapons possession (2 percent), and drug sales or possession (12 percent).

The great majority of these 310 rearrest cases were arraigned as lesser felonies or misdemeanors. (See table 6.4.) Thirty-seven percent of all rearrested offenders in the three boroughs combined

Table 6.2. *Total Number of Rearrests Sustained by Participants*

Days after date of sentence	Bronx	Brooklyn	Manhattan
0–30	21	11	21
31–60	29	21	24
61–90	25	7	22
91–120	15	14	12
121–150	14	12	15
151–180	17	18	12
Total arrests within 180 days	121	83	106
Total individuals in group	205	146	143
Average number arrests per individual	.59	.57	.74

SOURCE: Dates of sentence from project files; rearrest dates from New York City Criminal Justice Agency.
NOTE: Populations were identical to those described in table 6.1. All arrests followed by arraignment in the New York City Criminal Courts were counted here.

were charged at arraignment with class-D or E felonies; 48 percent were charged with misdemeanor offenses.

Persons who had been sentenced to community service and subsequently rearrested were often given jail sentences for their new offenses. (See table 6.5.) At the time of our checking the court records, 130 of the 212 individuals in all three boroughs had their first rearrest case reach final dispositions. Of these 130, 85 percent were convicted and 15 percent were dismissed outright or given an adjournment in contemplation of dismissal (ACD). (This gives us some indication of the extent to which rearrest rates overestimate the extent of crime.) Fifty-eight percent of the sentences imposed were to jail, although seven of the sixty-four offenders given jail terms were given credit for their pretrial time and released.

Table 6.3. *Type of Offense Charged at Arraignment Following Rearrest*

Type of charge	Bronx		Brooklyn		Manhattan	
Harm to persons or persons and property:						
Robbery	4	(3%)	10	(12%)	3	(3%)
Assault	3	(2)	1	(1)	3	(3)
Rape	1	(1)	—	—	1	(1)
Murder/att. murder	—	—	2	(3)	1	(1)
Arson	—	—	1	(1)	—	—
Reckless endangerment	—	—	—	—	1	(1)
Property/theft:						
Petit larceny	23	(19)	8	(10)	32	(30)
Grand larceny	34	(28)	19	(23)	19	(18)
Burglary and burglary tools	18	(15)	17	(21)	11	(10)
Possession stolen property	6	(5)	4	(5)	16	(15)
Forgery	—	—	1	(1)	—	—
Trespass	1	(1)	—	—	5	(5)
Criminal mischief	3	(2)	4	(5)	—	—
Jostling	3	(2)	—	—	1	(1)
Theft of services	1	(1)	—	—	1	(1)
Car theft	1	(1)	1	(1)	—	—
Public Order Offenses:						
Drug sales/possession	17	(14)	11	(13)	8	(7)
Weapons possession	4	(3)	1	(1)	—	—
Prostitution	—	—	—	—	2	(2)
Gambling	1	(1)	—	—	1	(1)
Resisting arrest/ contempt	1	(1)	1	(1)	1	(1)
Swindling	—	—	—	—	1	(1)
Traffic law viol.	—	—	1	(1)	—	—
Total arrests	121	(100%)	83	(100%)	106	(100%)
Charges unknown	—		1		—	
Total no. participants	205		146		143	

SOURCE: New York City Criminal Justice Agency.
NOTE: Percentages do not add exactly to 100 percent due to rounding.

Table 6.4. *Seriousness of Charges at Arraignment Following Rearrest*

Class of highest arraignment charge	Bronx		Brooklyn		Manhattan	
A felony	—	—	2	(2%)	1	(1%)
B felony	10	(8%)	11	(13)	1	(1)
C felony	7	(6)	6	(7)	8	(8)
D felony	24	(19)	27	(33)	16	(15)
E felony	20	(16)	11	(13)	17	(16)
A misdemeanor	59	(50)	24	(29)	58	(55)
B misdemeanor	1	(1)	2	(2)	5	(5)
Total arrests	121	(100%)	83	(100%)	106	(100%)
Total no. participants	205		146		143	

SOURCE: New York City Criminal Justice Agency.
NOTE: If cases had multiple charges, only the highest class arraignment charge was counted here.

Nineteen percent of those convicted were sentenced to a fine, often with a jail sentence specified as a penalty for failing to pay. Fifteen percent were given conditional or unconditional discharges; 7 percent received probation. Rearrested Manhattan participants were more likely to get jail sentences than participants from the other two borough projects, largely because they had longer and more serious prior criminal histories.

It is important to recognize that this pattern of recidivism characterized offenders sentenced to the institute project during a very specific period. The pattern may have changed in the months after the rearrest study was completed. Screening procedures in the Bronx and Brooklyn courts were modified in mid-1983, and these new procedures may have brought in participants whose subsequent recidivism was different. Probably more important for recidivism results, however, was the changing borough-by-borough contribution to the total citywide intake. The participants we tracked had all been sentenced to the project during the fourteen months prior to March 1982, and the Manhattan branch had opened only five-and-a-half months before the end of this period.

Table 6.5. *Disposition of Participants' First Rearrest Cases, by Borough*

Case outcome	Bronx		Brooklyn		Manhattan		Total	
Convicted and sentenced to:								
Discharge	7	(18%)	3	(11%)	7	(17%)	17	(15%)
Probation	3	(8)	3	(11)	2	(5)	8	(7)
Jail w/credit for time served	1	(3)	3	(11)	3	(7)	7	(6)
Jail	18	(45)	15	(54)	24	(57)	57	(52)
Fine or jail	11	(28)	4	(14)	6	(14)	21	(19)
Total sentenced	40	(100%)	28	(101%)	42	(100%)	110	(99%)
Dismissed/ACD	9		5		6		20	
Transferred to supreme court or grand jury	8		10		3		21	
Unknown/pending	22		17		22		61	
Total rearrest cases	79		60		73		212	

SOURCE: New York City Criminal Justice Agency.
NOTES: Only the disposition of the first rearrest is considered here.

This branch's share of the total participant population in the rearrest sample was relatively small as a consequence: only 29 percent of the citywide total. In the months after March 1982, Manhattan's share of the total project intake grew substantially. For example, during the year following March 1, 1982, the Manhattan Criminal Court had sentenced 46 percent of all community service participants in all three boroughs. This probably shifted the overall recidivism rate in the direction of the Manhattan pattern: a larger proportion of persons rearrested within six months of sentence and a higher average number of subsequent rearrests per offender. There were some other countertrends that worked against this result, however. These will be discussed more fully at the end of this chapter.

Could These Crimes and Rearrests Have Been Prevented?

That a substantial proportion of the participants in each borough were rearrested within six months of having been sentenced to the project is without doubt a depressing statistic. But could the courts have done better in the absence of the Vera Institute project? Would these offenders have been less likely to have been rearrested if their cases had been disposed in some other ways? How many of the crimes resulting in rearrests can really be attributed to imposing the community service sentence?

The best way to answer this question would be to conduct an experiment with some defendants chosen randomly for community service sentence and with others disposed of as judges saw fit. This would provide two groups to examine: "experimentals," or those sentenced to the project, and "controls," those sentenced otherwise. The subsequent arrests of individuals in both groups could then be tallied over a specified period and compared. Any differences in outcomes could be attributed quite clearly to the use of the community service sanction. Unfortunately for our purposes, however, such a research design could not be imposed upon the courts.

Not having had the opportunity to set up such an experiment, we decided to limit our analysis to the comparative crime-control effects of community service and of jail. If the use of community service had any impact at all on subsequent arrests, it was probably because jail sentences were not imposed. It is unlikely that the community service sentence differed significantly from other nonincarcerative sanctions in its impact on crime.

There are three principal ways that jail and community service sentences may influence offenders so that they behave in a law-abiding manner. One or the other sanction may deter, rehabilitate, or incapacitate offenders, thereby reducing or preventing their subsequent criminality. Deterrence strategies aim to "scare offenders straight," relying on punishment and privation for results.[6] Rehabilitation efforts also aim to turn offenders away from crime, but they typically rely not on punitive measures alone but on various kinds of programs to remedy offenders' handicaps, whether these are social, psychological, educational, vocational, or physical. Incapacitation strategies generally do not attempt to bring about long-term changes by winning offenders' hearts and minds, but aim only to remove or reduce their opportunities for crime. Execution incapacitates fully and permanently; imprisonment incapacitates almost completely, but only as long as prisoners are held behind bars. Other nonincarcerative sanctions, including community service, have some partial and temporary incapacitative results.

Comparing the Deterrent Effects
of Community Service and Jail

That jail sentences were not found to reduce subsequent arrests any better than community service sentences will undoubtedly strike many as perverse. Are not people deterred from crime by the prospect of punishment? And doesn't it follow that stiffer punishments deter more effectively than lesser ones? Even those who perform court-ordered community service sentences agree that jail is more punishing; our interviews with almost a hundred different participants confirmed this. (See chapter 5.) If punishments deter, wouldn't we then expect to find evidence of this most clearly in the actions of people who have been sentenced by the courts?

To see whether jail sentences would have been more effective deterrents than community service, we compared project participants with a group of offenders who were as similar as possible, but who had been given jail sentences. In the Bronx and Brooklyn courts, defendants found eligible for community service but subsequently rejected were used for this purpose.[7] For our analysis of rearrests, we tracked those rejected offenders who had been sentenced to jail. During the period running from December 5, 1980 to February 9, 1982, a total of fifty rejected defendants were sent to jail by the Brooklyn Criminal Court. In the Bronx, one hundred and seven rejected defendants went to jail after first having been declared eligible between October 24, 1980 and March 5, 1982 and then rejected.

In Manhattan a different selection procedure had to be used to create a comparison group. At the time when we were collecting rearrest information, the project in that borough had not been in operation long enough to generate a large pool of rejected defendants going to jail instead. As a consequence, the files of the New York City Criminal Justice Agency were used to build our comparison sample. Court dockets were searched systematically for all persons sentenced to jail during the first twenty-six days of June 1981. From this group, our researchers identified two hundred and sixty persons who met the two basic criteria employed by project court representatives in Manhattan when screening for initial eligibility.

Rearrest information was then obtained for all offenders in this three-borough sample who had been sentenced to jail. The files of the New York City Criminal Justice Agency were scanned for any cases in the lower criminal courts that had been initiated after the date of jailing. An arrest in any one of the city's five boroughs would have been turned up in this sweep, except perhaps for a few felony arrests that had been made after indictment and then arraigned for the first time in the Supreme Court. (If there had been any such arrests, they would have numbered no more than a very few; most offenders specialized in petty crimes of the sort not subject to pre-arrest investigations and indictments.) In order to compare the post-sentence experiences of these jailed offenders with those of community service participants, all offenders were excluded who had not had at least 180 days pass between the date of their release from jail and the time at which we collected rearrest information.[8] Of the fifty jailed Brooklyn offenders, only thirty-six had been released from jail more than 180 days earlier. In the Bronx, the corresponding number of offenders was eighty-one; in Manhattan, two hundred and forty-one.

Even though the two groups—participants and jailed offenders—in each borough were not selected by random assignment, they resembled each other very closely and the differences that existed between them were not substantial enough to invalidate the comparisons of rearrest rates. (See the Appendix for a fuller discussion of the groups' comparability.)

Table 6.6 shows the proportion of offenders in each borough arrested either within 180 days of sentencing to community service or 180 days of release from jail. In all three boroughs, the propor-

Table 6.6. Proportions of Participants and Jailed Offenders Rearrested Within 180 Days of Sentence or Release from Jail

Days between sentencing to community service or release from jail and first rearrest	Sentenced to community service			Sentenced to jail		
	Number participants	Percent	Cumulative percent	Number offenders	Percent	Cumulative percent
Bronx						
0– 30 days	18	9%	9%	5	6%	6%
31– 60	22	11	20	6	7	13
61– 90	14	7	27	3	4	17
91–120	12	6	33	2	3	20
121–150	6	3	36	7	9	29
151–180	7	3	39	4	5	34
Not rearrested within 180 days	126	62	101%	54	67	101%
Total	205	101%		81	101%	

Brooklyn

0– 30 days	8	6%	6%	6	17%	17%
31– 60	16	11	17	2	6	23
61– 90	6	4	21	2	6	29
91–120	9	6	27	2	6	35
121–150	8	6	33	2	6	41
151–180	13	9	42	1	3	44
Not rearrested within 180 days	86	59		21	58	
Total	146	101%	101%	36	102%	102%

Manhattan

0– 30 days	16	11%	11%	46	19%	19%
31– 60	15	11	22	23	10	29
61– 90	15	11	33	23	10	39
91–120	9	6	39	10	4	43
121–150	12	8	47	9	4	47
151–180	6	4	51	6	2	49
Not rearrested within 180 days	70	49		124	52	
Total	143	100%	100%	241	101%	101%

SOURCES: Participants' sentencing dates from project files; all other data computed from information supplied by N.Y.C. Criminal Justice Agency.

tions rearrested were remarkably similar for both participants and persons released from jail. Whereas 39 percent of those who had been required to perform community service work in the Bronx had been arrested on new charges within six months of sentence, 34 percent of those released from jail in that borough had been arrested again within six months of getting out. In Brooklyn, the proportions were 42 percent versus 44 percent, and in Manhattan, 51 percent versus 49 percent.

These small differences were probably not significant and can be partly attributable to error in measurements. For example, it was impossible to measure precisely the length of time between getting out of jail and the first rearrest. Available records did not reveal exactly how much time offenders had spent behind bars, and this had to be estimated using information collected by the New York City Criminal Justice Agency. Small errors in these estimates would have affected the reckoning of the proportion of ex-prisoners who had been rearrested within 180 days of being released. This range of error would not have changed the proportion rearrested more than a few percentage points in either direction, however.

A fair conclusion that might be drawn from these findings is that being sentenced to jail instead of community service produced no significant decrease in subsequent criminality, at least insofar as the proportion of persons rearrested indicates. This may seem surprising and counter-intuitive to many readers, but it is not difficult to explain. To the extent that people are deterred at all from committing crimes, it is the perceived likelihood of apprehension and punishment that turns people away from the crooked path to the straight and narrow. That is, calculations of risks and gains involve assessing the odds of getting away with the crime as opposed to getting caught. In the populations of offenders compared here, there is little reason to think that community service participants expected easier treatment upon subsequent arrests than jailed offenders. A sizable percentage of those sentenced to community service had been to jail before, and almost all had spent some time in pretrial detention. In other words, they all knew what the insides of jails looked like, and they knew that the likelihood of going back was high if they were arrested again. Even with a much publicized policy of using community service sentences more frequently for nonviolent property offenses, the odds of landing in jail would continue to be high for those offenders in either of the comparison groups. There is little reason to think that their assessment of future risk would be much affected by their having gone to jail for this offense instead of to the community service project.

Moreover, the sentence itself is not the only thing one hopes to avoid by going straight. From arrest up to the point of sentencing, the experience of being prosecuted can be terrifying and abusive. Defendants will usually spend some time in pretrial detention, which is often dangerous and almost always degrading; bail monies often have to be raised; lawyers' fees are sometimes larger than can be raised easily; defendants use up their credit with family and friends by leaning on them for help; and the psychic costs of arrest and prosecution are typically high because defendants face uncertain futures, imprisonment, and other deprivations of liberty and leisure. As Malcolm Feeley so aptly put it, "the process is the punishment," especially in the lower criminal courts.[9] Having served a community service sentence instead of having gone to jail is not likely to affect the offenders' subsequent assessment of his or her chances of avoiding this entire gauntlet of punishments, both pretrial and post-sentence.

How Many Arrests Could Have been Prevented by Warehousing Criminals?

Even if jailing offenders does not deter them from committing crimes any better than community service does, it does provide some respite from criminality while offenders are behind bars. Jail incapacitates criminals more effectively than a seventy-hour community service obligation, and some crimes are undoubtedly prevented as a result. But just how many of the participants' crimes would have been prevented if judges had not ordered community service?

The 494 participants we tracked were arrested a total of 310 times during the 180 days after being sentenced to community service. Within the first thirty days, there were fifty-three arrests. All of the crimes that led to these arrests could have been prevented if the participants would have been in jail for these thirty days.[10] Jailing for longer periods would have prevented even more rearrests.

Such calculations are quite irrelevant, however, for they suggest no realistic policies. Lawmakers could not adopt a policy of locking up all property offenders for thirty days, or any other fixed period of time, in the hope of preventing their crimes. This would be extraordinarily expensive, because there are vast numbers of offenders who would qualify for such mandatory sentences. It would also be terribly inefficient. To prevent one crime within a specified period of time, a great many persons would have to be jailed who would not have committed any crimes at all. If an incapacitation strategy is to be at all cost-effective, the courts must acquire the ability to predict reasonably well which offenders are likely to commit more crimes. Our own experience with trying to identify recidivism-prone participants leads us to expect little of such efforts.

Looking at the number of participants arrested within a certain number of days or months after their sentences also tells us nothing about how many of these crimes would have been averted if the courts had not sentenced the offenders to community service. Not all participants would have gone to jail. Many would have received a fine or some other nonincarcerative sentence and consequently would have been at liberty to break the law. In computing the incapacitative effect lost because the community service sentence was used, we have to take into account the actual frequency with which jail sentences would have been imposed, as well as the time these offenders actually would have spent behind bars.

One way to do this would be to identify which participants would otherwise have gone to jail, estimating how long they would have spent behind bars, and then to count the number of times they were actually rearrested within that period. Although we developed predictive models that were reasonably reliable in estimating the proportion of participants who would have gone to jail, they were useless in this analysis of recidivism. Not enough information was known about each of the participants in this rearrest study population to estimate the likelihood of imprisonment for each. (The estimates of how many persons would have gone to jail were essentially aggregate measures: percentages of the total population of participants who would have gone to jail, rather than offender-by-offender descriptions.) We also were unable to predict with any accuracy whatsoever the length of time individual offenders would have spent in jail. Trying to identify who would have gone to jail and for how long proved to be a hopeless exercise.

Lacking the ability to determine how jail sentences would have been imposed upon the participant populations in each borough, we developed estimates of the arrests that would have been averted for participants as a group, rather than on an individual basis. The first step in this calculation was to determine the average number of arrests per community service participant per day over the entire 180-day period following sentence. The second step was to estimate how many days within this 180-day period participants would have been incapacitated by a jail sentence, had community service not been ordered. Using these calculations, we then developed an estimate of the average number of arrests per participant that would have been prevented if the community service project had not existed. I have chosen to express these estimates as the approximate number of rearrests per one hundred participants sentenced to community service in each borough during the period examined here. The computations used to develop this estimate and the assumptions underpinning them are detailed in the Appendix.

In the Bronx, we estimated that 4.5 rearrests per one hundred participants would have been averted had the project not existed and judges sent some offenders to jail. In Brooklyn, 5.4 arrests per one hundred would have been averted; and in Manhattan, 25.0 arrests per one hundred. Because relatively few of the Bronx participants would have gone to jail and because they would have gone there for such short periods of time, the lost incapacitative effect was smallest in that borough. At the rate of 4.5 averted rearrests per one hundred participants, only nine (or 7 percent) of the total one hundred twenty-one arrests by all two hundred and five participants during the 180 days could have been averted if the courts had not sentenced these participants to the project. In Brooklyn, the loss in incapacitative effect was about the same. We estimated that a total of eight, or 10 percent of the total, rearrests in Brooklyn could have been averted. In Manhattan, the crime-control losses were considerably higher because judges more often used the project in lieu of jail and because sentences there would have been longer than in the other two boroughs. We estimated that twenty-five rearrests within the 180-day period could have been averted for each one hundred participants sentenced to the project. At this rate, thirty-seven (or 35 percent) of the one hundred and six rearrests incurred by the one hundred and forty-three participants within six months of sentencing could have been averted had judges not sentenced these participants to community service.

The citywide rate of rearrests that could have been averted depended upon the relative contribution of each borough's admissions to the total project intake. These proportions varied from one time period to another. During the twelve-month period running from 1 October 1981 to 30 September 1982, the Manhattan courts sentenced 335 persons to community service, which represented 49.6 percent of the total citywide intake. The Bronx courts sentenced 179 participants to community service, or 26.5 percent of the citywide total, and 161 persons were sentenced to community service in Brooklyn, or 23.9 percent. Extrapolating the borough-by-borough rates of averted rearrests per one hundred participants to these different intake levels, we estimated that approximately one hundred and one arrests, or fifteen per one hundred participants citywide, could have been averted if the courts had sentenced offenders during this period without recourse to the Vera Community Service Sentencing Project.

The roughness and volatility of these calculations should not be underestimated. They were based upon a pyramid of many assumptions and several rather loose estimates. We could not determine with accuracy and perfect vision what judges would have done in the absence of the community service project, and we could only hazard what amounts to a sophisticated guess. The estimates of how many days participants would have spent in jail—the essential determinants of the incapacitation effect—were constructed using many restrictive assumptions. There was no way to measure the range of possible error in the many estimates we employed. When each of these estimates was used to compute still other estimates, an aggregation of error may have occurred that would result in an even larger rate of error, ultimately yielding an

estimate that might be very shaky. This is not to say that the estimates are worthless or without grounding in data whatsoever.
There is simply no way to calculate exactly what would have happened if history had happened a different way—if judges had
made different decisions regarding community service. Any deter-
mination we can make is necessarily a guess, an estimate. Such estimates are needed because policy makers, judges, and project
managers need the best information available so that their decisions can be made as sensibly as possible. That need should not
lead them to etch these findings into stone, however, for their soft
underpinnings should be always recognized.

The Costs of Crimes That Could Have Been Averted

How grave were the offenses that could have been averted if
community service sentences had not been imposed? As shown
above in table 6.3, about three-quarters of the participants' rearrests within the 180 day-period resulted in arraignment charges
for nonviolent thefts. (In the Bronx, these charges amounted to 74
percent of the total; in Brooklyn, 66 percent; and in Manhattan, 80
percent.) Many of these offenses were petty thefts, involving such
crimes as taking ten dollars out of a taxi driver's ashtray, stealing a
twenty-dollar pair of shoes from a store, and possession of screw-
drivers and other such tools during an arrest on suspicion of burglary. Other offenses involved more expensive items. The average
cost of these property offenses could not be calculated from the
records that we examined, but a "ballpark" figure can be obtained
from other sources.

During 1981, the dollar value of items reported stolen by thieves
in all burglaries reported to the police in New York State was estimated at $1,383 per theft. For all other nonviolent property of-
fenses other than car theft that were reported to the police in that
year, the estimated value of lost goods was $412 per offense.[11] This
includes only those offenses reported to the police and, in all
probability, this figure probably overestimates the actual average
cost of all larcenies that were committed that year. Only about half
of all nonviolent offenses are reported to the police, and those that

are reported are probably the ones that involve the largest amounts of money and the most valuable goods. The average amount stolen per crime is therefore probably less than $400.

Between 12 and 19 percent of all participants' arrests, depending upon the borough, were for offenses against the public order—for example, prostitution, gambling, drug possession and sales, and weapons possession. Because these were not thefts, a dollar value cannot be easily assigned to them. The cost incurred by these crimes was not borne by individuals in most instances but by the society at large. (Perhaps this would be better phrased: lawmakers have determined that these offenses entail a cost to the society even though the individuals involved in such crimes usually have agreed to take part.) Nor can a dollar value be easily calculated for crimes of violence against persons. As table 6.3 shows, 6 percent of the Bronx rearrests were for crimes of violence, 17 percent of the Brooklyn arrests were also, and so were 9 percent of the Manhattan arrests.

In summary: the community service sentence is not a cure for crime, at least in the population of recidivist offenders (mostly thieves) that the New York City courts sentenced to the Vera Institute's project. Approximately 40 to 50 percent of those in our sample were rearrested within six months of having been sentenced. Most of these new charges were for the same kinds of crimes they had been charged with in the past. Unfortunately, jailing these offenders instead of ordering them to perform community service would not have been more effective in turning them away from crime and toward being law-abiding citizens. Once released from jail, people with backgrounds similar to those of our participants were also rearrested at almost identical rates as were our participants in each of the boroughs. It is therefore safe to conclude that the community service sentence exercises the same, if any, deterrent and rehabilitative effects on offenders as does a jail sentence.

This is not to say, however, that the use of the new sentence had no adverse effects on the subsequent criminality of offenders. Jails serve as warehouses, and even though they may do little or nothing to bring about a long-term change in offenders' propensities to commit crimes, they at least keep criminals off the streets for the duration of their sentences. Had the courts not been able to send persons to the Vera Institute of Justice's Community Service Sentencing Project during 1981–1982, some of these offenders would have been incapacitated by jail terms and their subsequent criminality would have been restrained for the length of those terms. Citywide, we estimate that about fifteen fewer arrests would have occurred for each one hundred participants sentenced to the Vera Institute's project had that project not existed. Again, the vast majority of the offenses that might have been prevented were nonviolent crimes against property, most of them involving losses of no more than a few hundred dollars.

This raises the question of whether the courts' use of the community service sentence in lieu of jail constitutes a prudent public policy. To answer this requires weighing several of the various financial and social costs of the sentence against the benefits that accrue from imposing the community service order. Such a reckoning is the subject of the following chapter.

Conclusion

Three broad conclusions can be drawn from our examination of the Vera Institute's experience with community service sentencing. First, community service is no panacea. It is not, as one enthusiast proclaimed several years ago, "an alternative to imprisonment which is positive from every point of view. . . ."[1] Although its use as a substitute for jail produces valuable returns, they come at a price.

Second, the experience shows that the community service sentence is a worthwhile addition to the repertoire of punishments available to the courts, despite the costs associated with it. Lawbreakers deserve to be punished, but the punishment should be proportional to the gravity of the crime. Relying upon jails to punish persons convicted of minor offenses is extraordinarily expensive and imposes a disproportionately punitive cost upon the taxpayer. Using jail cells for these lesser property offenders also diminishes valuable and finite public resources that are needed for persons convicted of more serious crimes. For these reasons, a closely supervised and heavily enforced obligation to perform unpaid labor is better suited to offenders convicted of nonviolent and relatively petty property crimes. Moreover, ordering criminals to perform restorative community services is appealing because it reflects a principle that is worth respecting: that victims' losses should be compensated, however indirect that compensation may be. That many people sentenced to community service cannot perceive the compensatory character of their labor does not negate the value of the principle.

Third, the institute's project demonstrates that the courts will use the sentence in many instances in which offenders would have gone to jail otherwise. Reforms aiming to substitute community-based sentences for imprisonment terms are not doomed to fail, as some disenchanted observers have been wont to argue.[2] The Brooklyn and Bronx units started off less than completely successfully. In the former, only about a quarter of those given the sentence would have gone to jail; in the Bronx, approximately a fifth. But changes instituted in mid-1983 brought about dramatic improvements. The sentencing patterns of the courts shifted and slightly more than half of those ordered to perform community service had been headed for jail. The institute thereby achieved its goal of having judges use the sentence as a substitute for jail half of the time and a substitute for lesser punishments the other half.

Some might argue that the institute's success was an easy one, especially with respect to judicial sentencing decisions, because the goals it set were too modest. That is, the institute did not aim to have the sentence used solely as an alternative to imprisonment. By declaring that a fifty-fifty ratio would be considered a success, the project's planners might be criticized for having made a safe bet. But even if the institute had aimed for 100 percent and achieved "only" 50, the results still would have been praiseworthy. As political scientists Jonathan Casper and David Brereton remarked in their analysis of criminal justice reforms, "small changes in expected direction are often interpreted as evidence of implementation 'failure' when existing theory about criminal court behavior suggests that such changes are quite consistent with 'success'."[3] This is especially true in efforts to reform sentencing decisions. Short of statutory changes mandating certain kinds of punishments (legislating mandatory life sentences for drug pushers, for example), there have been very few instances in which sentencing patterns have been dramatically altered by reforms aiming to change the way particular classes of offenders were sanctioned. "One result thus dominates the studies of sentencing reform impact," Jacqueline Cohen and Michael Tonry concluded in their analysis of sentencing reforms. "Regardless of the type or locus of the procedural change, no appreciable changes were found in the use of prison; whatever changes occurred were limited largely to case-processing procedures."[4] By this measure, the Vera Institute's experiment has been a roaring success.

Whether community service sentences should be used by courts as a substitute for jail is another matter, however. How one answers this question depends upon the values and principles one believes should guide the imposition of criminal sanctions. It also turns on whether the benefits outweigh or at least counterbalance the disadvantages associated with the use of the sentence. Such policy questions cannot be resolved entirely through cost/benefit analysis, because there are value choices that cannot be reduced to utilitarian terms, denominated in a common currency of dollars and cents. Specifying the advantages and disadvantages of the sentence in relation to other available alternatives does provide, however, a means of clarifying the different consequences of alternative choices for making policy decisions. Or, put another way, this information helps to reveal the consequences that flow from various policy decisions.

   The following pages are devoted to an examination of the trade-offs posed by the use of the community service sentence and a discussion of how the sentence should best be employed. I then turn to some concluding observations about what the Vera Institute experiment shows us about the nature of the courts, of sentencing decisons, and of the dynamics of the reform process.

The Principal Trade-Offs

   The main entries in a cost/benefit accounting of community service sentencing include the following on the credit side of the ledger: (1) offenders provide needed services to the community instead of idling their time away in jail at the taxpayers' expense; (2) the demand for jail cells is reduced, which in turn produces several valuable benefits to city government; (3) the introduction of a new intermediate-level punishment provides the courts with greater flexibility in scaling penal sanctions to different types of crimes and criminals.

   On the debit side are the two main costs associated with the use of the sentence in lieu of jail: (1) the direct dollar costs of operating the community service project, and (2) foregoing jail's incapacitative character, which results in a loss of the ability to prevent some crimes that will be committed if offenders are out on the street rather than behind bars.

The Value of Services Rendered

The most obvious benefit of the community service sentence is that offenders are not required to sit in jail at the taxpayers' expense, but are obligated to provide labor in payment for their crime. The value of this uncompensated service is considerable. Offenders sentenced to the Vera Institute project by the Bronx, Brooklyn, and Manhattan courts labored for a total of approximately 35,600 hours during the fiscal year ending 30 June 1982, about 52,700 hours in fiscal year 1983, and approximately 60,000 in fiscal year 1984. Putting a precise dollar value on this labor is difficult because it was performed outside a free market that would determine its market price. However, it is fair to estimate its value conservatively as averaging somewhere between the minimum wage and perhaps $4.50 per hour. At these rates, the dollar value of the services returned to the community during fiscal year 1982 by project participants would have been between $119,000 and $160,000. Because more offenders were sentenced to community service in subsequent years, the total value of the service rendered in these years would have been even higher: approximately $176,600–$237,200 in fiscal year 1983 and $200,000–$270,300 in fiscal year 1984. This represented a significant contribution to New York's neighborhoods.

Reducing Demand for Jail Cells

By imposing community service sentences, judges in the New York City Criminal Courts relieved some of the pressure on the city's overburdened jail system. This relief was brought about not only by channelling sentenced offenders away from jail cells into community service, but also by shortening the time that project participants spent in pretrial detention. For example, during the twelve months ending September 30, 1982, an estimated total of sixty-eight prisoner/years (the amount of space that would be required to jail sixty-eight persons for one full year) were saved by the use of the community service project. Most of these savings (about fifty-three prisoner/years) were due to reductions in the time that would have been required of sentenced prisoners. (See the Appendix for the methods and assumptions followed to develop these estimates.)

The savings in subsequent years were even greater. During fiscal year 1983, approximately eighty-nine prisoner/years were saved in the city's jails as a consequence of using the community service sentencing project. This increase occurred because the Manhattan branch had been open longer and had considerably expanded its intake, and judges in this borough used the community service sentence more often as a substitute for jail and for longer jail terms. During fiscal year 1984, the savings amounted to approximately one hundred and two prisoner/years because of the changes made in the Brooklyn and Bronx units' selection and sentencing procedures.

This reduced demand was a welcome development because the city's jails have been extremely crowded for the better part of a decade. Since 1974 when the federal courts found the city to be in violation of the Eighth Amendment's prohibition of "cruel and unusual punishment" because of the conditions in its jails, the city's managers have been under order to relieve prison overcrowding.[5] However, admissions to prison have continued to rise, and the Department of Corrections has been operating for the past several years close to or in excess of full jail capacity. Between fiscal years 1978 and 1983, for example, the number of prisoners under custody in the New York City jails grew 44 percent.[6] Although most of this increase was due to the rising number of persons held in pretrial detention, the courts also sentenced more people to jail: between fiscal years 1979 and 1983, the average number of sentenced prisoners under custody increased 29 percent.[7]

These strains have created a crisis in the management of the city's criminal justice system. One measure of this crisis was the extraordinary event that occurred in 1983: the Commissioner of Corrections was ordered by a federal judge to release several hundred pretrial detention prisoners to bring the jail population down to acceptable levels. Had the city's criminal courts not been using the community service sentencing project during this period, the demand for precious jail cells would have been even greater and the resulting crisis even deeper.

Even though a relatively large number of jail beds have been saved by the use of the community service sentencing project, this has not produced significant dollar savings. This is because the demand for cells far outstrips the available supply. Whenever space becomes available, it is filled immediately. Faced with a continuing and powerful demand for jail cells in New York City, there is virtually no prospect of reducing jail costs in the near future by sentencing even greater numbers of offenders to community service. At best, this would only slow the pace of the expansion of the system's capacities.

If community service sentences were imposed in relatively large numbers in an environment in which the demand for jail cells did not so massively overwhelm their availability, conditions would exist for reducing public expenditures for jails. However, these are only necessary and not sufficient conditions. Reduced demand does not necessarily translate directly into dollar savings. Most jail costs are relatively fixed, with the major share of them going to staff salaries, pensions, and fringe benefits. Reducing the prisoner population even by a very large amount would have little impact on the overall cost of operations, if policy makers choose to keep staffing at the present level. It is therefore wrong to assume that substituting community service sentences for jail terms will automatically save local governments the average cost of locking up a prisoner (about $30,000 per year during fiscal year 1983 or $38,500 during fiscal year 1984 in New York City, for example).[8] Some smaller savings may be produced because fewer prisoners require less food, medicine, and other such consumables, but exactly how big or small such savings would be is extremely difficult to determine. Much more substantial cost reductions can be achieved when the prisoner population declines to the point where entire cellblocks can be closed down and "destaffed," although this depends upon the architecture of the jail and the political environment within which correctional policy decisions are made. For the next several years in most localities throughout the country, the combination of rising prisoner populations, continuing litigation to remedy overcrowding and substandard jail and prison conditions, and powerful correctional officers' unions make it highly unlikely that jail and prison systems will be shrinking. All trends point in exactly the opposite direction.

Although community service sentences do not automatically result in lower operating costs for jails in New York City, substantial dollar gains may be realized by lowering the demand for cells and thereby slowing the pace of expanding the system. In response to severe overcrowding and its resulting lawsuits, the city began a crash program of jail construction and renovation, the largest capital expansion plan for corrections in its history. This will be very costly. The projected cost of construction, exclusive of financing charges, will be about $71,000 per bed, a bargain-basement price in the prison and jail industry.[9] This gives some indication of how much money the community service sentencing project could save the City of New York. Operating at the level it did during fiscal year 1984, approximately one hundred and two additional cell beds would have been required over the entire twelve months to house offenders who were instead sentenced to community service. To expand the jail system by this number would require a construction cost of approximately $7.2 million, and if one were to include the cost of financing this capital expenditure, the total would be more than double.

This points to one of the great advantages of using the community service sentence as a substitute for jail: expanding nonincarcerative sentences does not require sinking huge sums of money into buildings that will last decades or even centuries, as some have. The prison and jail business in this country is now experiencing a fast-growth period, but there is good reason to expect this demand to drop off by the end of the 1980s or early 1990s. Crime rates shot up when the baby boom generation reached the high-risk ages between the mid-teens and early twenties. By the mid-1970s, the number of people being imprisoned began rising quickly, as did the overall imprisonment rate, measured by the number of prisoners per hundred thousand U.S. residents. In 1980, the imprisonment rate had reached the highest level ever in our nation's history, and has continued to rise since then.[10] In part because this extremely large cohort of baby boomers has aged, crime rates have dropped. A downturn in demand for prison and jail cells may follow after a lag of several years, if lawmakers do not further stiffen sentencing policies and thereby stimulate demand further.[11] (Even though crime rates have been declining across the nation since 1980, imprisonment rates have continued to climb, partly because of demographics—the peak age for imprisonment is the mid-twenties, after criminally active offenders have accumulated a few convictions and have become more likely to receive imprisonment sentences for each subsequent offense—and because lawmakers in most jurisdictions have adopted tougher imprisonment policies.[12]) If city and state governments try to build all the jail cells needed to accomodate current demand, there is a possibility that they will be left with empty buildings—"white elephants"—a decade from now. If community service and other such intermediate-level punishments were used on a larger scale, the courts would have an enhanced capacity to get through the next several years without the city government having to commit itself to an even bigger capital investment plan.

Finally, there is yet another saving associated with using community service in lieu of jail, albeit one that is not denominated directly in dollars. By using community service in instances where offenders have been convicted of relatively minor property crimes, one frees up resources to deal with more serious offenders. In jurisdictions enjoying a glut of empty jail cells, the courts do not diminish their ability to punish the more deserving offenders by also locking up minor violators and petty criminals. However, in the more "normal" conditions of severe overcrowding and restricted resources that prevail in a great many localities, using scarce jail cells for lesser offenders does incur this cost.

The Costs: Dollars Spent For Community Service

The most easily calculated cost of the community service sentence is the expenditure by the Vera Institute of Justice for the project. During the institute's fiscal year 1982, it spent an average of $1,077 for each person sentenced to the project. The cost declined during the next twelve months to about $916 per participant, because the project became more established and intake rose to higher levels, resulting in a more productive ratio of staff to offenders. Most of this money came from public sources, and taxpayers ultimately paid most of the bill as a consequence. (During fiscal year 1983, all but 4 percent of the costs were recovered through contracts with state, city, and federal government agencies. The remainder was covered by a grant from a private foundation.)

Could this cost be cut? Certainly, if a different program design were adopted. For example, if the courts placed convicted offenders in other existing public agencies—say, the local Department of Parks—the specialized work crews and supervisory hierarchies that the institute project employs would not have to be created and paid for. Offenders would work alongside the paid work force and would be supervised by the existing staff. Because slightly more than half of the Vera Institute project's costs are associated with the supervision and administration of the service in the community, substantial savings could be incurred if the project were to be redesigned along these lines.

The Vera Institute strategy of creating closely managed work crews with their own institute-employed supervisors may not be necessary in instances in which white-collar or first offenders are given the sentence, but it seems to be necessary in New York City. By the end of 1984, approximately 3,200 criminal offenders had been supervised in institute work crews. It would have been enormously difficult to locate public and private agencies willing to absorb into their work force this many criminals, most of them thieves, many with long criminal records. Indeed, the task of finding willing agencies and then dealing with their complaints would probably require more energy and money than is needed to field the work crews as they are presently organized.

Costs could also be lowered at the front end if the institute removed its own full-time representatives from the courts. Slightly less than half of the project's costs are associated with the court representatives' screening, selection, and advocacy functions. Most projects elsewhere in the country do not follow such procedures, but instead announce the availability of the community service option and leave it to the courts to decide who is given the sentence. However, the risk of this laissez-faire approach is that judges will not consider the sanction or will be more likely to use it in cases where other nonincarcerative sentences would have been ordered. This is borne out by the institute's experience; many defendants referred to the project by judges are not headed for jail, according to court representatives and our own statistical assessments. Court representatives thus perform a crucial role in exercising quality control over the kinds of offenders given the sentence in order to assure that a sentence costing nine hundred to a thousand dollars is not used primarily for persons who would not otherwise have gone to jail.

In summary: both the court representatives' work as well as the close supervision performed by the work crews have been necessary elements of the project's success in the New York City courts. Some productivity gains might be realized, especially on the work sites, once the project becomes more established in each of the boroughs, and this may bring per capita costs down. Nonetheless, without a radical reorganization of the Vera Institute project, the price tag for each community service sentence will continue to range in the high three figures.

Crime Control Losses

The most difficult costs to bear, at least for the community at large, are the participants' crimes that could be prevented if jail sentences were imposed instead of community service. How many such preventable crimes take place depends upon how frequently the community service sentence is used in lieu of jail, how long the jail sentences would otherwise have been, and how frequently these criminals commited crimes while at risk. None of these factors are easy to measure with any precision, although, as reported in chapter 6, we developed some estimates of the incapacitative losses incurred by the Vera Community Service Sentencing Project during the twelve-month period ending 30 September 1982.

In Manhattan, where the courts were most likely to have imposed community service sentences as a substitute for jail during that period (and where the jail terms would have been the longest, on average), the use of the community service option "cost" the public approximately twenty-five crimes per one hundred project participants. In Brooklyn and in the Bronx, the estimated number of crimes that could have been averted by a jail sentence were much smaller: 5.4 per one hundred project participants and 4.5 per one hundred, respectively. This was due to the fact that during this period, judges in these boroughs were much less likely to have used the community service sentence as a substitute for jail and when the option was used as a substitute, the jail term that was displaced would have been shorter, on the average, than in Manhattan.

It is important to recognize that most of these "preventable" crimes were relatively minor ones. Of those project participants who were arrested again within 180 days of having been sentenced to community service, approximately three-quarters of them were charged with nonviolent crimes that were theft-related. A large proportion of these arrests were for shoplifting. Because we were not able to determine the estimated value of the items stolen, we could not develop accurate measures of the dollar cost of these crimes. However, the average loss from each nonviolent property offense in New York State during 1981 was estimated at about four hundred dollars, and it is safe to assume that the average cost of each property offense committed by project participants was no higher than this.[13] Another 12 to 19 percent of the charged offenses, depending upon the borough, were for offenses against the public order—drug possession or sales, prostitution, gambling, etc. The cost of these crimes is more difficult to reckon because they are less tangible. Finally, a relatively small proportion of the subsequent arrests were for crimes involving some degree of violence. (The proportions ranged from 6 percent in the Bronx to 17 percent in Brooklyn, and 9 percent in Manhattan.) Assigning a dollar cost to these offenses trivializes them, for the most significant costs are the traumas and injuries sustained.

Can Crime Control Losses Be Minimized?

The attractiveness of the community service sentence would be greatly enhanced if subsequent criminality could be reduced. Unfortunately, it does not appear that any significant reductions could be gained by redesigning the community service sentence itself. To be sure, the frequency of subsequent crimes could be reduced by locking participants into a jail cell at night after they have completed their daily service obligation, but this would transform the sentence into a jail term with a work-release component. Many benefits of the nonincarcerative community service sentence would be thereby obliterated.

The more obvious solution would be to change selection and sentencing policies so that offenders likely to be arrested again could be identified and sentenced to jail instead of community service. This would amount to a variant of what has been termed a "selective incapacitation" policy.[14] Such a policy would be feasible if the means existed to distinguish between future criminals and law-abiders. There's the rub, however: no methods now exist that provide us with the capability of predicting future criminality. We tried to develop an instrument to predict recidivism by examining a sample of 494 community service participants and exploring the factors correlated with their having been rearrested within 180 days of sentence. Only a few characteristics were found to be correlated statistically, and these associations were very weak. Taken separately or in combination, they were of no value in predicting future recidivism, at least as we were able to measure it by arrest incidents. Neither we, the courts, nor other criminologists possess the technology needed to implement a policy of selective incapacitation.[15]

Some could reasonably argue that the absence of such a capability suggests a more radical policy: to abolish altogether the community service project. If one cannot sort out the very bad apples from those that are not so bad, why not simply eliminate the possibility of a community service sentence and let the courts sentence criminals the way they did before the option existed? This would bring about a reduction in recidivism during the short term, because some offenders would be sentenced to jail and would be thereby incapacitated.

Such a course of action poses some difficult policy questions. If the program is to be abolished in order to strengthen the courts' crime control capabilities, should not all criminal sentencing decisions be grounded upon such a logic? If one is to apply incapacitation objectives to the relatively small population of offenders found eligible for the institute's community service project, why not apply it to all offenders convicted in the criminal courts?

The principal reason for not enshrining the incapacitation objective as the dominant one in sentencing decisions is that it would require massive amounts of money to implement. During 1983, approximately 114,220 persons were convicted in the lower criminal courts in New York City.[16] Most of them were charged with offenses that could have resulted in jail sentences had judges so wished. But the city has nowhere near that number of jail cells. It now has space for about twenty-five hundred sentenced prisoners. Current sentencing practices are such that the jails are already filled beyond their designed capacities, and if an incapacitation policy were adopted, the demand for jail space would be many times greater. Were judges to sentence with an eye first and foremost on the prevention of future crime, they undoubtedly would lock up far more people than necessary. This is because they would be hard pressed not to adopt the "better safe than sorry" rule, because they lack the ability to identify those offenders who are actually going to commit future crimes. The resulting burden on the city's jails would then be impossible to manage. Given the high cost of both jail construction and operation, a policy of incapacitation—whether "selective" or not—would force a massive transfer of tax dollars into the jail system while bleeding other government services.

The Case For Community Service

Even though community service is no panacea for the courts, there are compelling reasons why the imposition of the sentence should be supported. These are grounded in a few basic principles regarding the use of the criminal sanction generally.

First, the leading objective of the courts in matters of sentencing should be the punishment of offenders for their criminal conduct. The choice of those punishments should be governed by the rule of proportionality: that the severity of the punishment be matched to the gravity of the crime. This limiting principle is an ancient one, given expression thousands of years ago in the *lex talionis:* "eye for an eye, tooth for a tooth." Moreover, the choice of punishments should also be governed by the rule of parsimony: a preference for the least drastic alternative.

Second, whenever possible, punishments should be imposed in such a way that offenders can make amends to their victims, compensating them or otherwise restoring the status quo ante.

Third, utilitarian goals—imposing sanctions in order to control crime by virtue of deterring would-be offenders, incapacitating them, or rehabilitating them—should be considered secondary objectives, if they are considered at all. That is, the principle of commensurate deserts should not be violated by attempts to control crime through sentencing individual offenders.

Using the community service sentence to sanction criminals convicted of nonviolent crimes, especially of the lesser variety, is consistent with these principles. It is a punishment. Although judges may try to dress it up to make it appear rehabilitative (which may serve their interest to be doing something "for the offender's own good"), its punitive character is not easily disguised. Its inherently punitive quality is also not negated by the fact that more than half of the participants interviewed declined to describe it as punishment when asked. Given the choice they thought they faced in court—to plead guilty either to a jail sentence or to community service—it is not surprising that they defined the latter as a "lucky break" and the former as punishment. ("Punishment to me is being in jail with no chance at all," said one.) If they had been given the choice between community service and no obligation at all, it is clear that they would have chosen the latter. A substantial degree of coercion was required to compel their attendance, and this would not have been needed if the community service sentence were not perceived as punitive in some measure.

Being ordered to perform seventy hours of unpaid labor is also a commensurate retribution for committing relatively minor crimes not involving violence to persons. This is true, even if the sentence represented a stiffening of punishment for those who otherwise would have gotten less demanding penalties, and a lessening of punishment for those who would have gotten jail. Prior to the introduction of the new sentencing option, some lesser offenders were being punished insufficiently for their crimes because jail was not called for, given the minor character of their offenses, and the other available nonincarcerative sanctions (probation, fines) were seen as not appropriate. In instances in which offenders would have gone to jail in the absence of the project, the principle of proportionality is still respected by using the sentence, because most crimes committed by persons receiving short jail sentences are minor ones, not ones clearly warranting jail. Unless offenders have been convicted of a string of such crimes them, they are not usually jailed, at least in many jurisdictions. Consequently, locking up these offenders means that they are being punished at least as much for their persistent criminality—for their characters, that is—as for the crimes they have most recently committed. Because there should be a preference for matching the penalty to the offense rather than to the perceived nastiness or obduracy of the offender, ordering community service as punishment for nonviolent crimes seems patently reasonable.

This does not mean that community service is a justifiable punishment only for lesser crimes. Much more serious crimes can be punished legitimately by community service obligations that are more burdensome than those administered by the Vera Institute's project. There is no reason why people who steal very large sums of money, for example, could not be punished satisfactorily by having to contribute many hundreds or even thousands of hours of their labor. The community service sentence can easily be made more punitive and commensurate with the crime by expanding the obligation and coupling it with other penalties (fines, for example).

Moreover, there is no clear utilitarian justification for imposing jail sentences instead of community service orders. Judging from the comparisons shown in chapter 6, neither sanction does a good job at deterring or rehabilitating offenders. The frequencies of rearrests for offenders at risk were nearly identical whether they had been sentenced to community service or put behind bars and then released. Jail sentences do incapacitate offenders better, however, and some of the crimes that were committed by persons sentenced to community service could have been prevented by jailing them instead. But one cannot easily derive from these findings a policy based on utilitarian objectives. If the courts were asked to consider crime control purposes as paramount when determining sentences, and if the means of effecting that crime prevention was to be the incapacitation of offenders, the demand on jail cells would be many times larger than local governments could possibly manage. This is because there is no way of successfully discriminating those most likely to be future lawbreakers from those who would go straight. Lacking such an ability, judges would be constrained to lock up nearly all offenders. Such a strategy is impracticable.

Finally, does it make sense to spend the sums that would be required to keep these petty thieves away from other people's property? Should the public spend five thousand to ten thousand dollars to incapacitate offenders who are arrested for stealing items costing a few hundred dollars? Would not a better policy be to extract punishment in a financially less expensive manner (such as by ordering community service) and perhaps even expand the ability of victims to cover part of their losses by drawing from a crime victims' compensation fund?

For these reasons, community service sentences are, I believe, important additions to the panoply of punishments available to the courts and are worthy of support.

Some Thoughts On the Nature of Sentencing Decisions and Reforms

The Vera Institute's experience holds some broader lessons regarding the way criminal sentencing decisions can be reformed most efficiently. These apply not only to attempts to establish community service sanctions in other jurisdictions but also to other kinds of sentencing reforms as well. Even though the institute planners' strategies were designed to alter what they thought were the peculiar dynamics of the Bronx, Brooklyn, and Manhattan courts, the overall design of their intervention strategies was very similar to those followed elsewhere for other purposes. Consequently, our analysis of the Vera Institute reform has relevance for a wide variety of sentencing reforms.

We can also distill from our study some useful insights about how the criminal courts make sentencing decisions. Because reforms are based upon a number of specific assumptions about how the courts work, they serve in some ways as tests of these assumptions. That is, they succeed or fail in part because of the adequacy of the theories that underpin them.

The theory underlying the design of the Vera Institute reform strategy in the Bronx and Brooklyn projects was not an idiosyncratic or spontaneous invention of the planners. Rather, it was derived from contemporary social scientific analyses of the courts. Consequently, the initial failure of the Bronx and Brooklyn projects to achieve their principal objectives—the substitution of community service orders for short jail terms—has far-reaching consequences for our theoretical understanding of sentencing. The success of the Manhattan venture also has important implications for theory. How can one explain why this court responded so differently to the project's efforts?

In this section, I would like to delineate the key features of the reform strategies followed in each borough and review briefly the assumptions upon which they were based. I also examine the connection between these assumptions and social scientific theories of the court that have been advanced in the published literature. Finally, I conclude with some more general observations about reform strategies. Relatively little attention has been given to developing a theory of the reform process, even though much could be learned by considering it as a phenomenon in its own right with its own peculiar dynamics. With the intention of stimulating such as analysis, I sketch out a rough typology of reform strategies and examine briefly the usefulness of each type for changing sentencing practices.

Mistaking Courts For Organizations

When the Vera Institute planners set out to have the Bronx Criminal Court impose community service instead of jail sentences, they designed a strategy that focused on modifying the norms of the courthouse, both those embodied in codified law and the customary rules known to regular participants, but not written down anywhere. They sought and obtained a change in the penal laws of the state, but they recognized that this was not enough. The revised section of the penal code constituted no more than an enabling law, a statement that the legislature permitted community service sentences to be imposed for certain classes of offenses. To get the court to actually sentence offenders to community service, planners saw that they were also going to have to alter the unwritten rules of thumb, the "going rates," that have evolved to guide decision making in guilty plea negotiations.

To achieve this, the planning team pursued what was essentially an administrative reform strategy. They proposed a new rule: (1) that community service be used in lieu of short jail sentences when offenders are convicted of nonviolent crimes, and (2) that the sanction be imposed half of the time in cases for which jail would not have been called for, but for which other available punishments are ill-suited. (This latter part of the rule was not as clearly specified as the former.) To get the rule adopted as official policy, they obtained the approval of the district attorney and the administrative judge. Procedures were then designed to implement this policy. Project court representatives were charged with identifying candidates for the sentence, and eligibility criteria were established to guide their considerations. Once offenders were declared eligible, court representatives took their cases on a round of approvals to have all involved parties sign off on the proposed defendant. If approval was secured from the prosecutor and from the defendant and his or her attorney, the proposal was taken to the judge. The selection and sentencing process was designed, in short, as a quasi-bureaucratic routine.

This reform approach was grounded squarely in the dominant theories of social science concerning the courts. Although there exists no single unified theory of the courts (nor is there even a candidate for one), there does exist a conceptual paradigm that has exerted a powerful effect upon research over the past fifteen years. According to this paradigm, courts can be best understood as a species of organization, and, according to some scholars, as bureaucratic organizations. Proponents of this approach argue that we can learn a great deal about how the courts work by applying theories and insights developed in the studies of other formal organizations.

This line of analysis stems from Herbert Packer's seminal essay,

written in 1964, entitled "Two Models of the Criminal Process." [17]
Packer argued that two contradictory sets of beliefs and assumptions underpin the work of contemporary American courts. One
cluster forms what he termed the "due process model"; the other
constitutes the "crime control model." According to the due process model, defendants are assumed innocent until proven guilty;
facts and guilt are established by formal trial procedures; and defendants' rights are protected by a number of formal procedural
safeguards. In contrast, the crime control model assumes that defendants are guilty; adjudicative fact finding is held to a minimum
and more informal procedures are followed to establish what happened; and the primary job of the courts is understood to be the
extraction of guilty pleas from defendants. The overriding purpose
of this second model, Packer argued, is not to dispense justice so
much as to achieve the speedy prosecution of criminals in order to
control crime more effectively.

Packer did not delineate models of the courts' social organization—he was a legal scholar rather than a social scientist, and he
defined his task as clarifying the "animating presuppositions" and
values that underlie procedures—but he did liken the crime control model to the assembly line. Abraham Blumberg picked up this
analogy and ran with it in his book, published in 1967, *Criminal
Justice*.[18] Blumberg married Packer's insights to concepts that were
being developed in studies of formal organizations, thereby "so-
ciologizing" Packer. In so doing, he established a compelling conceptual paradigm—an imagery of the court, a cluster of concepts,
and an approach to analysis—that many researchers subsequently
adopted.

Blumberg conceived of large urban courts as having become bureaucracies not unlike large industrial firms. Under the pressure of
heavy caseloads, the goal of justice by due process had been displaced, Blumberg thought, by the demands of "efficient produc-
tion": the rapid disposition of criminal cases. As a consequence,
the informal organization of the courts—their plea bargaining routines—grew to dominate the courts' formal organization, which
was defined by written law, organization charts, and officially
promulgated rules and regulations. Judges and district attorneys in

this view have become bureaucrats who orient their activities toward encouraging quick case dispositions. Judges enforce compliance with productivity norms by disciplining lawyers and defendants who insist on exercising their rights to trial; for example, defendants who do not plead guilty are punished with heavier sentences. This creates in attorneys a "role strain," because they are, on the one hand, officers of the court, and at the same time they are also advocates for the defendant. To resolve the tension that this role conflict allegedly produces, Blumberg argued, they mostly side with the district attorney and the judge, thereby pledging their allegiance to norms stressing high productivity. Adversarial proceedings consequently give way to consensual working agreements between defense and prosecuting attorneys and the judge. Plea agreements are quickly arrived at by this "team." The defense attorney then has to run a "confidence game" on his client, manipulating him into going along with the deal by pleading guilty, believing that his interests have been represented well by his attorney.

This identification of plea bargaining with bureaucratic organization has unfortunately bedeviled much analysis. It has encouraged a misperception of how sentencing decisions are actually made in cases where dispositions are negotiated. It underrates the importance of adversarial negotiation in the choice of sentence. It also overemphasizes the importance of norms in determining sentences and overlooks the role of non-normative factors such as bargaining skill and power in its various forms (coercion, influence, etc.).

Bureaucracies, in their ideal form, are structured by procedural norms defined in such a way as to permit routine and speedy decisionmaking. Because procedures are spelled out in detail, the key decisions that officials make are the early classification of individual cases as belonging to one or another previously established category. Once cases are pigeonholed into categories, their subsequent processing follows a preordained path, permitting officials to "rubber stamp" them rather than give time-consuming attention to the peculiarities of each case. The nature of bureaucratic processing is inherently classificatory. Officials are given very little discretionary authority and are required to follow established procedures closely. (Thus the popular image of the bureaucrat as one unable to cut through the "red tape" of official procedure.)

Influenced by this imagery, scholars have too often seen plea bargaining as concerned almost exclusively with the definition of the facts—with the classification of the case in categories that will control the course of subsequent decisions—rather than involving decisions about what sentence to impose. Raymond Nimmer, for example, in his book entitled *The Nature of System Change: Reform Impact in the Criminal Courts* (1978), writes:

In many cases, dispositions are reached with little explicit negotiation or controversy; charge and sentence are determined by preexisting norms that have been described as "normal crime" categories. Such categorization, which may be quite specific, encompasses elements that are not in the criminal code but in practice describe recurrent crime patterns and system response. For example, one normal crime might be a subcategory of automobile theft: the taking of an automobile from a parking lot by a Caucasion high school student with recovery of the car unharmed, normally disposed of by a guilty plea to "joyriding" with one year of probation. Since any normal crime has a predetermined appropriate disposition, the only contested issue is whether a given offense fits into the normal category.[19]

This portrait of sentencing decisions is consistent with Max Weber's description of the modern judge as a "vending machine into which pleadings are inserted together with the fee and which then disgorges the judgment together with its reasons mechanically derived from Code."[20] According to this vision, sentencing is seen as the relatively mechanical application of norms to individual cases.

Because plea bargaining is frequently treated in the literature of social science as an alternative form of fact finding and charging, and not as sentencing, sentencing decisions in guilty plea cases are seen as fundamentally similar to decisions made after defendants have been convicted by trial. This is not to say that differences between the two are not recognized. For example, it is clear that the choice of sentence belongs solely to the judge in instances where the defendant has been convicted at trial, whereas other members of the plea bargaining "team" (as Blumberg called it) exert some control over the choice when guilty pleas are negotiated. Exactly how much control these other players have has been the subject of some debate in the literature.[21] However, the central task of sentencing is seen to be fundamentally the same, whether the conviction is established by trial or by plea: the application of general norms to individual cases.

Several scholars since Blumberg's time have correctly recognized that courts cannot usefully be considered bureaucracies, because they lack the hierarchical structure and other features definitive of that form.[22] Nonetheless, many continue to argue that courts are organizations of some sort. Eisenstein and Jacobs, for example, have defined the central organizational unit of the court as the "work group"—the network of attorneys, judges, clerks and other related personnel who regularly deal with one another in the courts.[23] This revision represents an important step in the right direction, moving away as it does from the imagery of the bureaucratic model, but it does not signify the abandonment of the basic theoretical paradigm. Courts are still considered a species of formal organization by many scholars. Guilty plea negotiations are still seen as being structured by informal norms; these "going rates" (or "tariff schedules," in British parlance) define the dispositional outcomes to be reached in different types of cases; and negotiations are still seen to be limited in most instances to fact finding and charging. And, importantly, sentences in cases involving guilty pleas are thought to be the products of consensual agreement rather than of adversarial contests.[24]

The design of the Vera Institute's reform approach was therefore consistent with the general thrust of prevailing social scientific theorizing about the courts. If the courts are indeed organizations (and to some observers, bureaucracies), an administrative reform strategy seems to be well-suited to the aim of changing the actual norms that govern decision making.

But in both the Bronx and Brooklyn, where the interventions of the project were designed essentially as administrative reforms, the institute failed to achieve substantial numbers of defendants sentenced to community service who otherwise would have gone to jail. The full story explaining why and how this resulted can be found in chapter 4, but the headline is quite short: project designers failed to appreciate the extent to which sentencing decisions, and not just fact finding and charging decisions, are influenced and even determined by adversarial negotiations. Those who designed the project certainly understood that plea bargaining occurs in the criminal courts and is the grease that makes them run. But, judging from their written statements and verbal accounts, they were much influenced by the court-as-plea-bargaining bureaucracy paradigm and, as a consequence, placed most of their stock in the redefinition of informal penal norms—the going rates—and the selection of offenders appearing to be otherwise headed for jail. This conception of the court partially blinded both the planners and even the managers who implemented the project. They didn't see clearly how their selection procedures fit into the prosecutors' plea bargaining strategies and how these strategies were undercutting their own organizational objective: to have the community service sentence imposed in a substantial number of cases in which defendants would otherwise have landed in jail.

The branch of the project established in the Manhattan Criminal Court enjoyed greater success in achieving this substitution of sentences because court representatives and managers positioned themselves differently in plea negotiations. As described more fully in chapter 4, this was partly as a result of planning, but in large part it was also fortuitous. Instead of working as a near subsidiary of the district attorney's office (which is a pretty accurate description of what the Bronx and Brooklyn branches became in the early stages of their existence), project officers in Manhattan struck a more independent stance. Prosecutors were not given the power to take a candidate out of the running for community service. Court representatives advocated the use of the sentence, often with great vigor, in direct communications with judges.

In Manhattan, the mode of the project's intervention into the courts evoked a battleground imagery rather than the bureaucratic/adminstrative mindset that prevailed in the Bronx and Brooklyn projects. This was partly because negotiations in Manhattan courtrooms were typically more openly contentious than in the other two boroughs. Judges, prosecutors, and defense attorneys frequently came to loggerheads over how defendants' cases were to be disposed. Indeed, every time judges sentenced a person to community service, they did so over the open and frequently strenuous objection of prosecutors, who read into the record the reasons for their office's disapproval. No accommodation was ever reached among prosecutors, project officials, and judges regarding the use of the sentence. In the other two boroughs, the adversarial character of plea bargaining was obscured by the district attorney's agreement as a matter of office policy to the use of the community service sentence. Additionally, the cultures of the Bronx and Brooklyn courtrooms are somewhat different from that of Manhattan's. The prevailing etiquette prescribes more cordial and outwardly accommodating relations among attorneys and judges. This is not to say that plea negotiations are not adversarial in these courts, for beneath the veneer of clubbiness, each of the parties do jockey to have their interests maximized.

The success of the Manhattan intervention suggests that a different model of the courts and of sentencing decisions is useful in explaining what we see. Instead of conceiving of the courts as bureaucracies, or even as organizations, it is more fruitful to see them as places—or "arenas," in Malcolm Feeley's felicitous phrase—in which individuals and representatives of different organizations meet to dispose of individual cases.[25] Describing these interactions more exactly—how they are routinely carried out, what kinds of rules structure them, and how non-normative factors impinge upon decisions—requires research that, oddly enough, is in rather short supply. Despite the voluminous amount of print that has been expended upon discussions of plea bargaining, most has been evaluative rather than descriptive, and very few scholars have undertaken a microscopic investigation of how guilty plea negotations actually proceed.[26] This is not the place to define at length an alternative approach to the analysis of courtroom interactions, but I can sketch out what I think some of the elements of such an approach should include, especially with regard to the process of deciding criminal sanctions.

A Battle Model of Negotiated Sentencing Decisions

First, sentencing decisions should be seen as more often the results of adversarial negotiation than the court-as-organization model would lead us to expect. Plea bargaining is not simply con-

cerned with establishing a definition of the facts. Instead, it is concerned first and foremost with shaping the outcome of the case—
the disposition, and in cases where defendants are likely to be
convicted, the sentence.[27] Blumberg's portrait of a conspiratorial
con game in which teams of players convince defendants to plead
guilty ignores the way in which adversarial relations pervade even
the informal plea bargaining processes. Bargaining is a process
whereby individual interests are meshed, producing a settlement
that does not necessarily signify the collapse of a vigorous defense
effort.[28]

Second, the normative context within which sentencing decisions are made is not so simple as the commonly held conception
of "going rates" suggests. Observers are correct in seeing that participants in the disposition process interact with one another in an
environment that is riddled with constraining norms, both those
written into law and customary ones that have emerged in the local
courts. But the existence of norms in these courts does not mean
that the outcomes of the disposition process are determined largely
by compliance with them. Imagine, for the sake of clarifying the
dynamics of such interactions, a card game: most games are structured by elaborate norms that cover all logical moves, but the outcome of the game—who wins or loses—is determined not by the
compliance with norms, but by the operation of non-normative
factors: the luck of the draw and players' skill in capitalizing upon
what they were given in their hands. Plea bargaining resembles
card games in certain respects. Norms structure the procedures to
be followed in negotiating the disposition of criminal cases. Some
substantive norms (which I like to call "penal norms") define the
matches between types of sanctions, crimes, and criminals that are
to be considered appropriate, legitimate, and fair. But these substantive penal norms are often quite broadly stated, specifying either general principles ("persons with longer criminal records
should be punished more severely, other things being equal"), or
specify ranges of permissible sanctions to be imposed. For example: "Burglaries of commercial establishments, committed at
night, are normally punished by a prison sentence of between one
and three years." Where a particular individual's sanction falls
within that range of morally acceptable alternatives is determined

largely by the luck of the draw (how solid the prosecutor's case is),
the relative skills of the prosecutor and the defense attorney, and
the ability of the defendant to withstand the pressures applied by
the prosecutor and sometimes by the judge.[29]

Regarding the defendant's ability to withstand pressure: recall
from chapter 3 that defendants' pretrial detention statuses were
found to be strongly predictive of whether or not a jail sentence
was imposed. This certainly reflects the fact that people who are
defined by prevailing penal norms as the most deserving of jail
sentences also are more likely to be given high bails and thereby
more often to be held in pretrial detention. I also think, however,
that there is strong evidence to support the proposition that being
in detention has the independent effect of weakening the defendant's bargaining position and thereby of increasing the odds of his
or her getting a jail term.[30]

A battle model of negotiated sentencing decisions will therefore
include concepts such as interests, recognizing that different players have differently defined values and objectives that they seek to
realize as successfully as possible; power and its kindred concepts—influence, coercion, and leverage; and the miscellaneous
factors that go toward affecting the distribution of power among
actors in the courthouse. These include the normative prescriptions that elevate power to authority (for example, written law
gives judges the ultimate power to determine sentences), as well as
the other non-normative factors that determine the strength or
weakness of an actor's bargaining position. These latter factors include the distribution of resources (for example, on the defendant's side, the ability to make bail or to hire a private attorney and
even investigators; and on the prosecutor's, the ability to put more
police investigators on the case to get stronger evidence or the ability to offer more lenient deals to co-defendants who agree to turn
state's evidence against their crime partners).

Moreover, I think that our general understanding of plea and
sentence bargaining could be expanded by turning not to studies
of formal organizations, but to research on negotiation and exchange.[31] These include studies of legislatures and how they arrive
at political decisions,[32] analyses of zero-sum and non-zero-sum
games,[33] and studies by political scientists of national defense pol-

icy making.[34] Any such theory-building enterprise needs to be founded upon descriptions of raw experience, however, and a point made earlier is worthy of repetition: we need to examine more closely the precise character of plea and sentence negotiations with an eye to describing as accurately as possible the nature of the interactions and the kinds of constraints that affect them.

Toward a Typology of Sentencing Reforms

This conception of sentencing decisions—what I have tentatively termed the battle model of competitive negotiations—also suggests a different way of thinking about reform strategies. Unfortunately, what might be called the science of sentencing reform is still in its infancy. The published literature is replete with studies of particular efforts to change the courts, yet few attempts have been made to move beyond the particulars in order to develop a more general understanding of the dynamics of court reform. Raymond Nimmer, one of the few who has given this matter sustained attention, observed in 1978 that:

[t]hough reform has been much discussed, it has seldom been considered as an independent phenomenon. Similarities of design, concept, implementation, and eventual impact, or lack of it, have been ignored or only superficially discussed. . . . In general, then, the patterns of reform of law-administering institutions are virtually uncharted.[35]

Nimmer, Malcolm Feeley, and others have begun to map that terrain, but we are still very far from having a comprehensive understanding of various reform strategies and their consequences.[36]

Among those who have discussed reforms more abstractly, the common tendency has been to classify strategies according to the rule-making agency that is being "targeted."[37] Following this line of reasoning, one can easily distinguish three types, corresponding to the tripartite division of governmental authority among the legislative, executive, and judicial branches. With regard to court reform, the legislative strategy seeks the revision of statutory laws or the allocation of public monies in a way that would further a particular purpose. Administrative strategies aim to revise the rules that prevail within governmental agencies. In a strict sense, this means the revision of official rules and regulations, but efforts to alter the customary rules of the court have also been classified as "administrative reforms," largely because the courts have been seen as organizations. The third broad class of reform discussed in the literature is what Stuart Scheingold has called a "strategy of rights."[38] Instead of establishing a rule at the legislative or administrative level, those pursuing this reform approach litigate in the courts to establish rules creating entitlements. Many of the procedural reforms of the due process revolution in the administration of justice that occurred during the past two decades—the right to an attorney, the right to a formal hearing in advance of parole revocation, etc.—resulted from such a reform strategy.

If, as I have argued above, the outcomes of sentencing decisions are determined not only by compliance with norms, but also by the distribution and exercise of power-related factors, this exclusive focus on rule-changing strategies misses an important aspect of the reasons why reforms succeed or fail. People who are on one or the other side of a reform initiative—the reformers themselves and those on the receiving end of the process—are generally attuned to matters of "turf," prerogative, and the like. Domains are often defined by promulgated rules, but not entirely so. In local court settings, they are often founded upon customary understandings and are defended by a variety of means. In other words, there is a "political" aspect of court reforms that involves battles over resources, prerogatives, and power. Changing established sentencing patterns not infrequently involves changing the distribution of power and resources within the courts. Viewing reforms solely as rule-changing efforts diverts attention away from a systematic consideration of these other factors.

Thinking about power, leverage, interests, and other such concepts sensitizes us to the aspects of reform efforts that make them successful. For example, one element of the Vera Institute's project that contributed substantially to its capacity to have otherwise jail-bound defendants sentenced to community service was the injection of "change-agents" into the courts who were charged with managing of the reform. These agents—the project's court representatives and their supervisors—were given a narrowly focused mission and had no other institutional interests to protect. This absence of cross-cutting obligations was important, for they could advocate the use of the community service sentence in a way that probation officers, for example, could not. (Probation officers, as their roles are presently defined, cannot advocate for a particular sentence in advance of a guilty plea. They may recommend a sentence when asked by the courts through the medium of a "pre-pleading investigation," but the written recommendations they submit are different in force from the oral presentations by the institute's project court representatives.)

Court representatives also had an ability to control the use of the community service sentence that stemmed from the institutional status of the project. Being an independent agency rather than a branch of government, the Vera Institute of Justice is under no obligation to the judiciary to take particular offenders. Court representatives have the ability to say "no" when others in the court want to use the community service sanction in ways that are inconsistent with the project's objectives.

This independent footing enables the court representatives to bargain. They control a resource that others want: their agreement to supervise convicted offenders so that the community benefits from their unpaid labor. Consequently, they can negotiate to some extent the terms of the sentence. They can, for example, control the number of hours that an offender will be required to work without pay (all those sentenced to the institute project are ordered to do seventy hours of labor). They can also trade one case for another. That is, court representatives may agree with either the judge or the district attorney to accept a certain number of offenders who otherwise would not have gone to jail on the condition that they obtain in return an equal number of persons who would have been jailed.

This ability to bargain and control the use of the sanction permitted the managers of the Bronx and Brooklyn projects to move "upscale" when the early results of the evaluation showed the sentence being used too often as an alternative, not to jail, but to other non-incarcerative dispositions. Prosecutors in these two boroughs learned that the project could operate effectively without their approval—the Manhattan branch demonstrated this very well—and in preference to losing control altogether, they agreed to loosen their restrictions on the use of the community service sentence.

Taking into account the political aspect of reforms (which is to say, that aspect involving the distribution of power) is especially important in understanding efforts to substitute nonincarcerative sanctions for jail and prison terms. This is because strategies aimed at changing rules—be they legislative, appellate, or administrative—are not particularly suited to this purpose. Legislatures are not likely to pass laws prohibiting imprisonment sentences. At best, they may prescribe that judges consider imposing the "least restrictive sanction consistent with the ends of justice," to use language that is in vogue among many reformers. Lawmakers typically restrict judicial discretion only when they seek to ensure the opposite result: the mandatory imprisonment of people convicted of certain offenses (usually those involving drugs, violent crime, the use of weapons, etc.).[39] But even in cases in which legislatures have tightened the statutes to sharply restrict judicial sentencing discretion, courts have frequently found ways to preserve the status quo and thereby frustrate reform goals.[40] This suggests that even legislative reform strategies have to attend to the distribution of incentives, resources, and power in the local courts if they are to be effective. This is more than a matter of changing the rules.

A strategy of rights, relying as it does upon appellate decisions, is of little use to reformers interested in changing the way sanctions are distributed among offenders. The courts have historically limited themselves to questions of procedure, rather than to the more substantive issue of determining who should and should not be sentenced to one or another type of sanction. Appellate judges have almost always deferred to the legislative branch for these determinations. The major exceptions to this are rulings on the death penalty, which has been subject to frequent judicial review. But on even this issue, the courts have supported legislatures' right to prescribe executions and have restricted themselves to questioning the procedures by which persons are sentenced to death.

The reasons why a strictly administrative strategy is ill-suited to sentencing reform should be clear from the discussion in the preceding pages. Courts are not organizations and they lack the hierarchical structures necessary for policy decisions to be implemented in individual cases. The outcomes of sentencing decisions that are enmeshed in guilty plea negotiations are determined by a much more complicated political process.

Describing this process and developing an adequate theory that explains why particular sentences are reached in individual cases is a research task that should have a high priority, if we as a society want to control the amount and kind of force that the state applies to its citizens in the form of criminal sanctions. In addition, we should learn more about the dynamics of reform strategies so that we can enhance our abilities to change the courts without generating unwanted side effects. The knowledge that would accrue from these two enterprises would benefit both scientists and policy-makers alike.

Appendix

Estimation Procedures:
Techniques and Assumptions

This appendix describes the statistical methods employed to develop estimates of (1) what proportion of project participants would have been sentenced by the courts in the absence of the community service option; (2) how much the demand for jail cells was reduced by judges using the sentence; and (3) how many crimes could have been prevented by jailing offenders rather than ordering them into community service.

Estimating the Proportions of Participants
Who Would Have Been Imprisoned

This analysis was undertaken in two stages for two different periods. The first involved an examination of all cases screened for eligibility by project staff in all three boroughs between 1 October 1981 and 30 September 1982. The second stage aimed to determine the effect of procedural changes that were instituted in the Bronx and Brooklyn units in the first half of 1983. For that analysis, case decisions were examined for all defendants screened for eligibility by the Bronx unit between 1 July 1983 and 31 December 1983, and in Brooklyn between 1 October 1983 and 30 September 1984. The methods and assumptions used for analyzing case decisions in both periods were identical. The following describes in detail the analysis of this first period and reports only the summary results of the analysis of the second.

To estimate the extent to which the community service sentence was used in each borough as a substitute for jail, the populations of defendants found eligible and subsequently rejected for community service were used to develop linear logistic regression models of judicial decisions regarding whether or not to impose an imprisonment sentence. These models were then used to estimate the proportion of project participants   219 who would have gone to jail in the absence of the community service sentencing project. Only cases that reached disposition in post-arraignment hearings were included in the analysis of the in/out decisions, because the constellation of factors associated with receiving a jail sentence were slightly different in the arraignment and post-arraignment stages. Because so few of the rejected defendants' cases reached disposition at arraignment, there were not enough in each borough to model the in/out decisions at this early stage of adjudication.

The dependent variable in the models was defined as a dichotomous one: being sentenced to jail as opposed to all other alternative modes of disposition. If the defendant had been sentenced to jail, the outcome variable was scored as a one; a non-jail disposition was scored as a zero. The independent variables included both interval and categorical ones, and all of the latter type were transformed into dummy variables for the analysis. A linear logistic regression procedure developed by Frank Harrell ("The LOGIST Procedure") was chosen because it is particularly well-suited to situations where the dependent variable is dichotomous and independent variables are interval and/or dichotomous.[1] The mathematical form of the model is as follows: Y denotes the dependent variable for the nth observation. The vector of the independent variables for the nth observation is $X_{n1}, X_{n2}, \ldots, X_{np}$. Furthermore, $X_nB = X_{n1}*B_1 + X_{n2}*B_2 + \ldots + X_{np}*B_p$ where $B = (B_1 \ldots B_p)$ denotes the vector of regression parameters. The model assumes that the probability that $Y_n = 1$ is $1/(1 + \exp(-ALPHA - X_nB))$ where ALPHA is the intercept parameter.

Because Harrell's LOGIST procedure only uses cases having values for all variables in the specified model, many defendants were deleted from the analysis because of missing information. To minimize the number of deleted cases, we aimed at finding a parsimonious solution to the estimating problem, which is to say, a model having as few predictive variables as possible, while retaining considerable predictive power. The decision rule followed to select variables for the first step in model building was that the probability associated with the zero-order correlation between the independent and dependent variable had to be 0.10 or less. (See table 3.2 in chapter 3 for the correlations.) Variables that showed no statistically significant higher-order correlation when included in the model were deleted, unless their inclusion increased the predictive strength of the model without substantially reducing the number of cases used by the LOGIST procedure. Care was taken to avoid using potentially collinear independent variables. The characteristics of the best-fitting models for each borough's rejected defendant pool are shown in table A.1.

An inspection of the columns for each borough reveals the strength and weaknesses of the three models. In the Bronx, for example, the model correctly predicted 87 percent of the in/out decisions for the post-arraignment rejected defendant pool—the population upon which the model was built. If one were to predict jail outcomes by flipping a coin, the proportion of predicted jailed defendants would be close to 50 percent. As shown in fifth row from the top in the left-most column of table A.1., only 17 percent of the Bronx rejected defendants received jail sentences. Flipping a coin would therefore overestimate the proportion of jail sentences by about 33 percent in that borough.

The model did a better job of prediction than the coin-toss method. It predicted that 10 percent of the rejected defendants disposed post-arraignment would have gone to jail, 7 percent fewer than the proportion actually jailed. It was far better in predicting the non-jail outcomes than the jail outcomes, for it correctly identified 96 percent of the defendants not given jail sentences, compared with only 60 percent of those receiving jail. The model erred in this direction because it made a strong presumption of no jail, an efficient strategy given that only 17 percent of the cases actually received a jail sentence. (The beta coefficient for the intercept in this model was strongly negative: −3.54.) The only factors that offset this strong presumption were: the defendants' being in pretrial detention (the beta for this variable was +2.83), the number of prior arrests, and the length of time between the last prior conviction and arraignment for the current offense.

When this model was applied to the project participants who had their cases disposed in post-arraignment hearings in the Bronx, it estimated that 15 percent of those participants would have gone to jail. Adjustments were made, using formulae derived from Bayes' Law, to compensate for the model's tendency to underestimate the proportion of rejected defendants who had gone to jail and overestimate the proportion who had not received jail sentences. This adjustment changed the estimated proportion of project participants who would have gone to jail in the absence of community service to 20 percent.

Using models developed separately for Brooklyn and Manhattan, and applying similar adjustments for under and overestimation, we estimated that approximately 28 and 66 percent, respectively, of the participants in these two boroughs who had their cases reach disposition in post-arraignment hearings would have gone to jail in the absence of the community service project. (Characteristics of the models for these two borough populations are described in columns two and three of table A.1.)

Notice that the estimated proportion of participants who would have gone to jail in each borough was almost identical to the proportion of rejected defendants who actually had been sentenced to jail (a finding that was useful in developing other estimates, as will be discussed below). In

Table A.1. Modeling the Imprisonment Decision:
Characteristics of the Models

	Bronx	Brooklyn	Manhattan
Rejected population used for modeling:			
Total cases with known outcomes	317	118	129
Number cases deleted	65	13	31
Cases used in modeling	252	105	98
Percent imprisoned	17%	27%	65%
Percent not imprisoned	83%	73%	35%
Characteristics of models:	COEFFICIENTS		
Intercept	−3.54 ***	−1.56 **	−.61
Predictive variables:			
In pretrial detention	2.83 ***	1.46 **	1.74 **
Number prior arrests	.03	.20 *	—
Days since last conviction and arraignment for instant offense	.0007 **	−.001 *	—
Days between arraignment and disposition	—	—	−.007
Ethnicity is white	—	−1.99	—
Imprisoned for most recent prior conviction	—	−1.06	1.0

the Bronx, for example, 17 percent of the rejects were given jail sentences. The model predicted, after adjustments, that 20 percent of the participants would have gone to jail had the community service option not been available. In both Brooklyn and Manhattan, the difference between the actual proportion of rejected defendants jailed and the estimated proportion of participants who would have been jailed was a mere one percentage point. This was because rejected defendants, as a group, were very similar to participants in the characteristics that were found to be predictive of receiving a jail sentence. Table A.2 compares participants with rejected defendants in each borough by several dimensions, including those used for modeling. An interesting conclusion can be drawn from this: to estimate the proportion of participants who would have gone to jail in the absence of the community service option, we could have used the actual

Table A.1. (continued)

	Bronx	Brooklyn	Manhattan
Percent rejects predicted imprisoned	10%	20%	71%
Percent rejects predicted not imprisoned	90%	80%	29%
Total correct predictions	87%	80%	78%
Percent imprisoned correctly predicted	60%	50%	88%
Percent not imprisoned correctly predicted	96%	91%	59%
r^2 of model	.28	.29	.28
Chi-square of model	59.9	34.8	28.5
Degrees of freedom	3	5	3
Estimated proportions of participants who would have been imprisoned:			
Before adjustments for error	15%	20%	71%
After adjustment	20%	28%	66%

*p ≤ .05
**p ≤ .01
***p ≤ .001

percentage of post-arraignment rejected defendants who had been given jail sentences.

A note on my assumptions about the direction of causality in the models: I chose to employ a linear estimation method because I assumed causality to be running in one direction only, without feedback loops. This assumption is certainly subject to challenge, especially because detention status was used as an independent variable. There exists a substantial debate in the research literature about the nature of the causal linkages between sentencing decisions and defendants' detention status. In most jurisdictions (including New York), the courts' bail decisions reflect to some degree the judges' predictions of whether imprisonment sentences will be imposed if defendants an convicted. Whether the defendant is detained or not therefore depends in part upon these predictions.[2]

Table A.2. *Characteristics of Participants and Rejected Defendants Whose Cases Were Disposed in Post-Arraignment Hearings*

	Bronx		Brooklyn		Manhattan	
	Partici-pants	Rejects	Partici-pants	Rejects	Partici-pants	Rejects
In pretrial detention	28%	25%	50%	36%	47%	70%
Avg. no. prior arrests	6	6	5	5	12	14
Avg. no. prior mis-demeanor convictions	2	2	2	2	6	8
Imprisoned for most re-cent prior conviction	40%	34%	39%	30%	41%	50%
Avg. no. days since most recent prior conviction	635	767	656	606	439	363
Class of highest arraign-ment charge:						
A felony	—	1%	—	—	—	—
B felony	1%	1	—	—	—	1%
C felony	6	6	2%	2%	—	—
D felony	38	30	52	52	1%	—
E felony	22	29	29	17	1	2
A misdemeanor	32	32	17	27	95	95
B misdemeanor	1	1	—	2	3	2
Violation	—	1	—	—	—	—
	100%	101%	100%	100%	100%	100%

SOURCE: Project files and data provided by the New York City Criminal Justice Agency.

Several researchers have argued that this accounts entirely for the observed correlation between detention status and sentencing outcomes.[3] Others have argued that detention status exerts an independent effect on the sentencing decision, influencing the type and perhaps the length of the sentence imposed.[4] The question remains an unresolved one in the scientific community.

My own earlier research and my reading of other studies leads me to suspect strongly that detention status does affect sentencing outcomes, largely because it influences the ability of the defendant to bargain for a more advantageous sentence, and conversely, because prosecutors and judges have correspondingly greater leverage over the defendant if that defendant is behind bars.[5] (See chapter 4 for a fuller discussion of this relationship.) This is not to say that judges' earlier predictions regarding sentences do not influence at all the defendants' subsequent detention statuses. Rather, I am arguing that a substantial proportion of the observed correlation between detention status and sentencing outcome is the result of the former affecting decisions about the latter. For this reason, I assumed that the behavioral system I was modeling was recursive and that a linear estimation procedure was well suited for it.

Nonetheless, I was concerned about the potential biasing effect of the detention variables' inclusion, because the disturbance terms of that variable and the sentence variable might be correlated. (Both may have been strongly influenced by the earlier bail decisions, which were not measured here.) To distill out these possible effects, I conducted the following test to determine whether the model should include or exclude the detention variable.

The pool of rejected defendants whose cases had reached disposition in post-arraignment hearings in the Bronx was split in two by means of random assignment. (This could not be done in the other two boroughs, because the rejected defendant populations were too small in each.) Using the first half of the data set (the "construction sample"), a best-fitting model was constructed that included the detention variable. This model was then applied to the cases in the second half of the data set (the "validation sample"), and the proportion of correctly predicted cases was noted. The value of the predicted dependent variable was correlated with the actual jail/no jail decision in the validation sample, and the simple r statistic was squared. This yielded two measures of how well the model with the detention variable fit the validation sample. A second model was then developed using the construction sample, this time including not the detention variable, but a predicted detention variable. This latter variable was developed by modeling whether the defendant was in pretrial detention (that is, by finding the best-fitting model that predicted that status) and then using the mathematical formula of the model to generate a predicted detention value for each case. This second model with the predicted detention variable was then applied to the cases in the validation sample and the goodness of the fit was measured by the proportion of correct predictions as well as by the r^2 statistic. The first model with the detention variable was found to fit the validation sample better, and it was therefore included in the models developed for each borough.

In retrospect, I realize that a potentially more effective strategy would have been to use other modeling techniques that are better suited to situations where the behavioral system might be nonrecursive. These include two-stage least squares regression and ordinary least squares regressions, which use instrumental variables.[6] It is possible that these techniques might have produced more robust estimates.

Arraignment-Disposed Cases: Estimating the Proportions Jailbound

The models were applied only to participants who had had their cases reach disposition in hearings subsequent to arraignment. A relatively large percentage of the offenders sentenced to community service during the period we examined was excluded: a total of 39 percent of the city-wide intake of the Vera Community Service Project during the twelve months ending September 30, 1982 consisted of persons sentenced at arraignment. (There were differences among the boroughs in the proportions of participants disposed at arraignment: 38 percent in the Bronx, 29 percent in Brooklyn, and 45 percent in Manhattan.) The ideal strategy would have been to model arraignment dispositions separately and apply these models to the participants sentenced at arraignment. Unfortunately, only 9 percent of all eligible defendants rejected during this period had had their cases reach disposition at arraignment. There were too few to model successfully.

Instead of modeling the in/out decision at arraignment in rejected defendants' cases and then using the resulting model to estimate the proportion of arraignment-disposed participants who would have gone to jail, we adopted a simpler method: we assumed that these participants would have gone to jail in proportions similar to those sentenced in post-arraignment hearings. In other words, the post-arraignment estimates were taken as our best estimates for all participants, regardless of when their cases reached disposition.

There is a soft spot in this logic that could not be hardened. The problem is that we cannot know how many participants would have had their cases disposed in some other fashion at arraignment had they not pleaded guilty to community service. Undoubtedly, some defendants would have had their cases closed out at arraignment, while others would have had their cases continued. How large both of these groups would have been has considerable relevance to our ability to estimate the impact of the project on the courts.

If participants pleaded guilty to the community service offer because it was too attractive to refuse (relative to other perceived alternatives, that is), then it is possible they would not have pleaded guilty at arraignment in the absence of this offer and instead would have held out for another equally favorable sentence. If the courts or the prosecutors had not been quickly forthcoming with such a sentence offer, many defendants would have withheld their guilty pleas and their cases would have been scheduled for later hearings. In instances in which this would have occurred, the proportion of jail sentences in this population would have been approximately the same as we estimated for the participants disposed in post-arraignment hearings. As table A.3 shows, arraignment-disposed participants did not have less serious criminal records and charges than those disposed in subsequent hearings. (Indeed, in Bronx and Brooklyn they had criminal records that were longer than those of participants disposed post-arraignment.) Unfortunately, we could not simply apply the post-arraignment statistical model to these participants to obtain an estimated probability of going to jail if they had been disposed in post-arraignment proceedings; a number of them would have gotten out of pretrial detention by the time their subsequent court dates arrived, which would have dramatically affected the accuracy of the models' projections.

There is another possible scenario that a large proportion of these arraignment-disposed participants might have followed, however. Their cases may have reached another type of nonincarcerative disposition at arraignment, even if the community service option had not been available. One possibility—which amounts to a kind of "worst case" scenario from the point of view of the project's managers—is that the participants were permitted to plead guilty to community service at arraignment primarily because prosecutors and judges wanted to get them out of the courts as quickly as possible, thereby rationing overburdened resources so that other more demanding and more serious cases could be given more concentrated attention. Following this train of logic, we would suspect that many participants would have been offered other attractive sentences if the community service option had not been available.

In our interviews with prosecutors in the Bronx and Brooklyn courts, it was clear that they often used the community service project as a channel for cases that were weak (the "garbage cases") or for defendants whose crimes were not very serious. This is one reason why so few of the participants in these boroughs would have gone to jail otherwise. But we found no evidence that they were any more likely to dump cases into community service at arraignment than in post-arraignment hearings. Judging from their prior criminal records and their charges, participants sentenced at arraignment seemed no more worthy of being dumped in greater proportions than those sentenced later. This is clear from table A.3. To be sure, we were not able to compare the strengths and weaknesses of the prosecutors' cases in these instances. There may have been some significant differences, but we found no indication in our interviews that these weaker cases were more prevalent among arraignment-disposed participants than others.

Prosecutors had no such power in Manhattan, but judges—the key gatekeepers—expressed great interest in getting quick dispositions at arraignment. But again, an inspection of table A.3 indicates that participants pleading guilty at arraignment were not significantly different from those pleading guilty at a later stage in this borough. This gives us no reason to think that participants pleading guilty to community service at arraignment would have avoided jail in any greater proportion than at later hearings.

Comparing participants whose cases had been disposed at arraignment with those disposed later shows that there was little difference between these two populations, but it does not show if the likelihood of being jailed was lower upon conviction at arraignment. If defendants, including participants, were "rewarded" with nonincarcerative sentences for having pleaded guilty at arraignment, we would expect to find different rates of imprisonment at the two stages of ajudication. Table A.4 compares in each borough the percentages of offenders sentenced to prison at arraignment and in post-arraignment hearings. The first row refers to the imprisonment rates of rejected defendants. The second row shows the rates for both participants and rejected defendants combined.

These comparisons provide no evidence that in the Bronx and Brooklyn courts there was a "discount" at sentencing for having pleaded guilty at arraignment. Only in Manhattan did there appear to be a lower likelihood of jail at arraignment. Even though Manhattan rejected defendants whose cases had been disposed at arraignment were nearly identical, as a group, to those whose cases had been disposed later, a smaller proportion received jail sentences at arraignment. This suggests that if arraignment-disposed participants in Manhattan had not pleaded guilty to community service, but would have had their cases disposed at arraignment anyway, a somewhat smaller proportion of them would have gone to jail, compared with the proportions disposed in post-arraignment hearings. Or put more succinctly: fewer than 66 percent of these participants would have gone to jail in Manhattan under these conditions.

I suspect, however, that relatively few of the Manhattan participants would have pleaded guilty to another nonincarcerative sanction at ar-

Those Sentenced in Post-Arraignment Proceedings

	Bronx		Brooklyn		Manhattan	
	Arraign-ment	Post-arraign	Arraign-ment	Post-arraign	Arraign-ment	Post-arraign
In pretrial detention	72%	28%	94%	50%	78%	47%
Avg. no. prior arrests	7	6	6	5	12	12
Avg. no. prior misdemeanor convictions	3	2	3	2	6	6
Imprisoned for most recent prior conviction	49%	40%	48%	39%	49%	41%
Avg. no. days since most recent prior conviction	663	635	731	656	523	439
Class of highest arraignment charge:						
A felony	—	—	—	—	—	—
B felony	—	1%	—	—	1%	—
C felony	1%	6	—	2%	—	—
D felony	25	38	49%	52	—	1%
E felony	21	22	32	29	1	1
A misdemeanor	52	32	19	17	92	95
B misdemeanor	—	1	—	—	7	3
	99%	100%	100%	100%	100%	100%

SOURCE: From project files and data supplied by the New York City Criminal Justice Agency.

Table A.4. *Comparing the Proportions Jailed at Arraignment and Post-Arraignment Hearings*

| | Proportions jailed | | | | | |
| | Bronx | | Brooklyn | | Manhattan | |
	Arraign-ment	Post-arraign	Arraign-ment	Post-arraign	Arraign-ment	Post-arraign
Rejects only	47%	19%	41%	26%	44%	62%
Rejects and participants combined	15%	14%	11%	13%	6%	26%

SOURCE: Project files; dispositional data supplied by the New York City Criminal Justice Agency.

raignment. Our interviews and observations revealed that defense attorneys usually brought the community service offer to the judge after other less onerous proposals had been turned down. If defendants had pleaded guilty, a large proportion of them would have pleaded guilty to a jail sentence. The majority of them probably would have had their cases scheduled for later hearings, and they would have gone to jail in proportions similar to those participants pleading guilty in later stages: approximately 66 percent.

In summary: it is reasonable to assume that in the absence of the community service alternative, participants who pleaded guilty at arraignment would have gone to jail in proportions similar to those that would have obtained had they been sentenced in subsequent hearings. Approximately 20 percent would have been jailed in the Bronx, 28 percent in Brooklyn, and 66 percent in Manhattan.

Similar analyses of decisions made in the Bronx and Brooklyn courts following the reorganizations there produced evidence that both borough units improved their jail-displacement rates. In the Bronx, the estimated rate was 52 percent; in Brooklyn, 57 percent. (Manhattan's performance was similarly examined during the period between 1 May–30 November 1984, not because there was any substantial reorganization to evaluate but for routine monitoring purposes. That analysis indicates that the Manhattan jail-displacement rate dropped somewhat, from approximately 66 percent in 1982 to 52 percent in this latter period.)

Estimating the Length of Imprisonment Sentences

As reported in chapter 3, we assumed that participants who would have gone to jail in the absence of the project would have received jail sentences of similar lengths to those of rejected defendants whose cases reached disposition in post-arraignment hearings. Our grounds for relying upon this assumption for our estimates were two. First, we had no better method of estimation. There were few rejected defendants sentenced to jail, and we were not able to develop statistical models of the sort used to estimate the proportions jailed. Second, we found, as described above, that our statistical models produced estimates of the proportions jailed that were almost identical to estimates that could have been drawn simply by looking at the proportion of rejected defendants jailed in each borough. This suggested that we could extrapolate from the dispositions of rejected defendants cases directly to participants, thereby obtaining a relatively accurate estimate. Thus, we assumed here that the length-of-sentence decisions in the participant population would also have been nearly identical to those in the sample of rejected defendants used for modeling.

We also assumed that participants who pleaded guilty at arraignment would have received similar sentences if the community service order had not been imposed. Our reasons for thinking this assumption justifiable were the same as those discussed above regarding the in/out sentencing estimates.

Therefore, we estimated that those participants considered in the October 1981–September 1982 period, who otherwise would have been sentenced to jail, would have received terms that averaged 75 days in the Bronx, 70 days in Brooklyn, and 143 days in Manhattan. During later periods (July–December 1983 in the Bronx, October 1983–September 1984 in Brooklyn, and May–November 1984 in Manhattan), those who would have gone to jail otherwise would have received sentences averaging sixty-seven days in the Bronx and Manhattan and sixty-five days in Brooklyn.

Estimating Time Actually Served in Jail

To determine the impact the community service sentencing project had on the correctional system, we needed to develop estimates of how much time participants actually would have spent in jail had they not been sentenced to community service. Court-imposed sentences are not typically served in full after the date of sentencing. Inmates receive varying amounts of time off for good behavior and whatever time they spent in pretrial detention is credited against their sentence.

The population used to develop estimates of how participants would have fared was, once again, the rejected defendants who had had their cases reach disposition in post-arraignment hearings. Lacking disciplinary records and other information from the New York City Department of Corrections, we assumed that all jailed rejected defendants had received their full allotment of time off for good behavior. (This accumulates automatically at the rate of one day off for two days without infractions.) The amount of time rejected defendants spent in pretrial detention was then estimated. For each rejected defendant who had received a jail sentence, we obtained case summary data from the New York City Criminal Justice Agency and used these to calculate the number of days each served in detention. In instances where defendants remained in detention the full period between arraignment and sentencing, we obtained exact measures. In cases where defendants had posted bail between scheduled hearings, we had to estimate the number of days they had served after their last recorded hearing before being released. (The case summary information we used listed the judges' bail-related decisions at each scheduled hearing, which permitted us to infer the defendants' detention statuses at each point.)

Finally, estimates of actual time served in jail after the date of sentencing were computed by subtracting good behavior time (one-third of the court-imposed sentence) and then further substracting from that the estimated number of days these rejected defendants spent in pretrial detention. These time-served figures were then averaged across all rejected defendants sentenced to jail in each borough. For the period October 1981–September 1982, the resulting estimates of average time actually served were thirty-nine days in the Bronx, forty-three days in Brooklyn, and seventy-three days in Manhattan. In the later 1983 and 1984 periods, the times averaged thirty-five days in the Bronx, forty days in Brooklyn, and fifty days in Manhattan.

As noted, these estimates were based on the jail sentences of rejected defendants whose cases had reached disposition in post-arraignment hearings. By extrapolating these estimates to all participants, regardless of whether they had been sentenced at arraignment or later, we probably underestimated the amount of time participants would have spent in jail after sentencing. If some participants had pleaded guilty to a jail sentence at arraignment, they would have accumulated no more than a few days in pretrial detention to credit against their sentences. There would be no overall difference in the number of days spent behind bars, however. What would differ would be the split between pretrial and post-sentencing time.

To compute the estimated total number of days that participants would have spent in jail had the community service project not existed, we made a series of calculations for each borough, shown in table A.5. These estimates were calculated for four different periods: 1 October 1981–30 September 1982 (the period used for developing the original estimates), New York City (and Vera Institute) fiscal year 1982 (1 July 1981–30 June 1982), fiscal years 1983 and 1984. During the first three periods, we assumed a constant rate of displacing jail sentences. During the fourth, we used estimates that were developed using exactly the same methods and assumptions employed in the analysis of the 1982 population.

Of the 676 participants sentenced to community service during the October 1981–September 1982 period, we estimated that 302 of them would have been sentenced to jail and that they would have spent a combined total of 19,479 days under sentence before being released. This equaled 53.4 prisoner/years. (Put another way, the New York City jails would have had used 54 beds for twelve months for these offenders, if the community service sentence had not been available.) During the first year ending 30 June 1982, the number would have been smaller: 14,870 days, or 40.7 prisoner/years. (This was due to the fact that the Manhattan unit was not open for the full year.) In fiscal year 1983, project participants would have spent an estimated 25,087, or 68.7 prisoner/years in jail following the date of sentencing, if they had not been ordered to perform community service. In fiscal year 1984, they would have spent 55.6 prisoner/years.

Estimating Pretrial Detention Time Saved by Use of the Project

Defendants who pleaded guilty to a community service sentence had their cases reach disposition more quickly, on the average, than defendants declared eligible by court representatives and subsequently rejected. As a consequence, they spent fewer days in pretrial detention. The extent to which the availability of the community service project was responsible for this short detention time is unclear, because some defendants who pleaded guilty to community service would have had their cases disposed on the same date even in the absence of the project. (This probably would have been most likely when the courts used community service sentences as an alternative to other nonincarcerative punishments.) However, it is safe to assume that the time required to reach a disposition would have been longer in a larger proportion of participants' cases had the community service alternative been absent.

Lacking any better estimator of how much time participants would

Table A.5. *Computing the Number of Days That Participants Would Have Spent in Jail After Sentencing Had the Community Service Sentence Not Been Imposed*

Time period	Borough	Annual intake	Est. proportion jailed	Est. no. jailed	Avg. no. days served	Est. no. prisoner/days
October 1, 1981– September 30, 1982	Bronx	180	20%	36	39	1,404
	Brooklyn	161	28	45	43	1,935
	Manhattan	335	66	221	73	16,140
	Combined total:					19,479
July 1, 1981– June 30, 1982	Bronx	182	20	36	39	1,404
	Brooklyn	166	28	46	43	1,999
	Manhattan	238	66	157	73	11,467
	Combined total:					14,870
July 1, 1982– June 30, 1983	Bronx	259	20	52	39	2,028
	Brooklyn	234	28	66	43	2,838
	Manhattan	420	66	277	73	20,221
	Combined total:					25,087
July 1, 1983– June 30, 1984	Bronx	205	59	121	35	4,230
	Brooklyn	273	57	156	40	6,273
	Manhattan	380	52	198	50	9,812
	Combined total:					20,315

SOURCE: Intake figures from project files.

have spent in pretrial detention had they not been sentenced to the project, we assumed that they would have experienced approximately the same fate as the rejected defendants. Table A.6 compares the average number of days spent in pretrial detention by both participants and rejected defendants and then computes an average difference within each borough. This difference represents the estimated average number of inmate/days averted by each participant's having pleaded guilty to the community service sentence. As the table shows, the average differences are computed for those defendants who were screened and found eligible for the project at arraignment and separately for those screened at any point afterwards. Multiplying the average number of saved detention days by the number of participants sentenced in each borough at either the arraignment or post-arraignment stage produces an estimated total number of detention days averted by the use of the community service project.

As noted in the section on estimating the jail time actually served after sentencing, the number of days some participants and rejected defendants spent in pretrial detention had to be estimated. Case summaries compiled by the New York City Criminal Justice Agency were used as the sole source of information on detention, and when defendants remained in jail for the full period between arraignment and disposition, an exact count of days behind bars could be made. In instances in which defendants had posted bail between scheduled hearings, we had to estimate the number of days they had served after their last recorded hearing before having been released. The case summaries listed judges' bail-related decisions at each hearing, and we assumed that defendants had been released midway between two hearings, if he or she was shown to have been at liberty by the time of the latter.

During the twelve months ending 30 September 1982, participants would have spent an additional estimated 5,319 inmate/days in pretrial detention had they been disposed the way rejected defendants were. This equaled 14.6 inmate/years, or the space required to house 15 inmates for a full year. Using identical methods and assumptions for the fiscal year 1983 and 1984 populations, we estimated that the use of the project saved approximately 20 inmate/years and 46.7 inmate/years, respectively.

Estimating the Relative Deterrent Effects of Community Service and Jail

As described in Chapter Six, we sought to determine whether a sentence to jail instead of community service would have made any ap-

Table A.6. *Estimating Pretrial Detention Time Saved by Sentencing to Community Service (October 1981–September 1982)*

Borough	Average days detained: rejects	Average days detained: participants	Average days detained: difference	Total est. inmate/days saved by participants
Defendants Screened at Arraignment				
Bronx	2.4	0.6 (n = 76)	1.8	136.8
Brooklyn	6.2	1.6 (n = 63)	4.6	289.8
Manhattan	7.6	0.4 (n = 162)	7.2	1,166.4
Defendants screened subsequent to arraignment				
Bronx	11.4	4.4 (n = 104)	7.0	728.0
Brooklyn	10.4	5.2 (n = 97)	5.2	504.4
Manhattan	21.9	7.4 (n = 172)	14.5	2,494.0
Total est. inmate/days pretrial saved by participants				5,319

SOURCE: Data provided by New York City Criminal Justice Agency.
NOTE: Rejected defendant populations include only those rejected defendants whose cases were disposed at the time of checking court records.

preciable difference in offenders' subsequent criminality. We posed two different questions. First, does a jail term deter future criminality more effectively than a community service sentence? (We assumed that any suppression that might be found to exist would be due to the deterrent effect of jail, rather than to the superior rehabilitative power of either sentence.) Second, do jail sentences, by virtue of their greater incapacitative functions, suppress crime more effectively in the short run, and if so, by how much? This section discusses the methods and assumptions used to address the first question, while those involved in answering the second question are examined in the following section.

The ideal method of comparing the deterrent effects of jail as opposed to community service sentences would be to devise an experiment in which offenders were chosen at random to receive one or the other sentence. This would maximize the likelihood of creating two groups of offenders that were identical in composition. Any observed difference in the rates of criminality following the imposition of the sentences could then be attributed with confidence to the effect of the sentence itself. Because we could not operate such an experiment (or a variant of it) in the courts, we compared instead participants sentenced to community service with those who were considered for the sentence but had then been rejected for it and sentenced to jail instead.

As shown in chapter 6, we found only narrow and probably insignificant differences in the proportions of offenders rearrested in the two comparison groups. One obvious conclusion is that jail had no significantly greater deterrent effect on subsequent criminality than community service. Our ability to trust the validity of such a conclusion turns on the similarity of these two populations, however. Because sentences were not imposed randomly, the possibility exists that the apparent lack of difference in the proportion of offenders rearrested was an artifact produced by the way in which the two populations were drawn. In other words: were there other differences in the two populations that biased the comparison either in favor of community service or jail?

Despite the lack of randomness in sentencing, jailed offenders in each borough, considered as a group, resembled participants quite strongly in their criminal histories and social backgrounds. (See table A.7.) On some dimensions, they were identical, while they were slightly different on others. To see which similarities and differences were likely to matter with regard to the probability of being rearrested within the six-month period, statistical tests were performed to identify characteristics associated with participants being rearrested within 180 days of release, in cases where offenders were jailed and released, and within 180 days of sentence in cases where community service was ordered. The results were quite disappointing, because very few characteristics were found to be even weakly correlated with rearrest. Of the twelve factors examined in each borough, only three were found to be associated with the rearrest of Bronx participants within the 180-day period: age at the time of screening for eligibility by Vera Institute project court representatives, last grade completed in school, and the length of time between the most recent prior conviction and arraignment on the charges that led to the community ser-

Table A.7. Comparing Persons Sentenced to Community Service with Those Sentenced to Jail, by Selected Characteristics

	Bronx	Brooklyn	Manhattan
	CSS/Jail	CSS/Jail	CSS/Jail
Average no. prior misdemeanor convictions	2.3/2.9	2.2/4.7	5.9/5.9
Average no. prior misdemeanor and felony convictions	2.7/3.3	2.5/5.5	6.2/6.3
Median no. days between most recent prior conviction and date of sentencing	436/448	308/326	231/NA
Proportion who received jail sentence for most recent conviction prior	38%/44%	46%/73%	42%/NA
Average age at time of screening	24/25	22/24	27/NA
Proportion white	9%/2%	9%/11%	10%/NA
Proportion employed	51%/51%	40%/58%	35%/NA
Proportion married (legally or common-law)	25%/NA	25%/NA	11%/NA
(Number of offenders)	(205/81)	(146/36)	(143/241)

SOURCES: New York City Community Service Sentencing Project files and New York City Criminal Justice Agency files.

NOTE: "NA" means that these data were not available. The median is computed by ranking all offenders in order of least to most (days between most recent prior conviction and date of screening, in this case), and then picking the number above which half of the group falls and below which the other half falls. This measure of a group's central tendency is unaffected by a few very extreme cases at either end of the range, unlike an average score. Employment status was obtained from the New York City Criminal Justice Agency's pre-arraignment interview with defendants, in which they were asked if they were employed at the time of their arrest in any capacity whatsoever.

vice sentence. (The twelve characteristics were the number of prior misdemeanor convictions, the number of prior felony convictions, having
gone to jail for the last conviction, the time elapsed between the time of
the most recent prior conviction and the arraignment on the charges that
led to the community service sentence, marital status, age, the highest
grade completed in school, length of time living at a current residence at
the time of screening by court representatives, gender, ethnicity, reported
employment status at the time of sentencing to community service, and
the seriousness of arraignment charges resulting in the community service sentence.) Jailed offenders were of similar ages and had about the
same time that had passed since the last prior conviction; the slight differences between participants and jailed offenders on these two measures
were insignificant, not only because they were so narrow, but also because
these factors were only very weakly correlated with being rearrested. No
information was available on the number of years that jailed offenders had
completed in school, but it was probably about the same as participants.
Again, this was only weakly correlated with being rearrested anyway.

In Brooklyn, only one factor—age—was found to be correlated with
rearrest, and it was a feeble association at that. Older participants were
slightly less likely to be rearrested (as in the Bronx). The average age at the
time of screening for community service was 22 years for participants and
23.7 years for jailed rejected defendants, a difference that was insignificant in its impact upon the likelihood of rearrest for both groups of
offenders.

In Manhattan, only the number of prior misdemeanor convictions was
found to be correlated with participants' rearrests, and this was a weak
association. (The more prior misdemeanor convictions, the greater the
likelihood of being arrested again within 180 days of sentence.) Both participants and jailed offenders in this borough had exactly the same average
number of misdemeanor convictions: 5.7 each.

In summary: our examination of both participants and jailed offenders
turned up nothing that indicated a systematic bias in the way these groups
were constituted, rendering jailed offenders more or less likely to be rearrested because of differing socio-economic conditions. Of course, we may
have missed identifying a key factor that distinguished the two groups,
but that is improbable. Previous studies of crime have not discovered a
cluster of factors that strongly predict who does and does not get arrested.
If there were any such selection bias operating in the sentencing decision,
it is hard to see how it would have had any bearing on the likelihood of
later arrests. Judges send persons to jail primarily because of their past
behavior and not because they can predict well what offenders' future be-

havior will be. To be sure, they often do impose sentences with a forward-looking orientation, trying to determine which offenders are more likely to cause trouble, but judges have no special lenses that permit them to see into the future. Whatever assessments of future danger they do make, these are based on a weighing of the same factors we examined—mainly prior criminal records. Because participants and jailed offenders had similar criminal histories prior to sentencing, judges would probably have forecast similar futures for both groups. Consequently, we have no reason to distrust a comparison of the post-sentence deterrent effects of these two groups in each borough.

Estimating How Many Crimes Could Have Been Averted if Participants Had Been Jailed

To estimate the number of crimes that could have been prevented by jailing offenders instead of ordering community service sentences, we first computed the average number of arrests (our measure of criminality) for each participant for each day during the 180 days following date of sentence to the project. We then employed the estimates (described above) of the number of days participants would have spent in jail had the project not existed. These two procedures yielded estimates of the numbers of arrests that would have been averted had the participants been jailed instead.

The method of calculating the daily average number of rearrests per participant is shown in table A.8.

It is important to note that this is not a measure of arrest rates per person for a specified time at risk. Some individuals were not at risk of committing new crimes during some segment of the 180-day period because they were locked up upon rearrest. The measure therefore represents the average number of rearrests per participant per day under the conditions that actually prevailed during the 180 days. (The decisive conditions here were the frequency of rearrest and the response by the courts to each arrest.)

The next step was to estimate the number of days that participants as a group would have spent in jail (and thereby would have been incapacitated) if community service sentences had not been imposed. In our earlier analysis described in chapter 3, we estimated that 20 percent of the Bronx participants, 28 percent of the Brooklyn participants, and 66 percent of the Manhattan participants would have gone to jail during the pe-

Table A.8. *Computing the Average Number of Arrests Per
Participant, Per Day, During 180-Day Period After
Sentencing to Community Service*

	Bronx	Brooklyn	Manhattan
Total number participants in sample	205	146	143
Days from sentence to end of six-month period	× 180	× 180	× 180
Total participant/days	36,900	26,280	25,740
Number rearrests within 180 days of sentence	121	83	106
Average number rearrests per participant/day	.0032791	.0031582	.0041181

riod between 1 October 1981 and 30 September 1982. We assumed that the same pattern would have held throughout the period during which the 494 participants in our rearrest sample were sentenced. This was not an unreasonable assumption, because the policies and procedures followed by the project's court representatives and the judges were not discernably different from one period to the other. The overall rate of displacing jailed offenders into the project would probably have been roughly constant in each borough.

We also made certain assumptions about the length of time participants would have spent behind bars had they been sentenced to jail. For reasons explained more fully above, we assumed that the participants who would have been sentenced to jail would have served approximately the same number of days as those served by rejected defendants who went to jail. In the pool used for modeling the imprisonment/non-imprisonment decision, we calculated that rejected defendants sent to jail in the Bronx served an average of thirty-nine days behind bars after the date of sentencing; in Brooklyn, the figure was forty-three days; and in Manhattan, seventy-three days. This counts time actually served before release, not the length of the court-imposed sentence. Because we did not obtain disciplinary records from the jails, we could not determine exactly how much

Table A.9. *Average Number of Days Held in*
Pretrial Detention, by Borough

	Rejects	Project participants	Average difference
Bronx	9.1	3.3	5.8
Brooklyn	9.2	4.2	5.0
Manhattan	17.0	4.5	12.5

SOURCE: Estimated from data provided by New York City Criminal Justice Agency.

time off the sentences were awarded for good behavior. We assumed that prisoners were awarded the full one-third off. We also subtracted the number of days served in pretrial detention, which in some cases had to be estimated. It was not unreasonable to assume that the participants we tracked for rearrests would have served sentences of approximately the same average length.

Participants also would have served more time in jail before sentencing had they not been ordered to perform community service. Defendants who "cop out" to community service generally speed up the disposition of their cases. If participants had not been sentenced to the Vera Institute project, they would have averaged slightly more time in detention. They would have been restrained from committing crimes in the community during this time as well. Consequently, we had to estimate the amount of additional pretrial detention time participants as a group would have incurred in the absence of the Vera Institute project.

In the population of rejected defendants and participants who had had their cases screened for eligibility between 1 October 1981 and 30 September 1982, we determined that Bronx participants spent an average of 5.8 fewer days in pretrial detention than rejected defendants. In Brooklyn, the corresponding savings per participant was 5.0 days; in Manhattan, 12.5 days. (See table A.9.) Again, we assumed the same patterns of disposition and detention would have been observed for all participants in the rearrest sample had community service sentences not been imposed.

Combining these three sets of measures, we then developed estimates of how many days would have been spent in jail by participants had the courts not used the community service options. These are expressed on the bottom row of Table A.10 as jail days saved per 100 participants.

Table A.10. *Estimating Number of Arrests That Would Have Been Averted Per 100 Participants if Community Service Sentences Had Not Been Imposed*

	Bronx	Brooklyn	Manhattan
Est. pretrial detention time saved:			
Number participants	100	100	100
Est. average detention days saved per participant	× 5.8	× 5.0	× 12.5
Est. total detention days saved per 100 participants	580	500	1,250
Est. post-sentencing jail time saved:			
Number participants	100	100	100
Est. proportion of jailbound participants	× .20	× .28	× .66
Est. number of participants who would have gone to jail per 100 participants	20	28	66
Est. sentence length (average number days)	× 39	× 43	× 73
Total est. days saved post-sentence per 100 participants	780	1,204	4,818
Est. total jail days saved:			
Pretrial detention days	580	500	1,250
Post-sentence jail days	+ 780	+ 1,204	+ 4,818
Est. total jail days saved per 100 participants	1,360	1,704	6,068
Est. number and percentage of re-arrests that could have been averted:			
Est. total jail days saved per 100 participants	1,360	1,704	6,068
Average number rearrests per participant day	× .0032791	× .0031582	× .0041181
Est. total crimes per 100 participants within 180 days that could have been averted	4.5	5.4	25.0

Notes

Chapter 1

1. James Beha, Kenneth Carlson, and Robert H. Rosenblum, *Sentencing to Community Service* (Washington, D.C.: U.S. Government Printing Office, 1977), 5–10.

2. Ibid., 1.

3. Mike Goff, "Harrington, firm to pay fines to home," *The Lincoln Star* (Nebraska), 28 September 1982; Roy Howard Beck, "Judge lets convicts say 'I'm Sorry'," *The United Methodist Reporter*, 23 December 1983.

4. "Insider Given U.S. Sentence," *The New York Times*, 26 August 1983.

5. Barbara Goldsmith, "The Meaning of Celebrity." *The New York Times Magazine*, 4 December 1983, 75.

6. Stephen Schafer, *Compensation and Restitution to Victims of Crime*, 2nd ed. (Montclair, N.J.: Smith Patterson, 1970).

7. See, for example, Fred E. Haynes, *The American Prison System* (New York: McGraw-Hill Book Company, Inc., 1939), chapter 14; David J. Rothman, *The Discovery of the Asylum* (Boston: Little, Brown and Company, 1971); and State of New York, *Report of the State Commission on Prison Labor* (Albany, N.Y.: The Argus Company, Printers, 1871). Around the turn of the century, many states amended their constitutions to limit the market for the goods produced by inmates, thereby reducing the intensity of labor in prisons.

8. In a few states, it could be imposed as a condition of probation. According to a 1949 Alaska statute, for example, judges could order offenders to clean up public recreational facilities or highways as a part of the probation sentence, if they had been convicted of littering such places. Alan Harland, "Court-Ordered Community Service in Criminal Law: The Continuing Tyranny of Benevolence?" *Buffalo Law Review* 29 (Summer 1980):428–429.

9. That community service orders have been expanded to probation

sentences does not invalidate this interpretation. California law did not yet permit community service as a free-standing sentence, which meant that the courts had to define it as a condition of probation. I think the creation of a special agency apart from the existing probation department indicates that the courts saw this as a distinctive sanction, rather than as just another form of probation.

10. Ken Pease and William McWilliams, eds., *Community Service By Order* (Edinburgh: Scottish Academic Press, 1980); K. Pease, S. Billingham, and I. Earnshaw, *Community Service Assessed in 1976*, Home Office Research Study no. 39 (London: Her Majesty's Stationery Office, 1977); John Harding, *Community Service Orders: Implications of the British Experience for the American Justice System* (Washington, D.C.: U.S. Government Printing Office, 1980); and Warren Young, *Community Service Orders* (London: Heinemann, 1979).

11. Kevin Krajick, "The Work Ethic Approach to Punishment," *Corrections Magazine* (October 1982), 8.

12. Peter R. Schneider, William R. Griffith, Anne L. Schneider, Michael J. Wilson, *Two-Year Report on the National Evaluation of the Juvenile Restitution Initiative: An Overview of Program Experience* (Eugene, Oregon: Institute of Policy Analysis, 1982), 1.

13. Alan Harland, "Court-Ordered Community Service," 430.

14. Schneider, *et al. Two-Year Report*, 14; Joe Hudson, Burt Galaway, and Steve Novack, *National Assessment of Adult Restitution Programs: Final Report* (Duluth, Minnesota: School of Social Development, University of Minnesota, 1980), 68.

15. Krajick, "The Work Ethic Approach," 9.

16. This is similar to what happened during the 1960s with bail reform practices. The concept of releasing defendants on their own recognizance (ROR) instead of making them post bail travelled faster than the actual organization of the agencies established to give judges information about defendants' community ties. Judges then began to employ ROR without relying upon agency assistance. See Wayne H. Thomas, Jr., *Bail Reform in America* (Berkeley and Los Angeles, California: University of California Press, 1976); Andrew Schaffer, *Bail and Parole Jumping in Manhattan* (New York: Vera Institute of Justice, 1970).

17. P. R. Schneider, A. L. Schneider, P. Reiter, C. Cleary, "Restitution Requirements for Juvenile Offenders: A Survey of the Practices in American Juvenile Courts," *Juvenile Justice* 28 (November 1977):47.

18. Hudson, *et al., Final Report*, 64–77; Schneider, *et al., Two-Year Report*, 9–23; Glen Cooper and Anita S. West, *An Evaluation of the Community Service Restitution Program: A Cluster Analysis* (Denver: Denver Research Institute, 1981).

19. Hudson, *et al.*, *Final Report*, 69–72.

20. Sheriff Douglas Call in New York State's Genesee County runs a community service project. Robert E. Taylor, "Instead of Jail, One County in New York Imposes Sentences of Work, Reparations, or House Arrest,'" *The Wall Street Journal* 23 December 1983.

21. See, for example, Harland, "Court-Ordered Community Service," 430. One community service program established to provide pretrial diversion is described in Joan Koffman, "Community Service Restitution: A Second Chance," *Today* (Northeastern University Alumni Magazine) 5, (June 1980):1–5. Judges in New York City also on occasion impose community service while suspending the formal imposition of sentence. Although there is no statutory authorization for this practice, it has been accepted by the various parties to the court. (There are serious problems, one could easily argue, with the constitutionality of such practices.)

22. This is the practice in New York State's Genesee County, for example. (See note 20.)

23. See, for example, Pat Choate and Susan Walters, *America in Ruins: Beyond the Public Works Pork Barrel* (Washington, D.C.: The Council of State Planning Agencies, 1981) and Robert E. Alcaly and David Mermelstein, *The Fiscal Crisis of American Cities* (New York: Vintage Books, 1977).

24. M. Kay Harris, *Community Service By Offenders* (Washington, D.C.: National Institute of Corrections, 1979), 2.

25. The law, passed in July 1982, authorizes judges to sentence young offenders sixteen years and older to between forty and two hundred and forty hours of community service. In a personal communication with me, a French official told me that the courts were not likely to sentence as many offenders to community service as the government had initially hoped.

26. It is impossible even to estimate the total number of criminal convictions in the United States during a given year because there exists no centralized agency to whom all jurisdictions report. The number must be in the millions, however. In New York State alone, for example, there were during 1977 approximately three hundred and thirty thousand people arraigned on criminal charges. The dismissal and conviction rates in the various town and village courts were not reported to the state government recording agency, but approximately 60 percent of all charges in the state's other courts resulted in convictions. If that rate held for all New York jurisdictions, there were approximately two hundred thousand convictions resulting from criminal charges in New York State alone during that twelve months. State of New York, The Judicial Conference and the Office of Court Administration, *Report of the Administrative Board of the Judicial*

Conference (Albany: Legislative Document no. 90, 1978), 56, 59, 62,; also State of New York, Department of Audit and Control, *1977 Analysis of Reports of Town Justices and Village Justices*, mimeographed, (Albany: Department of Audit and Control n.d.), 1.

27. National Advisory Commission on Criminal Justice Standards and Goals, *Corrections* (Washington, D.C.: U.S. Government Printing Office, 1973), 221.

28. Ibid., 223.

29. See American Bar Association, *Standards Relating to Sentencing Alternatives and Procedures* (New York: Project on Standards for Criminal Justice, 1969), sec. 2.3; American Law Institute, *Model Penal Code— Sentencing Provisions* (Philadelphia: American Law Institute, 1963), sec. 7.01; and National Council on Crime and Delinquency, *Model Sentencing Act* (Hackensack, N.J.: National Council on Crime and Delinquency, 1972), sec. 1.

30. The announcement of the Law Enforcement Assistance Administration's community service initiative stated that one of its goals was "to create an innovative alternative to the typical correctional processing of selected offenders. . . . The criminal justice system is expected to benefit from the lowered costs of non-incarceration." *Federal Register* 43 (1978): 32, 612. In the juvenile programs funded by the Office of Juvenile Justice and Delinquency Prevention, referral to community service was limited to adjudicated delinquents. This limitation, along with the stated goal of reducing the use of juvenile incarceration, made it absolutely clear that this agency was seeking to have the sanction used as a substitute for incarcerative punishments. For a discussion of how this policy objective was translated into program designs and selection criteria, see Peter Schneider, et al., *Two-Year Report*, 1–2, 61–64.

31. The Law Enforcement Assistance Administration, *A Partnership for Crime Control* (Washington, D.C.: LEAA, no date, circa 1976), 19.

32. Three of the four evaluation studies were not obliged to perform a rigorous impact analysis. See Schneider, et al. *Two-Year Report*, 61–76, for a discussion of their indirect, and to this reader, inconclusive approach to answering the question. Hudson and his colleagues (*Final Report*) and Cooper and West (*Evaluation of Community Service*) included no such systematic analyses in their research. The National Institute of Law Enforcement and Criminal Justice (the predecessor of the National Institute of Justice) pinned its hopes for a rigorous impact study on the research contracted with the Criminal Justice Research Center at Albany (forthcoming). Alan Harland, the project director, reports that their efforts to examine community service projects fell through for various reasons,

and that the forthcoming report deals only with monetary restitution projects as a result. (Telephone interview with Alan Harland, January 1984.)

33. Beha, et al., *Community Service*, 27.

34. Harland, "Court-Ordered Community Service," 443.

35. Eugene Doleschal, "The Dangers of Criminal Justice Reform," *Criminal Justice Abstracts* 14 (March 1982):135.

36. Sally T. Hillsman, "Pretrial Diversion of Youthful Offenders: A Decade of Reform and Research," *The Justice System Journal* 7 (Winter 1982):361–387.

37. Doleschal, "The Dangers of Reform," 148.

38. Pease, Billingham, and Earnshaw, *Community Service Assessed in 1976.*

39. Of the British practices, Harland writes: "The most optimistic estimates available, however, suggest that a majority of CSO cases would not have been incarcerated under traditional sentencing practices." "Court-Ordered Community Service," 448.

40. Hudson, et al., *Final Report*, 47.

41. Anne Newton, "Sentencing to Community Service and Restitution," *Criminal Justice Abstracts* 11 (1979):437.

42. Home Office, *Non-custodial and Semi-custodial Penalties* (London: Her Majesty's Stationery Office, 1970) para. 33.

43. K. Pease, P. Durkin, I. Earnshaw, D. Payne, and J. Thorpe, *Community Service Orders*. Home Office Research Studies, no. 29 (London: Her Majesty's Stationery Office, 1975).

44. "Turning Society's Losers into Winners," an interview with Dennis A. Challeen, *The Judges' Journal* 19, (Winter 1980):7.

45. Young, *Community Service Orders*, 38–46.

46. Hudson, et. al., *Final Report*, 19.

47. See, for example, Robert Martinson, "What Works?—Questions and Answers About Prison Reform," *The Public Interest*, 35 (Spring 1974): 22–54 and Douglas Lipton, Robert Martinson, and Judith Wilks, *Effectiveness of Correctional Treatment: A Survey of Treatment Evaluation Studies* (New York: Praeger Publishers, 1975). Some have criticized Martinson for having drawn such pessimistic conclusions from the data. See, for example, Ted Palmer, "Martinson Revisited." *Journal of Research on Crime and Delinquency* 12 (July 1975): 133–52, and Todd R. Clear, "Correctional Policy, Neo-Retributionism, and the Determinate Sentence," *The Justice System Journal* 4 (Fall 1978):26–48.

48: The opening pages of chapter 6 review what is known about this matter.

49. Challeen, "Turning Losers into Winners," 49.

50. All of the evaluations supported by the federal initiative make this assumption. See Hudson, et al., Final Report; Schneider, et al., Two-Year Report; Cooper and West, Evaluation of Community Service. Indeed, almost all observers classify it as a form of restitution.

51. An observer of the Monroe County (New York) courts told me of such sentences in a meeting in 1981.

52. A twenty-eight-year-old Hispanic man who had been arrested for stealing a radio from a car and who was subsequently sentenced to the Manhattan Community Service Sentencing Project. He was interviewed by my assistant, Antonio Valderrama, on 28 June 1982. Because he was promised anonymity, he and others interviewed in a similar way are known in our records by a number we gave them; this particular offender is known as number 7211.

53. A seventeen-year-old black male (number 7222), arrested for shoplifting and subsequently sentenced to the Manhattan project, who was interviewed by Antonio Valderrama on 22 June 1982.

54. Francis A. Allen, The Borderland of Criminal Justice (Chicago: The University of Chicago Press, 1964), 35–36.

55. Ruffin v. Commonwealth, 62 V. [21 Gratt.] 790, 796 (1871).

56. See, for example, Alvin J. Bronstein, "Offender Rights Litigation: Historical and Future Developments," in Ira P. Robbins, ed., Prisoners' Rights Sourcebook: Vol. II (New York: Clark Boardman Company, 1980), 9–28; and David Rudenstine, The Rights of Ex-Offenders (New York City: Avon Books, 1979).

57. American Bar Association, Standards, sec. 2.3.

58. "Especially, in view of the discretionary potential if used as an alternative to financial sanctions, serious thought must be given to the propriety of replacing one class of people bound to involuntary servitude on the basis of race by another class similarly bound on the basis of a criminal conviction and economic status." Harland, "Court-Ordered Community Service," 459.

59. Martinson's "What Works?" was perhaps the most influential of these manifestos.

60. See, for example, Andrew von Hirsch, Doing Justice, Report of the Committee for the Study of Incarceration, (New York: Hill and Wang, 1976); Citizens' Inquiry on Parole and Criminal Justice, Inc., Prison Without Walls: Report on the New York Parole (New York: Praeger Publishers, 1975); The Twentieth Century Fund Task Force on Criminal Sentencing, Fair and Certain Punishment (New York: McGraw-Hill Book Company, 1976).

61. One school, exemplified by those writers cited in note 60, argue for a "just deserts" principle derived from a retributionist perspective. Others argue for a "selective incapacitation" principle; see, for example, Peter W. Greenwood with Allan Abrahamse, *Selective Incapacitation* (Santa Monica, California: The Rand Corporation, 1982). James Q. Wilson, in his *Thinking About Crime* (New York: Random House, 1975), advocates a position based on both deterrence and incapacitation objectives.

62. See von Hirsch, *Doing Justice*, 118–123.

63. Quoted in Krajick, "The Work Ethic Approach," 7.

64. *Setting Prison Terms*, Bureau of Justice Statistics Bulletin (Washington, D.C.: U.S. Department of Justice, 1983), 3.

65. *Prisoners 1925–81*, Bureau of Justice Statistics Bulletin (Washington, D.C.: U.S. Department of Justice, 1982), 2.

66. *Prisoners at Midyear 1983*, Bureau of Justice Statistics Bulletin (Washington, D.C.: U.S. Department of Justice, 1983).

67. Margaret Cahalan, in her "Trends in Incarceration in the United States since 1880," *Crime and Delinquency* 25 (January 1979) 9–41, combines local jail and state/federal prison census figures to estimate trends in incarceration at all levels of government.

68. *Prisoners at Midyear 1983*, 1, for state and federal prison populations; local jail populations are extrapolated from a June 30, 1982 census, reported in *Jail Inmates 1982*, Bureau of Justice Statistics Bulletin (Washington, D.C.: U.S. Bureau of Justice, 1983). At this time, approximately one jail inmate was being held for every two state or federal prison inmates under custody.

69. American Civil Liberties Union National Prison Project, "Status Report—The Courts and Prisons," (Washington, D.C.: American Civil Liberties Union, 1983).

70. A recently published federal survey reported that construction costs per cell across the country ranged from a low of thirty-four thousand dollars to a high of one hundred and ten thousand dollars in 1982 dollars. Sue A. Lindgren, "The Cost of Justice," in Bureau of Justice Statistics, *Report to the Nation on Crime and Justice* (Washington, D.C.: U.S. Department of Justice, 1983), 93.

71. The estimate for New York State prisons is taken from the Correctional Association of New York, *Legislation to Manage the Prison Crisis* (New York City: Correctional Association of New York, 1984), 11. City jail figures are estimates. As I demonstrated in my earlier book on corrections costs—McDonald, *The Price of Punishment: Public Spending For Corrections in New York* (Westview Press: Boulder, Colorado, 1980)—the budget of the department charged with operating the jails reflects only a portion

of the true direct costs; other direct costs, most importantly, the pension and fringe costs of employees, are covered by other sections of the city budget. In the City of New York, *The Mayor's Management Report* (January 1983), 55, an average annual direct cost to the Department of Corrections per each city jail inmate during fiscal year 1982 was reported to be $20,255. A footnote indicated that the total cost to the city was estimated to be $29,200 that year. The direct cost to the Department was listed in a subsequent document—City of New York, *The Mayor's Management Report* (January 1984), 28—as being $20,800 in fiscal year 1983. Assuming the same proportion of costs borne by the Department of Corrections to total city costs, we can estimate that the latter cost was approximately $30,000 in that year. These figures, it should be noted, do not include the costs of construction or other more indirect costs that are incurred by locking people up (such as the cost of welfare payments by a family incurred when the breadwinner is locked up, etc.).

72. I know of no nationwide survey of per prisoner operating costs of jails and prisons, but I am sure that they vary greatly and that New York's costs are not terribly different from those found in many other jurisdictions.

73. "Nonjail Penalties Under Study by U.S.," *The New York Times*, 4 March 1983, 1.

Chapter 2

1. There are a number of Vera Institute of Justice reports that detail the project's progress. These include *The Bronx Community Service Sentencing Project: A Pilot Project* (New York: Vera Institute of Justice, 1980), which was later revised slightly by the addition of a new introduction and renamed *The New York Community Service Sentencing Project: Development of the Bronx Pilot Project* (New York: Vera Institute of Justice, 1981). Statistical reports from the institute are issued quarterly; the first covered the period October–December 1980. A few annual reports exist as well: Judith Greene, *The New York City Community Service Sentencing Project (Third Interim Report)*, issued in 1983, and the *Fourth Interim Report* printed in 1984. The interim reports included some of the preliminary findings from my research, many of which were revised after further analysis. Where contradictions exist between any of these interim reports and this book, the findings and conclusions presented here should be taken as the author's best and most supportable conclusions.

2. "Warren's" story is drawn from the Vera Institute of Justice, *The Bronx Community Service Sentencing Project*, 14–18.

3. New York law specifies that conditional discharges are authorized when the court "is of the opinion that neither the public interest nor the ends of justice would be served by a sentence of imprisonment and that probation supervision is not appropriate." At the time of sentencing, the judge may impose any conditions "as the court, in its discretion, deems reasonably necessary to insure that the defendant will lead a law-abiding life or to assist him in doing so." Persons convicted of a misdemeanor or violation and sentenced to a conditional discharge are required to remain under the court's jurisdiction for one year, unless the judge terminates the sentence earlier. If these conditions are not fulfilled, the judge is permitted to revoke the sentence and impose any legally available sanction in its place. (New York State Penal Law, sections 65.05 and 65.10.)

4. This tally was based on project records.

5. A good discussion of the English program can be found in Warren Young, *Community Service Orders* (London: Heinemann, 1979).

6. Joe Hudson, Burt Galaway, Steve Novack, *National Assessment of Adult Restitution Programs: Final Report* (Duluth, Minnesota: School of Social Development, University of Minnesota, 1980), 118.

7. That program is described in Lucy N. Friedman, *The Wildcat Experiment: An Early Test of Supported Work in Drug Abuse Rehabilitation* (Washington, D.C.: U.S. Government Printing Office, 1978).

8. New York State Penal Law, section 65.10.

9. The services performed since the onset of the community development funding is detailed every three months in the Vera Institute's *Community Service Sentencing Project: Quarterly Report on Service Activities*, (New York: Vera Institute of Justice).

10. This assumes seventy hours per completing participant.

11. Young, *Community Service Orders*, 26.

12. Hudson, Galaway, and Novack, *National Assessment*, 120–121.

13. Vera Institute, *The Bronx Community Service Sentencing Project*, 4.

14. I have not been able to locate the English document in which this seventy-hour average was reportedly mentioned, so I am not able to determine for which period and which region this average applied. Suffice it to say, however, that the planners picked seventy hours because this is the time they found that a population of English offenders serves, on the average.

15. In fiscal year 1983, it cost approximately thirty thousand dollars to house one prisoner for a year in the city's jails. See note 70 in chapter 1 for a discussion of how this cost was estimated.

16. Rhem v. Malcolm, 371 F. Supp. 549 (S.D.N.Y., 1974); Aff'd 507 F. 2d 33 (2d Cir., 1974).

17. Memorandum from David Condliffe, New York City Mayor's Office,

to Steve Sawyer, Deputy Criminal Justice Coordinator, New York City, 23 September 1977.

18. This perceived lack of options is not unique to New York. A 1983 report accompanying a U.S. Senate bill to recodify the federal criminal code declares: "Current law is not particularly flexible in providing the sentencing judge with a range of options from which to fashion an appropriate sentence. The result is that a term of imprisonment may be imposed in some cases in which it would not be imposed if better alternatives were available. . . . The statutes expressly suggest only a few possible conditions that may be placed upon a term of probation and do not provide specifically for alternatives to all or part of a prison term such as community service. . . ." U.S. Congress, Senate, *Senate Report on S.1762*, 98th Cong., 1st sess., 1983 p. 50.

19. Memorandum from Michael Smith, Vera Institute of Justice, to Kenneth Schoen, Edna McConnell Clark Foundation, 1 June 1979.

20. A fuller discussion of the decisions regarding the legal status of the project can be seen in The Vera Institute of Justice, *The Bronx Community Service Sentencing Project: A Pilot Project*, 71–72, and footnote no. 2 on p. 5.

21. An ACD is permitted by the NYS Criminal Procedure Law (section 170.55) and is a means by which the court can adjourn a case "with a view to ultimate dismissal of the accusatory instrument in furtherance of justice." Any time within a period of six months, the prosecutor can restore the case to the calendar. The ACD is therefore used as a way to flush the minor cases out of the courthouse, while retaining some power over the defendant for a period of time in hopes of keeping him or her on the straight and narrow path.

22. See the evaluation of the project by Sally Hillsman Baker and Susan Sadd, *Diversion of Felony Arrests: An Experiment in Pretrial Intervention* (Washington, D.C.: National Institute of Justice, 1981).

23. Actually, one should distinguish between the fates of phases one and two of the Court Employment Project. The first began when the project was designed as a pretrial diversion program in 1967. As a direct result of the findings produced by the evaluation research by Baker and Sadd, cited in note 22, the project was radically redesigned. Because that research found that C.E.P. was not functioning to divert cases from further prosecution, C.E.P. abandoned its mission as a pretrial agency and chose instead to focus its organizational energies on persons already sentenced to jail or prison. In cases where C.E.P. thought that their services could be valuable to offenders, judges were asked to defer the imposition of an imprisonment sentence, with the condition that offenders participate in

C.E.P.'s employment and education programs. By moving the point of intervention to a later stage in the adjudication process, C.E.P. officials hoped to increase substantially the probability that their program would be used in cases in which offenders would otherwise have gotten imprisonment sentences. This second phase of C.E.P.'s existence began in 1979 and was made final in the summer of 1980, when foundation and New York City government funds were obtained for a twelve-month demonstration of the redesigned program. For a fuller discussion of this transition, see Vera Institute of Justice, *Status Report: Program Development Activities of the Vera Institute of Justice* (New York: Vera Institute of Justice, 1983), 35–38.

24. The early history of the bail project can be obtained from Lee S. Friedman, "The Evolution of a Bail Reform," *Policy Sciences* 7 (1976): 281–313, and Vera Institute of Justice, *Further Work in Criminal Justice Reform* (New York: Vera Institute of Justice, 1977), 8–25.

25. Vera Institute, *The Bronx Community Service Sentencing Project: A Pilot Project,* footnote 2 on p. 5.

26. New York State Penal Law, section 65.10.

27. Section 65.10 of the Penal Law was amended again in 1981 to permit this. The pertinent sections of the amended law read as follows: "Except as otherwise required by section 60.05, the court may impose a sentence of conditional discharge for an offense if the court, having regard to the nature and circumstances of the offense and to the history, character and condition of the defendant, is of the opinion that neither the public interest nor the ends of justice would be served by a sentence of imprisonment and that probation supervision is not appropriate." (section 60.05) "Section 65.10. Conditions of probation and conditional discharge: 1. In general. The conditions of probation and conditional discharge shall be such as the court, in its discretion, deems reasonably necessary to insure that the defendant will lead a law-abiding life or assist him to do so. 2. Conditions relating to conduct and rehabilitation. . . . (h) Perform services for a public or not-for-profit corporation, association, institution or agency. The court may establish provisions for the early termination of a sentence of probation or conditional discharge pursuant to the provisions of subdivision three of section 410.90 of the criminal procedure law after such services have been completed. Such sentence may only be imposed upon conviction of a misdemeanor, violation, or class D or class E felony, or a youthful offender finding replacing any such conviction, where the defendant has consented to the amount and conditions of such services. . . ."

28. I am not familiar with any survey that lists project-by-project the

leading program objectives, but my reading of the literature reveals that offender rehabilitation ranks among the top objectives in most programs, even if the managers of these programs declare themselves interested in providing community service for punishment's sake.

29. Vera Institute of Justice, "Application for federal assistance from the Law Enforcement Assistance Administration" (March 31, 1978), 11–12.

Chapter 3

1. Personal communication from Michael Smith to the author in a meeting during 1983.

2. Because anonymity was promised to all those interviewed for this research, each respondent was identified by a number rather than a name. These numbers were assigned in the order that the statements appear here in the text and do not correspond with any hierarchy in the courts or other agencies. These comments come from interviews by A. T. Wall with three Bronx Criminal Court judges: judge 1, 8 February 1982; judge 2, 2 February 1982; judge 3, 4 March 1982.

3. For a fuller discussion of the interrelationship between guilty plea negotiations and sentencing decisions, see Douglas McDonald, *On Blaming Judges* (New York: Citizen's Inquiry on Parole and Criminal Justice, Inc., 1982).

4. See *Experimentation in the Law*, Report of the Federal Judicial Center Advisory Committee on Experimentation in the Law (Washington, D.C.: Federal Judicial Center, 1981). For an example of a powerful experiment, see Sally Hillsman Baker and Susan Sadd, *Diversion of Felony Arrests: An Experiment in Pretrial Intervention.*

5. Frank Harrel, "The LOGIST Procedure," (Cary, N.C.: The SAS Institute, Inc., 1980).

6. Computed from data obtained by means of a telephone conversation with the State of New York Office of Court Administration, February 1983.

7. For those untutored in the language of statistics, an explication of the table may be helpful. To the right of each characteristic listed in table 3.2 is a number stated in decimal terms, which is the correlation coefficient, or the measure of how strongly the particular characteristic was associated with being sentenced to jail. Perfect correlation is represented by a value of 1.00; a complete absence of a correlation is indicated by a 0.00 value. Therefore, the larger the number, the stronger the correlation. The asterisks next to the coefficients signify the odds of obtaining this result if the variables were not correlated in the larger population of cases. Three

asterisks show that the odds of this correlation resulting from sampling fluctuations were extremely low: less than one in one thousand. Two asterisks indicate somewhat higher odds: less than one in one hundred, but not less than one in one thousand. One asterisk indicates that the odds of this observed relationship being due to chance were five in one hundred or less (but not less than one in one hundred). Some characteristics have coefficients with negative values, which means that they were associated with *not* going to jail. For example, white defendants were significantly less likely to receive a jail sentence than blacks or Hispanics, although the odds that this pattern of association may have been due to chance was reasonably high in both Bronx and Manhattan courts.

8. "Time served" sentences were considered non-jail sentences for our purposes here, even though they were legally classified by the courts as a jail sentence. There were two reasons for doing this. First, "time served" means that the offender walked out the door with no further obligation to the court. In practical terms, it is the equivalent of a discharge. Defendants have often spent many days in pretrial detention awaiting the resolution of their case, and judges have determined that the defendants' obligations have already been fulfilled, without their having to report to probation offices, pay fines, or adhere to other burdensome obligations. Second, we were interested in examining the extent to which community service sentences reduced the demand for jail cells both before and after disposition. If "time served" sentences were counted as both pretrial and post-trial time, they would have been counted twice. We therefore chose to count days served in jail before disposition as pretrial detention time. A jail sentence was defined as one in which the offender was required to spend additional time behind bars after sentencing.

9. Bronx Criminal Court, judge 4, interviewed by A.T. Wall, 13 August 1982.

10. Brooklyn prosecutor 1, in an interview with me and Selma Marks, 3 December 1981.

Chapter 4

1. In many instances, a number of different reasons were given, but the court representative recorded the one that seemed the most important. Also note that the percentages rejected by each party to the negotiation, as shown in tables 4.2 and 4.3, are different from those shown in table 4.1. This is because table 4.1 counts all eligible defendants, whereas tables 4.2 and 4.3 count only persons found eligible and then rejected.

2. This imagery continued to be used for a few years after the develop-

ment of the Bronx and Brooklyn projects and was frequently employed in planners' discussions with me of their objectives.

3. Abraham Blumberg, *Criminal Justice* (Chicago: Quadrangle Books, 1967).

4. Vera Institute of Justice, *The Bronx Community Service Sentencing Project—A Pilot Project*, footnote 3 on p. 7.

5. Ibid.

6. Ibid., 8.

7. In a private conversation, one of the planners also told me that they had been told by someone whose authority they respected that the prosecutors "ran the show" in the Bronx Criminal Court.

8. See, for example, Arthur J. Hoane, *Strategems and Values: An Analysis of Plea Bargaining in Urban Criminal Courts*, (Ph.D. diss. New York University, 1978); Malcolm Feeley, *Court Reform on Trial* (New York: Basic Books, 1983); and his article, "Plea Bargaining and the Structure of the Criminal Process," *The Justice System Journal* 7 (Winter 1982):338; and Roberta Rovner-Pieczenik, *The Criminal Court: How It Works* (Lexington, Ma: Lexington Books, 1978).

9. A fuller exposition of this line of analysis can be found in my Ph.D. dissertation, *Morals and Marketplace: Criminal Sentencing Practices in Three New York Counties* (New York: Columbia University, 1983), and in my book *On Blaming Judges: Criminal Sentencing Decisions in New York Courts* (New York: Citizens' Inquiry on Parole and Criminal Justice, Inc., 1982).

10. Although trials achieve great visibility in the press, the vast majority of convictions involve guilty pleas. During 1981, for example, there were 884 trials conducted in the lower criminal courts of the Bronx, Brooklyn, and New York (Manhattan) counties, resulting in 429 convictions. During the same twelve months, 72,991 cases resulted in defendants pleading guilty. Guilty pleas therefore produced 99.4 percent of all convictions in 1981. State of New York Office of Court Administration, *Report of the Chief Administrator of the Courts, 1981* (New York: 1982), 47. These three boroughs were not abnormal in this regard, for guilty plea rates have been very high for decades, not only in New York City but elsewhere in the state. In his path-breaking 1929 study, *Politics and Criminal Prosecution* (New York: Minton, Balch and Company), Raymond Moley found that by 1850, half of all convictions in the state were by guilty plea. The plea rate drifted upwards in the following decades, hitting 90 percent in 1926. For a more recent analysis of plea and sentencing bargaining in New York State, see Douglas McDonald, *On Blaming Judges*, especially chapter 2.

11. Plea rates from New York State, The Judicial Conference and the Office of Court Administration, *Twenty-Third Annual Report* (Albany, N.Y.: State of New York, 1978), 97. These official reports show the numbers of convictions by plea and by trial, but they do not reveal whether these pleas were negotiated. The exact proportion of these pleas that were negotiated is not easy to discern, but it is undoubtedly very high. For a fuller discussion of negotiations in New York, see McDonald, *On Blaming Judges*, cited above.

12. Brooklyn prosecutor 1, in 3 December 1981 interview.

13. Prosecutors 2 and 3, in separate interviews with A.T. Wall on 8 February 1982.

14. Prosecutor 3 in a 3 March 1982 interview by A.T. Wall.

15. Prosecutor 1, in 3 December 1981 interview.

16. Prosecutor 4, interviewed by A.T. Wall on 17 February 1982.

17. Prosecutor 3, quoted in notes kept by A.T. Wall as a record of his observations as he watched cases being decided in the Bronx Criminal Court on 7 December 1981.

18. The first statement was made by Bronx prosecutor 5, in response to a court representative's request to consider a defendant for community service. A.T. Wall was observing case processing that day (17 December 1981) and recorded it. The second statement was given in A.T. Wall's interview with Bronx prosecutor 2 on 8 February 1982. The third statement is by Brooklyn prosecutor 1, in a 3 December 1981 interview with me and Selma Marks.

19. The first statement was made by Bronx prosecutor 2 in a 8 February 1982 interview by A.T. Wall. The second statement was made by Bronx prosecutor 3 in a 8 February 1982 interview by A.T. Wall. The third statement was made by Brooklyn prosecutor 6 in Wall's interview on July 1982. The fourth statement was made by Bronx prosecutor 7 in A.T. Wall's interview on January 29, 1982.

20. Bronx prosecutor 8, interviewed by A.T. Wall on 19 February 1982.

21. Brooklyn defense attorney 1, in an interview conducted by A.T. Wall on 2 July 1982.

22. State of New York Office of Court Administration, *Report of the Chief Administrator of the Courts, 1981* (New York: State of New York 1982), 47.

23. Bronx prosecutor 4, in A.T. Wall's 1 March 1982 interview.

24. Bronx prosecutor 3, in A.T. Wall's interview on 2 February 1982.

25. Telephone conversation with a former director of the Brooklyn Community Service Project, during the fall of 1983.

26. These remarks were made by three different court representatives

in response to queries by A.T. Wall when he was observing their work. All were promised anonymity so that they would be free to share their thoughts with the evalution team. The first statement was made by Bronx court representative 1 on 15 December 1981; the second statement was made by Brooklyn court representative 2 on 27 April 1982; the third by Bronx court representative 3 on 28 December 1981.

27. Bronx defense attorney 2, in 21 January 1982 interview with A.T. Wall.

28. Bronx defense attorney 3, in A.T. Wall's interview on 22 January 1982.

29. Bronx defense attorney 4, in A.T. Wall's 20 January 1982 interview.

30. Bronx defense attorney 4, in Wall's 19 January 1982 interview.

31. Bronx defense attorney 3, in Wall's 22 January 1982 interview.

32. Brooklyn defense attorney 5, in Wall's 9 July 1982 interview.

33. Brooklyn defense attorney 6, in an interview by A.T. Wall on 24 August 1982.

34. Bronx defense attorney 2, in Wall's 21 January 1982 interview.

35. Brooklyn defense attorney 7, in interview with A.T. Wall on 21 January 1982.

36. Bronx defense attorney 4, in Wall's 20 January 1982 interview.

37. Ibid.

38. Ibid.

39. Bronx attorney 3, in Wall's 27 January 1982 interview.

40. Bronx defense attorney 8, in an interview with me and A.T. Wall on 19 January 1982.

41. Brooklyn defense attorney 1, in an interview conducted by A.T. Wall on 2 July 1982.

42. State of New York, Report on the Chief Administrator, 47.

43. New York County (Manhattan) Criminal Court, judge 5, in interview with A.T. Wall on September 23, 1982.

44. Ibid.

45. New York County Criminal Court, judge 6, in A.T. Wall's interview on 24 September 1982.

46. New York County Criminal Court, judge 7, in Wall's 22 September 1982 interview.

47. New York County Criminal Court, judge 8, in Wall's 29 September 1982 interview.

48. Judge 7, 22 September 1982.

49. Judge 8, 29 September 1982.

50. Attorney 9, interviewed by A.T. Wall on 5 October 1982.

Chapter 5

1. Bronx County Criminal Court, judge 2, in A.T. Wall's interview on 1 March 1982.

2. Quoted in Kevin Krajick, "The Work Ethic Approach to Punishment," *Corrections Magazine* 8 (October 1982), 10.

3. See, for example, Elaine Hatfield and Mary K. Utne, "Equity Theory and Restitution Programming," in Burt Galaway and Joe Hudson, eds., *Offender Restitution in Theory and Action* (Lexington, Massachusetts: Lexington Books, 1978), 73–88.

4. These and all subsequent statements by persons sentenced to community service are taken from the transcripts of Antonio Valderrama's interviews with them, all of which were conducted between late June and early September 1982. Because we assured these offenders anonymity, we cannot identify them by their names. Instead, each will be identified here by the numbers we assigned all offenders whose cases were examined for research purposes, by the charges lodged against them at time of arrest, and by their age, gender and ethnicity.

The statements quoted in this section were made by (in order of their presentation in the text): offender 4213, thirty-year-old Hispanic man, charged with car theft; 4218, a thirty-two-year-old black man, charged with grand larceny for stealing a ring from a store; 4220, an eighteen-year-old black man charged with grand larceny (shoplifting from a department store); 7249, a thirty-three-year-old black man charged with shoplifting; 4223, a seventeen-year-old black man charged with grand larceny (auto theft); 7232, a twenty-three-year-old black man charged with attempting to steal a car; and 7240, a twenty-eight-year-old black man charged with possession of burglars' tools.

5. Offenders: 4236, a twenty-three-year-old black male charged with possession of stolen property; 7229, a twenty-six-year-old black woman charged with stealing a television and money from an acquaintance; and 7268, a thirty-five-year-old black man charged with shoplifting.

6. Offenders: 7262, a seventeen-year-old black man arrested for shoplifting; 7268, a thirty-five-year-old black man charged with shoplifting; 7273, thirty-six-year-old black man charged with shoplifting; 7289, a twenty-seven-year-old Hispanic man charged with breaking into a van and stealing a hand truck; 7290 a thirty-one-year-old black man charged with petit larceny for an offense not further specified; 7297, a twenty-nine-year-old black man charged with a forged endorsement and theft of another person's check; 7599, a twenty-eight-year-old Hispanic male, arrested for possession of stolen property (a crate of brass knobs); 7295, a

twenty-one-year-old Hispanic man, charged with attempting to steal a car battery; 7255, a twenty-five-year-old Hispanic woman charged with shoplifting; 7249, a thirty-three-year-old black man charged with shoplifting; 7221, a twenty-eight-year-old Hispanic man charged with stealing a radio from a car; 4224, a twenty-year-old black man charged with stealing a tire from a van; and 4222, a thirty-year-old black woman arrested for attempted petit larceny.

7. Offenders: 7228, a twenty-eight-year-old black woman; 7231, a twenty-one-year-old black woman charged with stealing a television and money from an acquaintance; 7235, a thirty-six-year-old Hispanic male arrested for possession of burglary tools while hovering around a car that the police suspected he was trying to steal; and 7283, a thirty-eight-year-old Hispanic man charged with stealing a bicycle tire.

8. Offenders: 4223, a seventeen-year-old black man charged with grand larceny auto theft; 4226, a nineteen-year-old black man arrested for unauthorized use of a vehicle and grand larceny car theft; 7211, a twenty-eight-year-old Hispanic man charged with stealing a radio from a car; 7237, nineteen-year-old black man; 1614, a thirty-six-year-old Hispanic man charged with burglary; and 1607, a twenty-six-year-old Hispanic man charged with possession of a stolen car.

9. Offender number 4219, a twenty-year-old black man charged with robbing a jewelry store.

10. Offender number 1609, a twenty-one-year-old black man charged with grand larceny, auto theft.

11. Offenders: 1609, a twenty-one-year-old black man charged with grand larceny for auto theft; 4212, an eighteen-year-old black man arrested for shoplifting from a department store and charged with grand larceny; 7230, an eighteen-year-old Hispanic man caught by police while acting as a lookout in a car theft and charged with grand larceny; 7211, a twenty-eight-year-old Hispanic man charged with stealing a radio from a car; 7232, a twenty-three-year-old black man charged with attempting to steal a car; 7240, a twenty-eight-year-old black man charged with possession of burglary tools; 7251, a twenty-five-year-old Hispanic man charged with pickpocketing; and 7259, a seventeen-year-old Hispanic woman charged with shoplifting and also prosecuted for two other outstanding warrants for shoplifting.

12. Offenders: 7255, a twenty-five-year-old Hispanic woman charged with shoplifting; 7240, a twenty-eight-year-old black man, charged with possession of burglary tools; 7265, a forty-eight-year-old Hispanic man charged with jostling; 7289, a twenty-seven-year-old Hispanic man arrested for breaking into a van and stealing a hand truck; and 7274, a thirty-

year-old black man charged with purse snatching and jumping the turnstile in the subway.

13. Offenders: 7283, a thirty-eight-year-old Hispanic man, charged with petit larceny (theft of a bike tire); 7272, a thirty-three-year-old black man, shoplifting and menacing; 1600, a thirty-three-year-old black man, grand larceny for auto theft; 1614, a thirty-six-year-old Hispanic man, burglary; 7297, a twenty-nine-year-old black man, forging another person's signature on a stolen check; and 7293, a forty-year-old black man, for shoplifting.

14. Offenders: 1613, a thirty-one-year-old Hispanic man, caught while working as the lookout man in a marijuana sale and charged with drug sale; and 1607, a twenty-eight-year-old Hispanic man charged with possession of a stolen car.

15. Offenders: 7269, a twenty-six-year-old black woman, shoplifting; 7284, a forty-two-year-old Hispanic man, possession of burglar's tools; 7232, twenty-three-year-old black man, attempted car theft; 4212, a seventeen-year-old Hispanic man, charged with grand larceny for auto theft; 1605, a seventeen-year-old black woman, arrested for unauthorized use of a vehicle; and 7292, a twenty-nine-year-old black man, arrested for using a slug in a subway turnstile and prosecuted for that offense as well as others committed in the past for which arrest warrants were issued.

16. Offender 7283, a thirty-six-year-old black man charged with stealing a bike tire.

17. Offenders are not the only ones holding this opinion. The identification of punishment with jail has long roots in American culture. Throughout the colonial period in America, punishment was seen as the infliction of pain and death. Sentences were suspended as acts of "grace." Shortly after the American Revolution, the number of crimes that could result in execution was cut back from over a hundred to a handful, and imprisonment became the punishment of first resort, in principle if not in actual frequency of use. Probation, where it exists as a legally defined sanction, owes its origins to the impulse to legitimize the suspension of sentences. In some states, all "sentences" continue to be defined in law as terms of incarceration, and sometimes a fine, and most other sanctions can be ordered only after the imposition of sentence is suspended. In one such state, this writer heard several prominant judges and lawmakers refer to imposing probation as an "act of judicial grace" rather than as a "sentence"; it is quite possible that they would also have defined probation, not as punishment, but as beneficial social service and discipline.

18. Offenders: 7211, a twenty-eight-year-old Hispanic man who was arrested for stealing a radio from a car; 7261, a twenty-three-year-old black

man charged with possession of stolen property and jostling; 7281, a thirty-seven-year-old Hispanic man charged with attempted auto theft, petit larceny, and criminal mischief; 7292, a twenty-nine-year-old black man arrested for using a slug in a subway turnstile and prosecuted for that offense as well as others committed in the past for which arrest warrants were issued; 7293, a forty-year-old black man arrested for shoplifting; and 4218, a twenty-two-year-old black man charged with grand larceny for stealing a ring from a store.

19. Offender 7241, a thirty-five-year-old American Indian, charged with selling marijuana and prosecuted for that offense as well as for an outstanding shoplifting charge.

20. Offenders: 7291, a twenty-nine-year-old black man, arrested for shoplifting; and 7595, a twenty-nine-year-old Hispanic man, arrested for trying to steal a car battery.

21. Offenders: 7262, a sixteen year-old black man arrested for shoplifting; 7273, a thirty-six-year-old black man charged with petit larceny for stealing magazines from a newstand; 7274, a thirty-year-old black man charged with snatching a purse and jumping a subway turnstile; 7287, a forty-eight-year-old Hispanic man charged with petit larceny for "stripping" a building, probably vacant; and 7593, a nineteen-year-old black man charged with something involving the breaking of windows.

22. Offenders: 1607, a twenty-eight-year-old Hispanic man charged with possession of stolen property; 7595, 28-year-old black man, charged with possession of stolen property; and 4225, a twenty-year-old black man, charged with stealing a station wagon.

23. Offenders: 4220, an eighteen-year-old black man charged with grand larceny for stealing from a department store; 7218, a twenty-eight-year-old white woman arrested for jostling; 1567, a forty-year-old black man charged with criminal trespass; 4210, a twenty-eight-year-old black man charged with attempted burglary; 4226, a nineteen-year-old black man charged with car theft; and 7243, a 25-year-old black woman charged with shoplifting.

24. Offender number 7235, a thirty-six-year-old Hispanic man, charged with possession of burglar's tools.

25. Offenders: 7274, a thirty-year-old black man charged with snatching a purse and jumping a subway turnstile; 4236, a twenty-eight-year-old black man arrested for possessing stolen property; and 1604, a twenty-four-year-old black man charged with petit larceny.

26. Offenders: 1612, a thirty-three-year-old black man, charged with possession of stolen property; 4234, a twenty-two-year-old Hispanic male, arrested while standing lookout for a car theft; 7251, a twenty-five-

year-old Hispanic man charged with picking someone's pocket; 7262, a seventeen-year-old black man, arrested for shoplifting; 7269, a twenty-six-year-old black woman, arrested for shoplifting; 7276, a twenty-six-year-old black man, arrested for shoplifting; and 7291, a twenty-nine-year-old black man, also arrested for shoplifting.

27. Offenders: 7283, a thirty-eight-year-old Hispanic man charged with stealing a bike tire; 1609, a twenty-one-year-old black man arrested for possession of a stolen car; 1614, a thirty-six-year-old Hispanic man charged with burglary; 7231, a twenty-one-year-old black woman charged with stealing a television and money from an acquaintance; 7240, a twenty-eight-year-old black man arrested for possessing burglar's tools; 7273, a thirty-six-year-old black man charged with stealing magazines from a newstand; and 7281, a thirty-seven-year-old Hispanic man charged with attempted car theft, criminal mischief, and petit larceny.

28. Offender 7243, a twenty-five-year-old black woman, charged with stealing a dress from a department store.

29. 7243's companion in crime, offender 7242, a twenty-one-year-old black woman, who was arrested with her and charged with stealing dresses.

Chapter 6

1. Joe Hudson, Burt Galaway, and Steve Novack, *National Assessment of Adult Restitution Programs: Final Report* (Duluth, Minnesota: University of Minnesota School of Social Development, 1980), 19.

2. Worries about increased recidivism seem to animate at least some of the opposition to the use of community service. For example, the district attorney's office in Manhattan has adopted a policy of opposing the use of community service sentences in lieu of jail terms, and judging from statements made by prosecutors in this office, one of their primary concerns is for the recidivism of offenders sentenced to the Vera Institute projects.

3. K. Pease, S. Billingham, and I. Earnshaw, *Community Service Assessed in 1976* (London: Her Majesty's Stationary Service, 1977), 11–18. The comparison group included offenders whose average age was significantly higher than participants, and because age was found to be correlated with reconviction rates, the authors rightly warned that any conclusions based on the reported data were "limited."

There exists yet another study that employed a comparison group. The research was done by the Minnesota Department of Corrections in 1977, but it was not published. The only documentation of it published in print is a brief summary of findings and methods in Joe Hudson and Steven Chesney, "Research on Restitution: A Review and Assessment," in Burt Galaway and Joe Hudson, eds., *Offender Restitution in Theory and Action* (Lexington, Massachusetts: Lexington Books, 1978), 138–143. The group of offenders that was examined in this study included people required to pay restitution after having been released on parole. Only nine of the sixty-two offenders in this group performed community service instead of paying monetary restitution. These findings are therefore not directly relevant to our examination of community service. (This study also relied on comparisons between groups that may have been dissimilar in significant ways.)

4. Indicative of our communal ignorance on this matter is the treatment of it in Hudson, Galaway, and Novack's *National Assessment of Adult Restitution: Final Report.* Commissioned by the National Institute of Justice to summarize and evaluate the state of current knowledge, it included no sustained discussion of recidivism. There are simply no data to summarize, other than those reported in these studies.

5. A very large number of crimes are not reported to the police, and of those reported, only a fraction of them result in an arrest. A 1977 study of victimization in New York State, conducted by the U.S. Bureau of the Census for the U.S. Department of Justice, discovered that only 32.1 percent of all "personal crimes" (which included rapes, robberies, assaults, purse-snatching, and pickpocketings) were reported to the police. Of all crimes against households (burglaries, household larcenies, and car thefts), 46.4 percent were reported. (U.S. Department of Justice, Bureau of Justice Statistics, *Criminal Victimization of New York State Residents, 1974–1977,* (Washington, D.C.: U.S. Government Printing Office, 1980), 54. Of the crimes that are reported, a relatively small proportion are "cleared" by an arrest of a suspect. In New York City during 1981, for example, only 12 percent of all reported burglaries were cleared by an arrest, 15 percent of all reported larcenies, and 7 percent of all motor vehicle thefts. New York State Division of Criminal Justice Services, *Crime and Justice Annual Report, 1981,* (Albany, N.Y.: State of New York) 25.

6. This is called "specific deterrence" to distinguish it from the general deterrent effect on the public at large.

7. As described in chapter 2, the screening process worked to sort defendants into two categories: participants and rejected defendants. Court representatives employed by the institute first identified defendants who met certain rigid requirements: they had to have at least one prior adult criminal conviction, and they could not have been arrested for crimes involving crimes against a person or weapons offenses. Defendants who made this first-level cut were considered "paper eligible," and they were

then considered in greater detail by the various parties to the plea negotiations. Any party could request that a defendant be dropped from further consideration. Rejected defendants' cases were then disposed of by the courts using the other available options.

8. Dates of release from jail had to be estimated, because they could not be obtained easily. New York City Criminal Justice Agency files showed the actual lengths and dates of sentences imposed by the courts. Offenders usually do not serve their full sentences, however, because they get credit for time spent in pretrial detention and for good behavior while under sentence. We therefore subtracted from each offender's sentence the number of days spent in pretrial detention, which had to be estimated in some instances from the New York City Criminal Justice Agency's data. Lacking any information at all about offenders' disciplinary records while in jail, we assumed for the sake of analysis that all had received the maximum amount of "good time" permitted: one day off for every two days spent behind bars. Subtracting these two figures produced an estimated date of release from jail for all offenders.

9. Malcolm Feeley, *The Process is the Punishment* (New York: Russell Sage Foundation, 1979).

10. Phrased in this way, we assumed that all arrests had been triggered by crimes, which of course was not always the case. At least 10 percent of the arrests resulted in the dismissal of charges, usually because the evidence for a crime was insufficient. If we had defined "crime" here as an arrest that led to a conviction, the total number of crimes would have been lower during the 180-day period. This criterion could not be used, however, because the ultimate disposition of arrests was known in only 61 percent of the arrest cases at the time the N.Y.C. Criminal Justice Agency's files were scanned for information about subsequent arrests.

11. Calculated from tables and graphs in *New York State Crime and Justice Annual Report*, (Albany, N.Y.: New York State Division of Criminal Justice Services, 1981), 25, 33, 35. This may overstate the actual amount of loss, because crime victims not infrequently pad their claims for insurance purposes.

Conclusion

1. Anne Newton, "Sentencing to Community Service and Restitution," 437.

2. For example, see Eugene Doleschal, "The Dangers of Criminal Justice Reform," 148.

3. Jonathan Casper and David Brereton, "Evaluating Criminal Justice

Reforms," (Paper presented at the Law & Society Association Meetings, Denver, Colorado, June 1984), 3.

4. "Sentencing Reforms and Their Impacts," Jacqueline Cohen and Michael H. Tonry, in *Research on Sentencing: The Search for Reform*, ed., Alfred Blumstein, Jacqueline Cohen, Susan E. Martin, and Michael Tonry, vol. 2 (Washington D.C.: The National Academy Press, 1983), 438.

5. Rhem v. Malcolm, 371 F. Supp. 549 (S.D.N.Y., 1974) Affirmed 507 F. 2d 33 (2d Cir., 1974). Because the city's jails were not able to expand quickly enough to handle their increased admissions, something had to give. One ongoing "adjustment" has been the shortening of jail sentences. The average number of days served for a jail sentence has dropped considerably since its two-decade high point in the early 1970s; the average length of stay for a sentenced prisoner in 1983 was 49 days, compared to 130 days in 1971. (Computed from information provided by the New York City Department of Corrections.)

6. Computed from figures provided by the New York City Office of Managment and Budget in a telephone conversation on 12 December 1984.

7. Ibid. The increase from 1978 or from earlier years cannot be easily computed because until 1979, parole violators placed in custody counted as sentenced inmates, even though most of them awaited transfer back to state prison. Beginning in 1979, these violators were counted separately.

8. See note 70, chapter 1, for a discussion of how the fiscal year 1983 cost was derived. The estimate for fiscal year 1984 was computed from figures developed by Diane Steelman in her *New York City Jail Crisis: Causes, Costs, and Solutions* (New York: The Correctional Association of New York, 1984). The $38,500 cost represents the amount Steelman estimated, minus the cost of debt service.

9. City of New York, *Mayor's Management Report* (January 1984), 17. As of early 1984, the City of New York had committed itself to spend $277 million in order to create a total of 3,896 beds in its jail system at an average cost of $71,100 per bed. Although two new jails will be built from scratch, the city will rely mostly upon renovation of standard buildings and modular expansion of already existing jails.

10. *Report to the Nation on Crime and Justice* (Washington, D.C.: U.S. Department of Justice, Bureau of Justice Statistics, 1983), 81.

11. Ibid., 9, for a discussion of crime rates.

12. For an analysis of age and imprisonment, see Alfred Blumstein, Jacqueline Cohen, and Harold D. Miller, "Demographically Disaggregated Projections of Prison Populations," *Journal of Criminal Justice* 8, (1980): 1–26. Since the mid-1970s, many states have adoped mandatory sentenc-

ing laws for a variety of crimes and determinate or fixed sentencing codes (most of which prescribe tougher "fixed" sentences for convicted persons). See *Setting Prison Terms*, Bureau of Justice Statistics Bulletin (Washington, D.C.: U.S. Department of Justice, 1983).

13. Calculated from tables and graphs in *New York State Crime and Justice Annual Report*, (Albany, N.Y.: New York State Division of Criminal Justice Services, 1981), 25, 33, 35.

14. Most proponents of selective incapacitation advocate its application to predatory street crimes, such as robbery and burglary. See Peter Greenwood and Allan Abrahamse, *Selective Incapacitation*. For a critique of this proposed policy, see Andrew von Hirsch and Don M. Gottfredson, "Selective Incapacitation: Some Queries About Research Design and Equity," *New York University Review of Law and Social Change*, 12, (1983—1984):11—52.

15. For an excellent review of actuarial and clinical methods of predicting future crime, see John Monahan, "Prediction of Crime and Recidivism," *Encyclopedia of Crime and Justice* (New York: Free Press, 1983). Also see von Hirsch and Don M. Gottfredson, "Selective Incapacitation."

16. The exact count cannot be made, because the courts tally docketed cases rather than individual offenders. During 1983, there were convictions recorded in 125,642 arrest cases; persons brought into court by summons were not counted here, because they were the least likely to receive jail sentences. The rule of thumb is that the ratio of docketed cases to defendants is approximately 11 to 10. Using this rule, we estimated that 125,642 cases represented approximately 114,220 persons. Arrest caseload statistics were obtained by a telephone interview with the New York State Office of Court Administration.

17. Herbert Packer, "Two Models of the Criminal Process," *University of Pennsylvania Law Review* 113 (1964):1—68.

18. Abraham Blumberg, *Criminal Justice*.

19. Raymond Nimmer, *The Nature of System Change: Reform Impact in the Criminal Courts* (Chicago: The American Bar Foundation, 1978), 38.

20. Max Weber, *On Law in Economy and Society*, (trans. Edward Shils and Max Rheinstein, (New York: Simon and Schuster, 1954), 354.

21. To call this a "debate" misrepresents somewhat the discussion in the literature. Several scholars have proposed different typologies to describe the various forms of judge/prosecutor/defense attorney interactions in plea bargaining. See, for example, Albert Alschuler, "Trial Judge's Role in Plea Bargaining, Part I," *Columbia Law Review* 76 (1976):1059; Donald Newman, "Pleading Guilty for Consideration: A Study of Bargain Justice,"

Journal of Criminal Law, Criminology, and Police Science 46 (1966):780. Some have gone further to argue that the development of plea bargaining has brought about the usurpation of sentencing authority by prosecutors. For example, Eugene H. Czajkoski, "Exposing the Quasi-Judicial Role of the Probation Officer," Federal Probation 37 (1973):9–13. What is at issue here is the extent to which prosecutors' sentencing recommendations constrain judges' sentencing decisions, and the extent to which judges themselves are constrained by whatever tentative sentence "promises" they have made in exchange for the offenders' agreement to plead guilty. For an analysis of the legal and organizational constraints on sentencing decisions in both of these circumstances, see Douglas McDonald, On Blaming Judges, chapter 2. At bottom, the extent to which judges' sentencing decisions are constrained by the actions of other parties depends upon the peculiar character of the plea negotiations, and substantial variation exists among jurisdictions in the ways these negotiations are carried out.

22. Lawrence B. Mohr, "Organizations, Decisions, and Courts," Law & Society Review 10 (1976):621–642; Austin Sarat, "Understanding Trial Courts: A Critique of Social Science Approaches," Judicature 61 (1978): 318; Malcolm Feeley, Court Reform On Trial: Why Simple Solutions Fail (New York City: Basic Books, Inc., 1983), 17–18.

23. James Eisenstein and Herbert Jacob, Felony Justice (Boston: Little Brown, and Company, 1977).

24. In many studies, the precise character of the negotiations—whether they are consensual or competitive or some mix of the two—is not really examined in great detail. For example, Eisenstein and Jacob, in Felony Justice, describe sentencing decisions as "group products," and they argue that prosecutors and defense attorneys constrain judges' decisions in important ways (267–268). The extent to which these interactions are consensual and norm-guided or more openly competitive, driven by opposing goals and interests, is not made clear in their analysis and there exists, as a result, an unresolved tension in their work. I think that I am fair in seeing their characterization as leaning heavily in the direction of Blumberg's notion of sentencing as a "team conspiracy."

25. Feeley, Court Reform on Trial. Mohr, in his "Organizations, Decisions, and Courts," suggested that theories of inter-organizational relations might be better suited to explaining court decisions. For a more extended treatment of the courthouse-as-arena idea, see Arthur Joseph Hoane, Strategems and Values: An Analysis of Plea Bargaining in Urban Criminal Courts (Ph.D. Diss. New York University, 1978).

26. See the works of Albert W. Alschuler: "The Prosecutor's Role in

Plea Bargaining," *University of Chicago Law Review* 36 (1968):50; Alschuler, "Trial Judge's Role in Plea Bargaining," Alschuler, "The Defense Attorney's Role in Plea Bargaining," *Yale Law Journal* 84 (1975):1179. See also Milton Heumann, *Plea Bargaining* (Chicago: University of Chicago Press (1977); and Douglas Maynard's recent ethnomethodological investigation, in which he undertakes a truly microscopic analysis of taped guilty plea exchanges: *Inside Plea Bargaining: The Language of Negotiation* (New York City: Plenum Publishing Corporation, 1984).

27. Many observers call this "sentence bargaining" to distinguish it from "plea bargaining," although the latter term is typically used to refer to guilty plea negotiations of all sorts. The key question has to do with the meaning of the negotiation, whether it is over what to charge or how to sentence. Even in instances in which the conviction charge is the subject of negotiation, consideration of sentence is overriding; defendants seek charge reductions only because they want to limit the sentences that will be imposed subsequently.

28. See Malcolm Feeley, "Plea Bargaining and the Structure of the Criminal Process," *The Justice System Journal* 7 (1982):338; Douglas McDonald, *On Blaming Judges*, chapter 2.

29. This analytic approach is elaborated more fully in McDonald, *On Blaming Judges*, and Douglas McDonald, *Morals and the Marketplace: Criminal Sentencing Practices in Three New York Counties* (Ph.D. diss., for Columbia University, 1982).

30. See chapter 5, "Pretrial Detention and Sentencing," in McDonald, *On Blaming Judges*.

31. For example, Peter Blau, *Exchange and Power in Social Life* (New York City: John Wiley and Sons, 1964).

32. James Coleman, "Theory of Collective Decisions," *American Journal of Sociology* 71 (1966):615; James Coleman, "Collective Decisions," in M. Turk and R.L. Simpson, eds., *Institutions and Social Exchange* (Indianapolis: Bobbs-Merrill, 1971).

33. E.g., Thomas C. Shelling, *The Strategy of Conflict* (London: Oxford University Press, 1963); A. Rapoport, *Fights, Games, and Debates* (Ann Arbor, Michigan: University of Michigan Press, 1974).

34. Roger Hilsman, *The Politics of Policy-Making in Defense and Foreign Affairs* (New York: Harper & Row, 1971); Charles Lindblom, *The Policy-Making Process* (Englewood Cliffs, N.J.: Prentice-Hall Inc., 1968); Graham Allison, *The Essence of Decision* (Boston: Little, Brown, and Co., Inc., 1971).

35. Nimmer, *The Nature of System Change*, 193, 195.

36. Malcolm Feeley, *Court Reform on Trial*, especially chapter 7. Also

see Jonathan Casper's review of Feeley's book: "The Impact of Criminal Justice Innovation: Feely on Court Reform," *American Bar Foundation Research Journal* (1983):959–965.

37. Feeley, *Court Reform on Trial*, and Nimmer, *The Nature of System Change*.

38. Stuart A Scheingold, *The Politics of Rights: Lawyers, Public Policy, and Political Change* (New Haven: Yale University Press, 1974).

39. As of January 1983, all but three jurisdictions (Vermont, Utah, and the federal system) had laws that prescribed mandatory prison terms for violent crimes, habitual offenders, narcotic/drug law violations, and/or handgun/firearm violations. Bureau of Justice Statistics, "Setting Prison Terms" (Washington, D.C.: U.S. Department of Justice, 1983).

40. Milton Heumann and Colin Loftin, "Mandatory Sentencing and the Abolition of Plea Bargaining: The Michigan Felony Firearm Statute," *Law & Society Review* 13 (1979):393–430; The Association of the Bar of the City of New York and the Drug Abuse Council, Inc., *The Nation's Toughest Drug Law: Evaluating the New York Experience* (Washington, D.C.: U.S. Government Printing Office, 1977).

Appendix

1. Frank E. Harrell, Jr., "The LOGIST Procedure," SUGI Supplemental Library Users' Guide (Cary, N.C.: The SAS Institute, Inc., 1980).

2. The bail decision does not necessarily determine detention status, because whether detained defendants make bail depends upon whether they or someone else can and will come up with the money required to post bond or pay a cash alternative directly to the court, where such cash alternatives are permitted.

3. William M. Landes, "Legality and Reality: Some Evidence on Criminal Procedure," *Journal of Legal Studies* 3, (1974): 287–338; William M. Rhodes, "A Study of Sentencing in the Hennepin County and Ramsey County District Courts," *Journal of Legal Studies* 6 (1977):333–353.

4. For example, John S. Goldkamp, *Two Classes of the Accused: A Study of Bail and Detention in American Justice* (Cambridge, Mass.: Ballinger Publishing Co., 1979); Robert Hermann, Eric Single, and John Boston, *Counsel for the Poor* (Lexington, Mass.: Lexington Books, 1977).

5. Douglas McDonald, *Morals and the Marketplace*, 209–237; this analysis was reworked somewhat and published in my *On Blaming Judges*, 85–108.

6. David R. Heise, *Causal Analysis* (New York: John Wiley & Sons, 1975).

Index